ALL THE FINGERS ON HIS LEFT

W9-CYH-623

He'll murder
us all again

there really is
no way out

fear remains...

Razors.
Tampons.
Thread.
Needles.
ugh Syrup.
erosene.
Rope.
ct Tape.

Ghost Stories

BY

RICK CHILLOT · MATT FORBECK · GEOFF GRABOWSKI ·
MATTHEW MCFARLAND · ADAM TINWORTH · CHUCK WENDIG

Prologue: CLUTCH

> "Only the hand that erases
> can write the true thing."
> — Meister Eckhart

Someone had sliced open Ted's forearms from wrist to elbow. They had pulled back the skin and pushed aside muscles and tendons, torn through nerves and blood vessels, until they exposed the yellow-white of bone. They had filled the cavities with carpet tacks, sewing needles, shards of a glass and razor blades. Then they had squeezed muscle, tendon and sinew back together, pulled the skin tight, and sewn it all together again without leaving a single stitch mark. Now Ted could feel the hundreds of jagged edges and merciless needles tearing into his arms as he typed, ripping into him like tiny teeth.

He pushed himself away from the desk, massaging one wrist and then the other. "Carpal tunnel syndrome…." Ted muttered. "Should have its own telethon, like MS." He checked the clock. He'd been typing for two hours. That was an improvement. A month ago, five minutes at the keyboard would have left him in pain for the rest of the day. It seemed the vitamins and wrist exercises were actually helping.

Opening the FedEx box Arnie had sent made Ted forget about his condition for a while. According to Arnie's last email, a real-estate contact had hooked him up with a well-off widow preparing to move to an old-folks' home. A widow usually knew the value of her own treasures, but could easily be talked into unloading her husband's stuff at a fraction of its actual price. "For grave robbers, we're pretty lucky," Arnie had once said. "We don't even get our hands dirty."

By late afternoon, Ted had priced several fly-rod reels and sent email queries to three collectors who'd fight for them like hyenas over a dead antelope. He'd listed 10 mint-condition LPs for online auction. He'd thrown out six water-stained copies of *Reader's Digest*. (What was Arnie thinking?) And he'd closed back up a desk lamp, three fountain pens, seven porcelain figurines and two wristwatches for later appraisal.

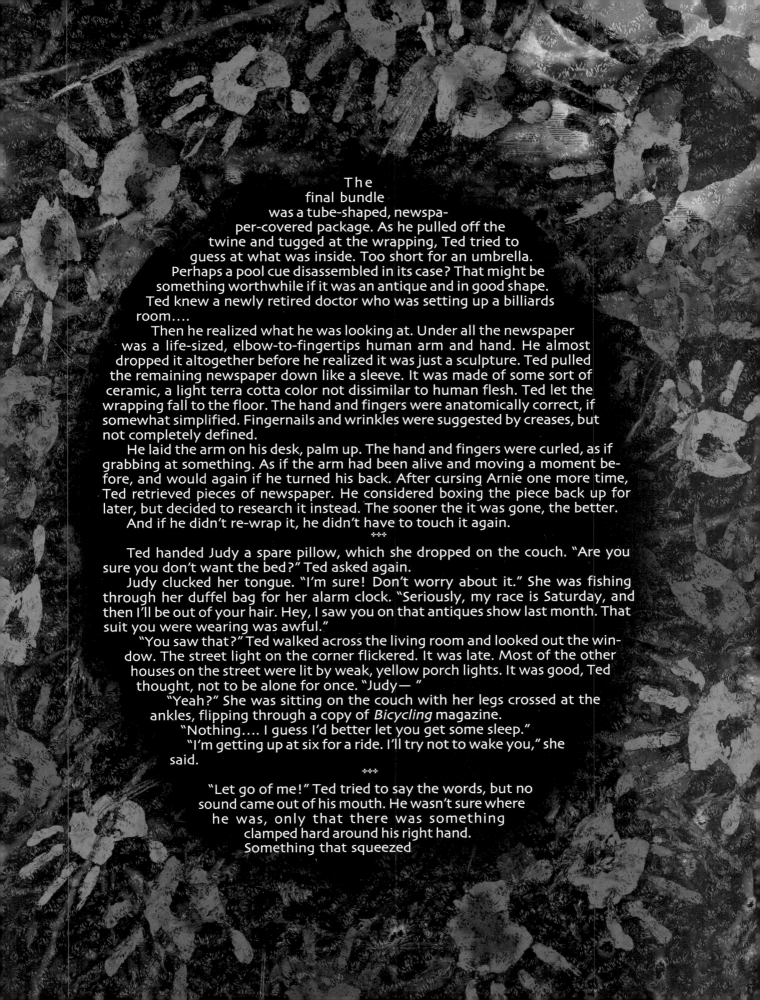

The
final bundle
was a tube-shaped, newspa-
per-covered package. As he pulled off the
twine and tugged at the wrapping, Ted tried to
guess at what was inside. Too short for an umbrella.
Perhaps a pool cue disassembled in its case? That might be
something worthwhile if it was an antique and in good shape.
Ted knew a newly retired doctor who was setting up a billiards
room....

Then he realized what he was looking at. Under all the newspaper
was a life-sized, elbow-to-fingertips human arm and hand. He almost
dropped it altogether before he realized it was just a sculpture. Ted pulled
the remaining newspaper down like a sleeve. It was made of some sort of
ceramic, a light terra cotta color not dissimilar to human flesh. Ted let the
wrapping fall to the floor. The hand and fingers were anatomically correct, if
somewhat simplified. Fingernails and wrinkles were suggested by creases, but
not completely defined.

He laid the arm on his desk, palm up. The hand and fingers were curled, as if
grabbing at something. As if the arm had been alive and moving a moment before, and would again if he turned his back. After cursing Arnie one more time,
Ted retrieved pieces of newspaper. He considered boxing the piece back up for
later, but decided to research it instead. The sooner the it was gone, the better.

And if he didn't re-wrap it, he didn't have to touch it again.

❖❖❖

Ted handed Judy a spare pillow, which she dropped on the couch. "Are you
sure you don't want the bed?" Ted asked again.

Judy clucked her tongue. "I'm sure! Don't worry about it." She was fishing
through her duffel bag for her alarm clock. "Seriously, my race is Saturday, and
then I'll be out of your hair. Hey, I saw you on that antiques show last month. That
suit you were wearing was awful."

"You saw that?" Ted walked across the living room and looked out the window. The street light on the corner flickered. It was late. Most of the other
houses on the street were lit by weak, yellow porch lights. It was good, Ted
thought, not to be alone for once. "Judy— "

"Yeah?" She was sitting on the couch with her legs crossed at the
ankles, flipping through a copy of *Bicycling* magazine.

"Nothing.... I guess I'd better let you get some sleep."

"I'm getting up at six for a ride. I'll try not to wake you," she
said.

❖❖❖

"Let go of me!" Ted tried to say the words, but no
sound came out of his mouth. He wasn't sure where
he was, only that there was something
clamped hard around his right hand.
Something that squeezed

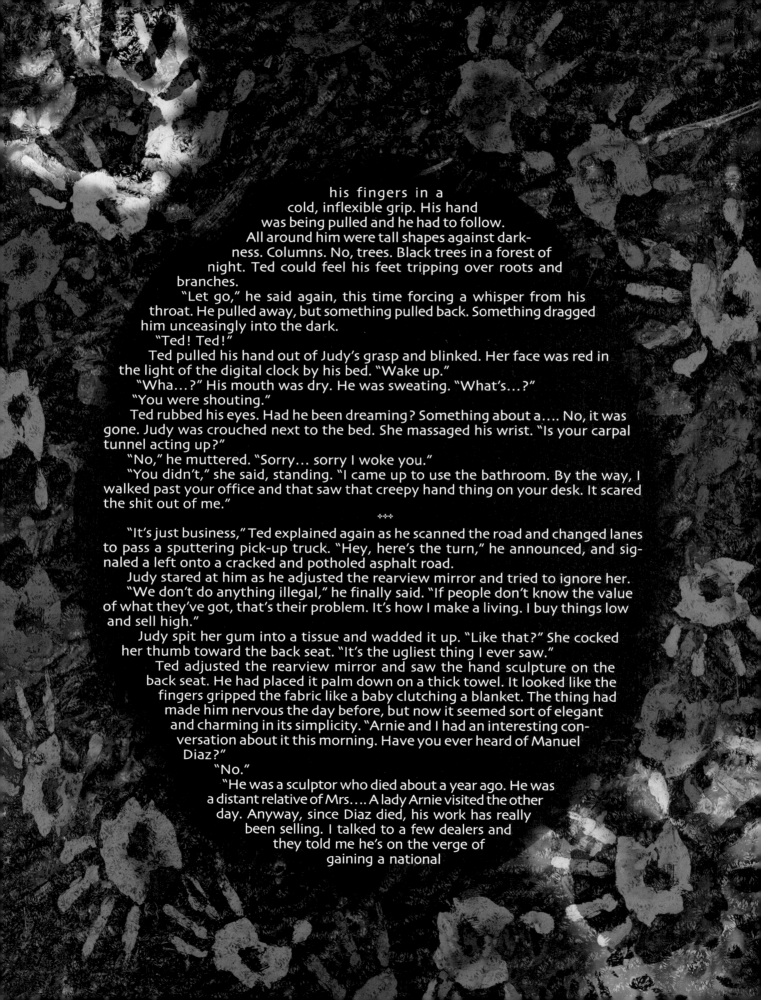

his fingers in a
cold, inflexible grip. His hand
was being pulled and he had to follow.
All around him were tall shapes against darkness. Columns. No, trees. Black trees in a forest of
night. Ted could feel his feet tripping over roots and
branches.

"Let go," he said again, this time forcing a whisper from his
throat. He pulled away, but something pulled back. Something dragged
him unceasingly into the dark.

"Ted! Ted!"

Ted pulled his hand out of Judy's grasp and blinked. Her face was red in
the light of the digital clock by his bed. "Wake up."

"Wha...?" His mouth was dry. He was sweating. "What's...?"

"You were shouting."

Ted rubbed his eyes. Had he been dreaming? Something about a.... No, it was
gone. Judy was crouched next to the bed. She massaged his wrist. "Is your carpal
tunnel acting up?"

"No," he muttered. "Sorry... sorry I woke you."

"You didn't," she said, standing. "I came up to use the bathroom. By the way, I
walked past your office and that saw that creepy hand thing on your desk. It scared
the shit out of me."

***

"It's just business," Ted explained again as he scanned the road and changed lanes
to pass a sputtering pick-up truck. "Hey, here's the turn," he announced, and sig-
naled a left onto a cracked and potholed asphalt road.

Judy stared at him as he adjusted the rearview mirror and tried to ignore her.

"We don't do anything illegal," he finally said. "If people don't know the value
of what they've got, that's their problem. It's how I make a living. I buy things low
and sell high."

Judy spit her gum into a tissue and wadded it up. "Like that?" She cocked
her thumb toward the back seat. "It's the ugliest thing I ever saw."

Ted adjusted the rearview mirror and saw the hand sculpture on the
back seat. He had placed it palm down on a thick towel. It looked like the
fingers gripped the fabric like a baby clutching a blanket. The thing had
made him nervous the day before, but now it seemed sort of elegant
and charming in its simplicity. "Arnie and I had an interesting conversation about it this morning. Have you ever heard of Manuel
Diaz?"

"No."

"He was a sculptor who died about a year ago. He was
a distant relative of Mrs.... A lady Arnie visited the other
day. Anyway, since Diaz died, his work has really
been selling. I talked to a few dealers and
they told me he's on the verge of
gaining a national

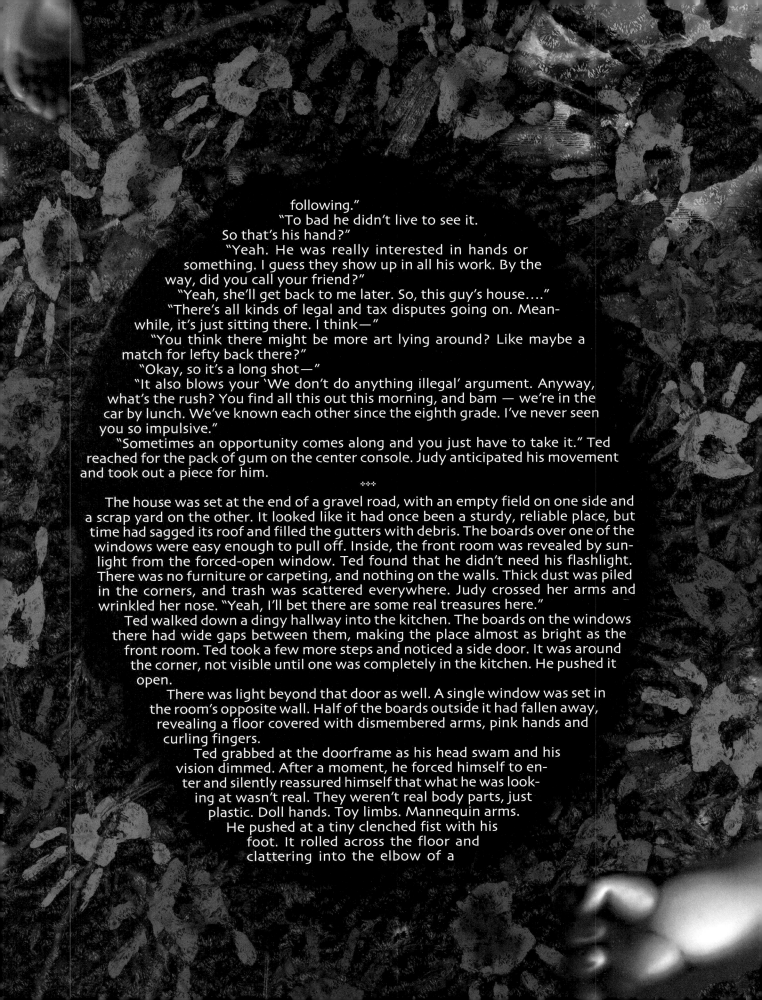

following."

"To bad he didn't live to see it. So that's his hand?"

"Yeah. He was really interested in hands or something. I guess they show up in all his work. By the way, did you call your friend?"

"Yeah, she'll get back to me later. So, this guy's house...."

"There's all kinds of legal and tax disputes going on. Meanwhile, it's just sitting there. I think—"

"You think there might be more art lying around? Like maybe a match for lefty back there?"

"Okay, so it's a long shot—"

"It also blows your 'We don't do anything illegal' argument. Anyway, what's the rush? You find all this out this morning, and bam — we're in the car by lunch. We've known each other since the eighth grade. I've never seen you so impulsive."

"Sometimes an opportunity comes along and you just have to take it." Ted reached for the pack of gum on the center console. Judy anticipated his movement and took out a piece for him.

•••

The house was set at the end of a gravel road, with an empty field on one side and a scrap yard on the other. It looked like it had once been a sturdy, reliable place, but time had sagged its roof and filled the gutters with debris. The boards over one of the windows were easy enough to pull off. Inside, the front room was revealed by sunlight from the forced-open window. Ted found that he didn't need his flashlight. There was no furniture or carpeting, and nothing on the walls. Thick dust was piled in the corners, and trash was scattered everywhere. Judy crossed her arms and wrinkled her nose. "Yeah, I'll bet there are some real treasures here."

Ted walked down a dingy hallway into the kitchen. The boards on the windows there had wide gaps between them, making the place almost as bright as the front room. Ted took a few more steps and noticed a side door. It was around the corner, not visible until one was completely in the kitchen. He pushed it open.

There was light beyond that door as well. A single window was set in the room's opposite wall. Half of the boards outside it had fallen away, revealing a floor covered with dismembered arms, pink hands and curling fingers.

Ted grabbed at the doorframe as his head swam and his vision dimmed. After a moment, he forced himself to enter and silently reassured himself that what he was looking at wasn't real. They weren't real body parts, just plastic. Doll hands. Toy limbs. Mannequin arms.

He pushed at a tiny clenched fist with his foot. It rolled across the floor and clattering into the elbow of a

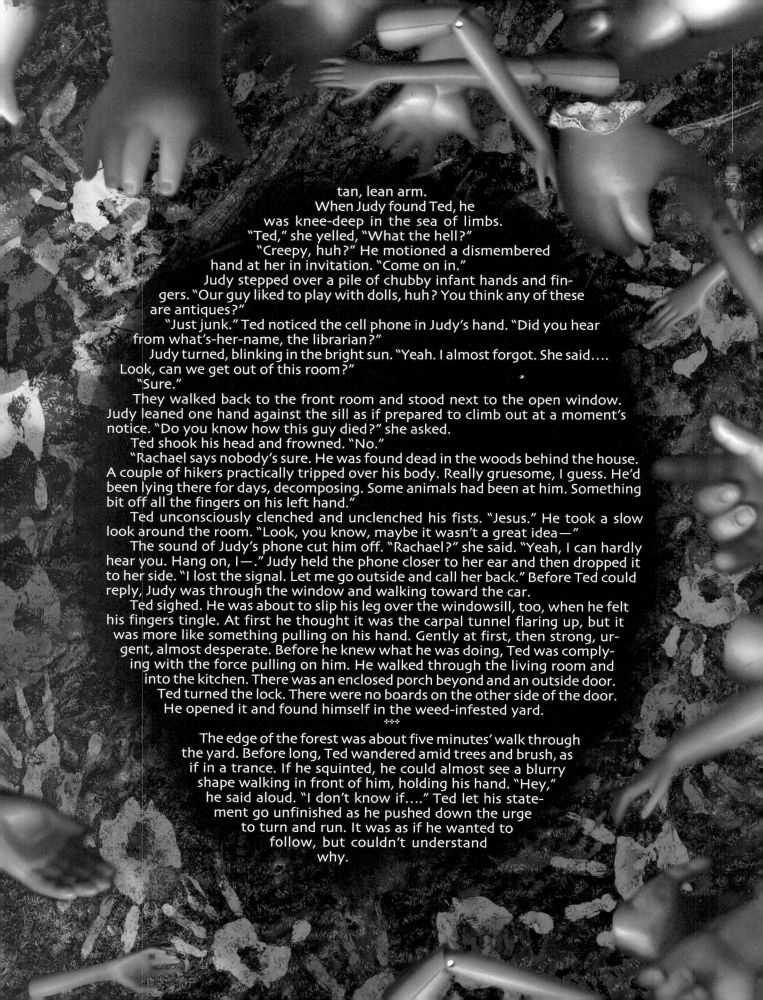

tan, lean arm.

When Judy found Ted, he was knee-deep in the sea of limbs. "Ted," she yelled, "What the hell?"

"Creepy, huh?" He motioned a dismembered hand at her in invitation. "Come on in."

Judy stepped over a pile of chubby infant hands and fingers. "Our guy liked to play with dolls, huh? You think any of these are antiques?"

"Just junk." Ted noticed the cell phone in Judy's hand. "Did you hear from what's-her-name, the librarian?"

Judy turned, blinking in the bright sun. "Yeah. I almost forgot. She said.... Look, can we get out of this room?"

"Sure."

They walked back to the front room and stood next to the open window. Judy leaned one hand against the sill as if prepared to climb out at a moment's notice. "Do you know how this guy died?" she asked.

Ted shook his head and frowned. "No."

"Rachael says nobody's sure. He was found dead in the woods behind the house. A couple of hikers practically tripped over his body. Really gruesome, I guess. He'd been lying there for days, decomposing. Some animals had been at him. Something bit off all the fingers on his left hand."

Ted unconsciously clenched and unclenched his fists. "Jesus." He took a slow look around the room. "Look, you know, maybe it wasn't a great idea—"

The sound of Judy's phone cut him off. "Rachael?" she said. "Yeah, I can hardly hear you. Hang on, I—." Judy held the phone closer to her ear and then dropped it to her side. "I lost the signal. Let me go outside and call her back." Before Ted could reply, Judy was through the window and walking toward the car.

Ted sighed. He was about to slip his leg over the windowsill, too, when he felt his fingers tingle. At first he thought it was the carpal tunnel flaring up, but it was more like something pulling on his hand. Gently at first, then strong, urgent, almost desperate. Before he knew what he was doing, Ted was complying with the force pulling on him. He walked through the living room and into the kitchen. There was an enclosed porch beyond and an outside door. Ted turned the lock. There were no boards on the other side of the door. He opened it and found himself in the weed-infested yard.

·:·

The edge of the forest was about five minutes' walk through the yard. Before long, Ted wandered amid trees and brush, as if in a trance. If he squinted, he could almost see a blurry shape walking in front of him, holding his hand. "Hey," he said aloud. "I don't know if...." Ted let his statement go unfinished as he pushed down the urge to turn and run. It was as if he wanted to follow, but couldn't understand why.

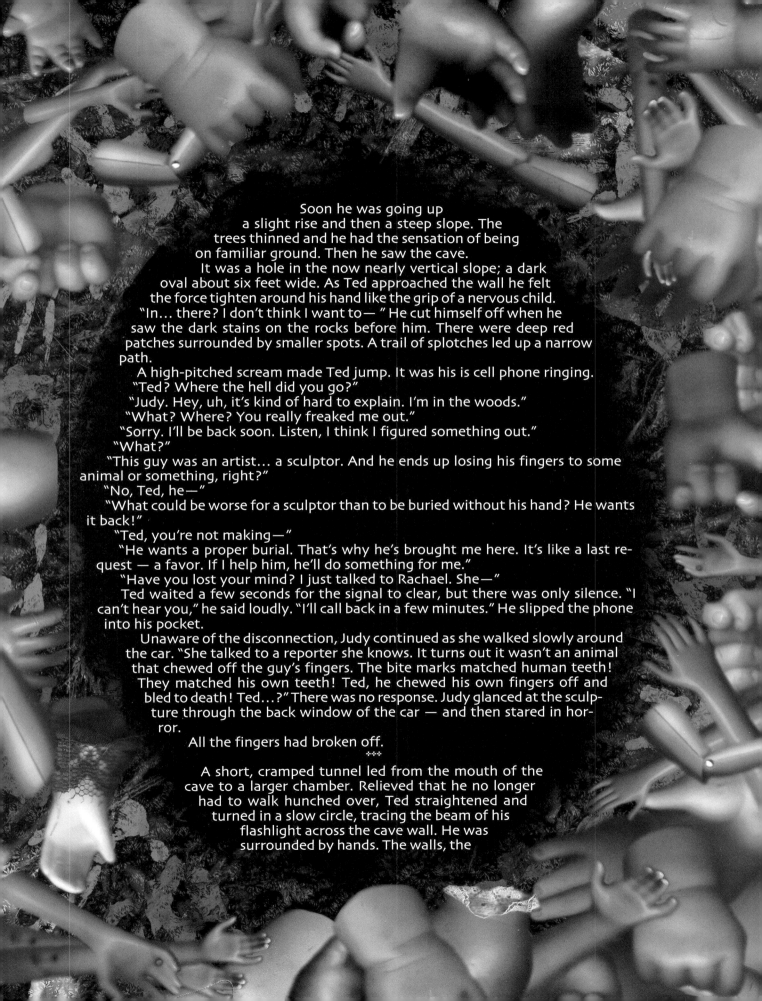

Soon he was going up
a slight rise and then a steep slope. The
trees thinned and he had the sensation of being
on familiar ground. Then he saw the cave.
It was a hole in the now nearly vertical slope; a dark
oval about six feet wide. As Ted approached the wall he felt
the force tighten around his hand like the grip of a nervous child.
"In… there? I don't think I want to— " He cut himself off when he
saw the dark stains on the rocks before him. There were deep red
patches surrounded by smaller spots. A trail of splotches led up a narrow
path.
A high-pitched scream made Ted jump. It was his is cell phone ringing.
"Ted? Where the hell did you go?"
"Judy. Hey, uh, it's kind of hard to explain. I'm in the woods."
"What? Where? You really freaked me out."
"Sorry. I'll be back soon. Listen, I think I figured something out."
"What?"
"This guy was an artist… a sculptor. And he ends up losing his fingers to some
animal or something, right?"
"No, Ted, he—"
"What could be worse for a sculptor than to be buried without his hand? He wants
it back!"
"Ted, you're not making—"
"He wants a proper burial. That's why he's brought me here. It's like a last re-
quest — a favor. If I help him, he'll do something for me."
"Have you lost your mind? I just talked to Rachael. She—"
Ted waited a few seconds for the signal to clear, but there was only silence. "I
can't hear you," he said loudly. "I'll call back in a few minutes." He slipped the phone
into his pocket.
Unaware of the disconnection, Judy continued as she walked slowly around
the car. "She talked to a reporter she knows. It turns out it wasn't an animal
that chewed off the guy's fingers. The bite marks matched human teeth!
They matched his own teeth! Ted, he chewed his own fingers off and
bled to death! Ted…?" There was no response. Judy glanced at the sculpture through the back window of the car — and then stared in horror.
All the fingers had broken off.
✦✦✦
A short, cramped tunnel led from the mouth of the
cave to a larger chamber. Relieved that he no longer
had to walk hunched over, Ted straightened and
turned in a slow circle, tracing the beam of his
flashlight across the cave wall. He was
surrounded by hands. The walls, the

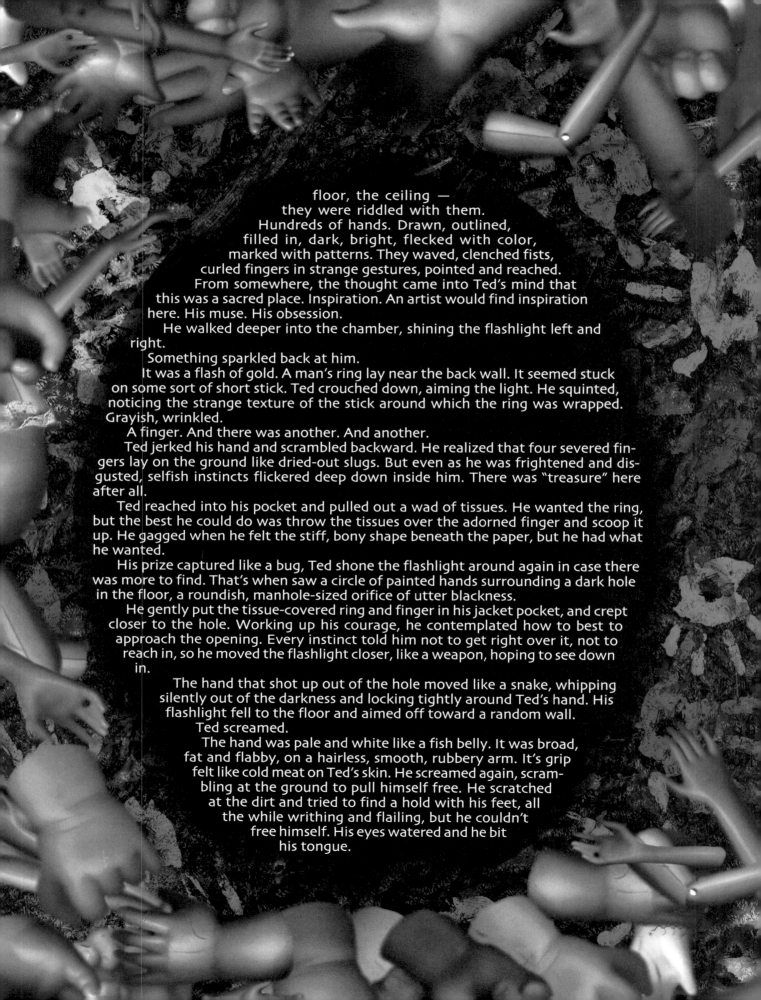

floor, the ceiling —
they were riddled with them.
Hundreds of hands. Drawn, outlined,
filled in, dark, bright, flecked with color,
marked with patterns. They waved, clenched fists,
curled fingers in strange gestures, pointed and reached.
From somewhere, the thought came into Ted's mind that
this was a sacred place. Inspiration. An artist would find inspiration
here. His muse. His obsession.

He walked deeper into the chamber, shining the flashlight left and right.

Something sparkled back at him.

It was a flash of gold. A man's ring lay near the back wall. It seemed stuck on some sort of short stick. Ted crouched down, aiming the light. He squinted, noticing the strange texture of the stick around which the ring was wrapped. Grayish, wrinkled.

A finger. And there was another. And another.

Ted jerked his hand and scrambled backward. He realized that four severed fingers lay on the ground like dried-out slugs. But even as he was frightened and disgusted, selfish instincts flickered deep down inside him. There was "treasure" here after all.

Ted reached into his pocket and pulled out a wad of tissues. He wanted the ring, but the best he could do was throw the tissues over the adorned finger and scoop it up. He gagged when he felt the stiff, bony shape beneath the paper, but he had what he wanted.

His prize captured like a bug, Ted shone the flashlight around again in case there was more to find. That's when saw a circle of painted hands surrounding a dark hole in the floor, a roundish, manhole-sized orifice of utter blackness.

He gently put the tissue-covered ring and finger in his jacket pocket, and crept closer to the hole. Working up his courage, he contemplated how to best to approach the opening. Every instinct told him not to get right over it, not to reach in, so he moved the flashlight closer, like a weapon, hoping to see down in.

The hand that shot up out of the hole moved like a snake, whipping silently out of the darkness and locking tightly around Ted's hand. His flashlight fell to the floor and aimed off toward a random wall.

Ted screamed.

The hand was pale and white like a fish belly. It was broad, fat and flabby, on a hairless, smooth, rubbery arm. It's grip felt like cold meat on Ted's skin. He screamed again, scrambling at the ground to pull himself free. He scratched at the dirt and tried to find a hold with his feet, all the while writhing and flailing, but he couldn't free himself. His eyes watered and he bit his tongue.

"Please," Ted whispered hoarsely, and then all he could make was a low moaning sound. The repulsive, alien hand pulled him closer.

He clawed at the thing with his free hand. Then pushed backward in the dirt, splitting his nails and making them bleed. But he was losing the grotesque tug of war, his hand almost gone down the hole.

Then a shadow broke the halo of light cast by the flashlight, the silhouette of a person appearing against the far wall. Ted croaked. It was hard to speak, hard not to make any sound that wasn't a guttural chuff of fear. "Judy... help."

Then Ted realized what he was looking at. It was the silhouette of a man. Its arms hung by its sides, the shadow of one hand showing only ragged stumps instead of fingers.

Ted blinked against the tears, gasped for breath, lurched his head closer to his captured hand... and began to bite.

Credits

Written by: Rick Chillot, Matt Forbeck, Geoff Grabowski, Matthew McFarland, Adam Tinworth and Chuck Wendig

World of Darkness created by Mark Rein•Hagen.

The Storytelling System is based on the Storyteller System designed by Mark Rein•Hagen.

Developed by: Ken Cliffe

Editor: Ken Cliffe

Art Director: Rich Thomas

Layout & Typesetting: Ron Thompson

Interior Art: Sam Araya, Jim DiBartolo, Anthony Granato, August Hall, Michael William Kaluta, Joshua Gabriel Timbrook and Jamie Tolagsun

Front Cover Art: Brecky Jollensten

Front & Back Cover Design: Becky Jollensten, matt milberger and Ron Thompson

For use with the
World of Darkness Rulebook

1554 Litton Dr
Stone Mountain, GA
30083
USA

© 2004 White Wolf Publishing, Inc. All rights reserved. Reproduction without the written permission of the publisher is expressly forbidden, except for the purposes of reviews, and for blank character sheets, which may be reproduced for personal use only. White Wolf, Vampire and World of Darkness are registered trademarks of White Wolf Publishing, Inc. All rights reserved. Storytelling System, Vampire the Requiem, Werewolf the Forsaken, Mage the Awakening and World of Darkness Ghost Stories are trademarks of White Wolf Publishing, Inc. All rights reserved. All characters, names, places and text herein are copyrighted by White Wolf Publishing, Inc.

The mention of or reference to any company or product in these pages is not a challenge to the trademark or copyright concerned.

This book uses the supernatural for settings, characters and themes. All mystical and supernatural elements are fiction and intended for entertainment purposes only. This book contains mature content. Reader discretion is advised.

For a free White Wolf catalog call 1-800-454-WOLF.

Check out White Wolf online at
http://www.white-wolf.com; alt.games.whitewolf and rec.games.frp.storyteller

PRINTED IN CANADA.

Ghost Stories

Table of Contents

Introduction

The Unseen World

The abandoned house at the end of the street that all the kids fear. Old lady Creedy was born, lived and died there, but she never left. Her spirit lingers on, protecting the home from neighborhood intruders, and guarding her lifelong secret in the attic.

The bend in State Road 67, where all those accidents have occurred. Sure, there are no streetlights that far out, and the turn is sharp, but they say 12 people have died there in the past 50 years. Is it possible that the road is really so dangerous, or are the whispered rumors true? Do the ghosts of past victims haunt the bend and lure other drivers to their doom?

The legend of Arnold Miller, colonial shipwright during the American Revolution. They say he was a master craftsman, but an angry drunk. It was no surprise, then, that he killed his wife when he found her lying with another man. It was no surprise that he fled aboard one of his own ships. It was no surprise that was caught, tried and executed at sea. Now he wanders the maritime shoreline, looking for a way to escape the authorities who he believes still hunt him, and to exact his revenge of any "harlot" he happens upon.

The world we know is rife with stories of the mysterious, the unknown and the terrifying. They say such legends are based on kernels of truth, and in the World of Darkness that cliché is laden with terrifying truth. Horrid things lurk amid the shadows. Unspeakable entities stalk beyond our sight and reckoning. Inhuman predators hide in our midst, picking and choosing among us at will, like wolves among the herd.

There's no way for humanity to understand the secret, hidden truths that are kept from us. We can't even discern between folklore, urban legend and reality. So who are we to recognize undead predators, ravenous beasts or otherworldly creatures when they exist beyond our perception and comprehension? The best that ordinary, mundane people can do is listen to instinct and deep-rooted ancestral memory. The feeling that makes the hair on the back of our necks stand up, that momentarily draws our attention to something that moved but is now gone, that intuitively makes us want to run when we know *something* is nearby. We think we're at the top of the food chain, but in fact we're a few of links down. We're hunted just as the rabbit and mouse are hunted. Those animals instinctively know it, and on some fundamental level so do we, if only we'd allow ourselves to accept it. Instead, we fill ourselves with false pride, certain that we're the King of the Beasts. In truth, there are beasts out there that we can't even imagine… and their reign is supreme.

Ghost Stories

While people have little or no sense of what monsters lurk in the dark places, we do have something of a grasp on the concept of ghosts. After all, ghosts are assumed to be us, simply dead. Imagining the possibility of spirits can help us feel better about the hereafter. It can give us some relief to know that after death, some people linger. The vast unknown of death is defined somewhat by the world that we do understand; some people who die stay here, the place we know. And they stay for reasons we can grasp — unfinished business, a craving for revenge, unrequited love.

My father's spirit in arms! all is not well;

I doubt some foul play: would the night were come!

Till then sit still, my soul: foul deeds will rise,

Though all the earth o'erwhelm them, to men's eyes.

— William Shakespeare, *Hamlet*, Act I, Scene II

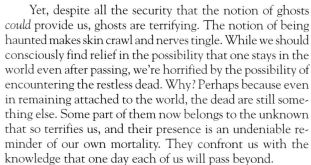

Yet, despite all the security that the notion of ghosts *could* provide us, ghosts are terrifying. The notion of being haunted makes skin crawl and nerves tingle. While we should consciously find relief in the possibility that one stays in the world even after passing, we're horrified by the possibility of encountering the restless dead. Why? Perhaps because even in remaining attached to the world, the dead are still something else. Some part of them now belongs to the unknown that so terrifies us, and their presence is an undeniable reminder of our own mortality. They confront us with the knowledge that one day each of us will pass beyond.

And so we get ghost stories. Tales that have foundation in a reality we think we can trust, but that extend into realms that can only be imagined. And by telling ghost stories, we allow ourselves to suffer a small death each time, imagining what the next world could be like and what our experience with it might be. Ghost stories therefore help us come to terms with what awaits.

In Storytelling games, ghost stories are ideal scenarios to play with ordinary, mundane, mortal characters. Those protagonists probably aren't yet immersed in the truths of vampires, werewolves, mages or other things. They don't know how truly precarious their existence is. But they, like players, can imagine ghosts and at some point find the open-mindedness or courage to confront such beings directly. Encounters with the restless dead give mundane characters a glimpse into the depths of the supernatural. The existence of spirits suggests that other kinds of beings could exist as well, but ghosts in particular immerse the uninitiated into the secret world in small steps. Yesterday, ghosts were kids' stories. Today, the spirit of a dead loved one is a cold reality. Tomorrow, who knows what will possible?

Stories of the Dead

World of Darkness: Ghost Stories is a collection of five scenarios for you to play with your troupe. This book is intended exclusively for Storytellers, not for players. Each story assumes that players' characters are ordinary people without any supernatural capabilities, and without much or any understanding of the unknown. Indeed, each story could be the launching point for an entire chronicle. Characters could start out as mundane here, be shown a sliver of the truth, and be consumed with or consumed by the supernatural hereafter. They might start as regular folks only to turn into the undead, shapeshifters, mysterious beings or their own ghosts later on. Or characters could remain human, but with an ever increasing grasp of what it means to be inhuman. All of the stories presented here could be played in your chronicle, with the protagonists developing into astute occultists, determined monster hunters, raving madmen or decaying corpses.

The only other book you need to play any of these stories is the **World of Darkness Rulebook**. Specific rules for handling ghosts that are referenced pervasively here can be found in the Storytelling Chapter, pp. 208-216. Some of those rules — and sample ghosts for your easy reference — are also provided in handy guides at the end of this Introduction.

While all of these scenarios abide by those rules, you don't have to. Your spirits can bend some rules, ignore others or exist beyond them all. Why do your ghosts need to be able to range only a few yards from their anchors, for example? Maybe they can travel for miles. Or maybe just one of them can, and that's what makes her such a threat to investigators. The fine point is, ghosts are close to humanity, but are still part of the unknown. While the rulebook may outline how to handle spirits in general, no set of rules should define them completely. Such limitations actually make ghosts *known*, and that means they aren't scary. When players think they have a lock on how characters should handle a spirit, because the players have read the rulebook, defy their expectations by letting your ghosts do things that aren't written down anywhere. That's when both characters *and* players face the unknown.

Ghost Stories offers the following five scenarios.

Chapter 1: Dust to Dust is about a forgotten town that seeks to reclaim its former glory — at the expense of anyone who resides in it. Consider this the story of a ghost town updated to the 21st century.

Chapter 2: The Terrifying Tale of James Magnus confronts characters with the legacy of a twisted and abusive man. They deal with the home in which he murdered his wife and killed himself, but which he never left.

Chapter 3: No Way Out reveals the ramifications of suicide, and the anguish that results when a desperate effort to escape life's problems only binds one to them in the afterlife.

Chapter 4: Roots and Branches explores the cycle of abuse that results from murder, when people killed in the vicinity of a tree turn its branches into a web that ensnares the dead. Murder begets murder as the tree's hunger for more victims grows.

Chapter 5: Holy Ghost illustrates humanity's lack of faith, and the danger of passion taken too far. Even acts of mercy, generosity and sacrifice, performed for the best of reasons, can keep a soul from its final reward.

Storytelling Ghost Stories

Tales of departed spirits are among the oldest forms of horror stories. They resonate with us because the horror inherent to them is so basic — death and the unknown. What happens to the human soul after death remains a mystery despite thousands of years of searching, worship, theory and mythology. The best that any living person can do in the face of the inevitable is accept it.

But it's not that simple. Fear remains, and to relieve it somewhat, we tell stories. Running a World of Darkness story featuring ghosts is one method of confronting the horrific possibilities of the great beyond, and of having an evening's fun in the bargain. But a ghost story experienced in a book, film or even around a campfire is a very different thing than one experienced in a roleplaying game. This Introduction is intended for Storytellers and focuses on how best to retain the mood and themes of a ghost story while providing maximum enjoyment to players.

Setting the Stage

A ghost story in a roleplaying game begins well before the characters ever come onto the scene. It gets underway when the ghost is created, with the death of a human being. The characters probably don't witness this death. (If they do, or even cause it, the ghost story takes a different spin that we'll discuss later.) Even so, it's important that you, the Storyteller, understand what happened. When designing a ghost story for your troupe, it's helpful to write down what really happened as opposed to what the characters can find out during their investigation, or what the ghost can tell them. In films and novels, the viewer is typically treated to information that the characters do not and cannot know, and thus has a better sense of what's going on than the characters do. In Storytelling games, however, viewers (i.e., players) normally know only as much as their characters do. It's therefore critical that you know in advance what the truth is and how much of it you want to reveal.

Means of Death

So, where did the ghost in your story come from? What killed the person? A few basic possibilities include:

• **Murder:** The wrongfully killed do not rest easy. Murder victims make classic ghosts. They're usually angry, and passion for spirits is power. But simply saying that a ghost was a murder victim isn't nearly enough. The victim of a serial killer faces a much different death than the victim of a scheming spouse or relative who's after insurance money. Someone murdered in the heat of passion by a jealous lover or by a complete stranger suffers the same end result as someone who passes peacefully, but the differences in the way such deaths affect a ghost and her anchors are critical to resolving her story.

A violent murder normally leads to a violent ghost. People whose lives are ripped away aren't usually introspective, forgiving or curious. They respond to intrusion and questions with anger. Summoning such a ghost through a medium might result in the host lashing out with whatever weapons are at hand, or collapsing from the sheer malice of the spirit that she accepts into herself.

A murder victim's anchors are likely to include the person who killed her, the place where she was killed, and/or the weapon used to do the deed. Some powers appropriate to a murder victim (as described in Chapter 8 of the **World of Darkness Rulebook)** are Ghost Sign, Magnetic Disruption, Telekinesis and Terrify.

• **Suicide:** On one hand, a person who takes his own life probably doesn't want to hang around any

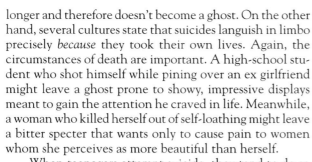

longer and therefore doesn't become a ghost. On the other hand, several cultures state that suicides languish in limbo precisely *because* they took their own lives. Again, the circumstances of death are important. A high-school student who shot himself while pining over an ex girlfriend might leave a ghost prone to showy, impressive displays meant to gain the attention he craved in life. Meanwhile, a woman who killed herself out of self-loathing might leave a bitter specter that wants only to cause pain to women whom she perceives as more beautiful than herself.

When teenagers attempt suicide, they tend to do so as a solution to an immediate problem that's perceived as insurmountable. Such attempts are normally one-time occurrences. Adults, however, are much more likely to make multiple attempts. For characters investigating the ghost of a teen suicide, the "trigger" event might not seem earth shattering or even relevant, but the teen (and thus the ghost) was willing to end his life over it. That makes for a spirit passionate about even childish subjects such as *perceived* neglect, loneliness or unrequited love. Ghosts that result from adult suicides can be stern and determined as a result of their deaths. Despite their best (and perhaps repeated) efforts to escape their problems, they linger in the world. That engenders resentment and the drive to see life's problems resolved once and for all.

Ghosts of suicides typically cling to the people, places or things that caused them so much grief in life. They might exhibit the Ghost Speech, Phantasm and Compulsion powers.

• **Accidental Death/Natural Causes:** Most of the time, when someone dies it isn't by design. Bad luck, carelessness or the ravages of time claim them. This is an extremely broad category with regard to ghosts, and includes any person whose death wasn't the result of someone's willful act.

When designing a ghost in this category, consider whether anyone else was involved in the person's passing. Someone who died in a five-car pile-up might haunt that stretch of highway, forever looking for the person who rear-ended her (and taking her frustration out on anyone driving a similar car). Or she might hunt down each of the other people involved in the accident, whether or not they caused it or were fellow victims. A person who died from an accidental gunshot wound (a hunting incident, perhaps) is likely to fixate on the person who pulled the trigger, much as a murder victim would. The difference is that even if the ghost takes revenge, he isn't likely to find satisfaction in it — the death wasn't personal, so the resolution isn't personal. The ghost simply transfers his hatred to someone else, probably someone with a quality in common with the person who shot him.

Victims of disease or other natural causes don't usually become ghosts, because they have time to recognize their impending demise and come to terms with it. Occasionally, however, a person is so attached to life that time spent sick only reinforces her fear and anger. Such ghosts can defend the area in which they died, unwilling to let go of the last place they beheld with earthly eyes.

Common powers for ghosts claimed by natural causes or accidents vary widely. A spirit haunting the factory in which she passed might possess Magnetic Disruption and Telekinesis, while the ghost of a person who died of exposure in a forest might exhibit Ghost Sign and Animal Control.

• **The Supernatural:** Ghosts of people killed by supernatural beings (while they ostensibly qualify as murder victims) merit special mention. Such spirits serve as a good "gateway" into the deeper mysteries of the World of Darkness. The ghost of a vampire's victim not only provides the same story potential as a murder victim, but also gives the characters the chance to discover that vampires exist, which in turn might allow for characters to *become* vampires. (Incidentally, consider how that ghost of a vampire victim might react if the people she haunts wind up becoming the things she despises.)

Ghosts of those claimed by the supernatural don't always remember what killed them, and certainly don't have any special insight into the societies of vampires, werewolves or other beings. They might, however, be forced to serve such creatures, meaning the characters can take on the challenge of freeing them from their slavery *and* allowing them to pass on. This, in turn, probably earns the protagonists the enmity of the shadowy killer, leading to further stories.

If you choose to introduce the ghost of someone who knew about supernatural beings, whether the person died at those creatures' hand or not, understand that the focus of your story immediately shifts from "ghost as a dead person" to "ghost as vehicle for other creatures." That changes the themes of a ghost story considerably. Normally, ghost stories reflect our fears of death and ultimately our own humanity. A story in which a ghost is a product of something or someone who was already immersed in the unknown does not teach the same morals. It acts as a cautionary tale, instead — "Stay away from the unknown or you'll suffer the same fate."

Designing a Ghost

Once you know how your dead person became a spirit, consider what her spirit is like. Ghosts in literature aren't always self-aware, and most are utterly focused on their own needs and desires to the point that they carry those obsessions to illogical and frightening extremes. Very few have the emotional or psychological stability necessary to think like a living human, but some do, and are capable of complex plans. When designing your ghost story, consider the following points for the spirit(s) involved.

• **Motivation:** Most ghosts have unfinished business, goals which, if achieved, allow or force them to move on to whatever awaits the dead. Even if a ghost has no actual desire to move on (which most don't, even if they're aware of the possibility), it still pursues its unfinished business. Sometimes the goal is simple and understandable. A murder victim might want to see her killer brought to justice, while a father who died in an accident many miles from home might simply want to see his children again. Meanwhile, the ghost of someone executed for murder might want to see every witness of his execution brutally murdered in turn, which probably isn't something that characters are prepared to help accomplish.

When deciding what a ghost wants or needs to pass on, be specific. In the above example of a woman who wants to see her killer brought to justice, what does "brought to justice" mean? Does the killer have to die? Be convicted? Simply arrested? What if he has to admit to what he did and feel remorse? Decide what emotion(s) the ghost displays in her unfinished business. If a murder victim acts out of spite or hatred, her version of "justice" isn't as forgiving as that of a spirit acting out of the desire to see a loved one protected. Remember that ghosts have Virtues and Vices, and these traits can go a long way toward determining goals.

• **Self-awareness:** A classic element of ghost stories, and one that often appears in films, is the notion that a ghost doesn't realize he's dead. He sees only what he needs to in order to convince himself that life continues as normal, and he doesn't acknowledge any evidence to the contrary. If more than one ghost dies in the same event or shares a similar outlook, they might all haunt the same area, none of them understanding the truth of their situation.

Other ghosts know they're dead, but clearly don't quite grasp what it means (if they did, they would have passed on). Some ghosts know they're dead and stuck on Earth, unable to move on unless they complete some task. Some extremely self-aware ghosts even understand what that task is. Others have only a vague sense that they've died, but are so focused on their goals (sometimes as simple as "causing pain" or "terrifying children") that they can't confront their own demise. When running a ghost story, consider where on this spectrum your ghost falls, and more importantly what reaction she's likely to have when characters expose her to the truth. Some ghosts lash out at the news, some use it as a motivation to pass on and some ignore it completely.

• **Capabilities:** A ghost's traits are a good barometer of what it's capable of doing, but be specific. As written, the Phantasm Numen allows a ghost to create an illusion of anything it wishes. But why does the ghost create illusions at all? Does it realize that it does so, or is use of Phantasm simply an unconscious means for the ghost to ignore the evidence of time passing, freezing it in its own era forever? Likewise, a spirit with a high Power rating is capable of ranging far from an anchor, but if it also has a low Finesse rating, it can't perceive the living very well. This sort of point spread is effective to represent wandering ghosts such as the clas-

sic "phantom hitchhiker." Know what the numbers mean in rules terms, and then decide what they mean in relation to your antagonist.

• **Communication:** In theory, all ghosts can manifest before the living. As stated in the **World of Darkness Rulebook**, manifestation can take many forms. A ghost might create cold spots, frost on windowpanes, bursts of static electricity or any other appropriate indication of its presence. Why do ghosts communicate in such obscure fashions? One possibility is that they wish to frighten the living (and sometimes that's the case). Another is that they don't know any other way to be heard. This can be extremely frustrating for characters, as they realize that something is trying to get their attention. Imagine how frustrating it is for the ghost, though. She knows only that she must make contact and can't understand why her subjects don't react the way she intends.

Ghosts do not immediately develop a complete understanding of their powers upon death (and, of course, haven't read the rulebook). A spirit might not realize that it can form a human-looking apparition until someone asks it to, or it might have so little self-awareness that its manifestations are unconscious. A ghost with the Vice of Sloth might be too lazy to manifest in any concrete form, while one with the Virtue of Faith might want to avoid demonstrating its own inherent blaspheme.

Decide under what circumstances your ghost can and does communicate with others, and what manifestation methods it prefers besides appearing as a phantom. Remember, too, that communication is a two-way street. Consider how the characters can reach the spirit. Some ghosts respond if addressed by name, some have to be scolded like children, while others must be approached respectfully. Any such "rules" are requirements that the ghost itself concocts, but if the characters want to see results (and want to avoid a powerful entity unleashing its full might on them), they search out and respect the spirit's chosen methods of discourse.

Introducing the Ghost

Ghost stories typically begin in one of two ways. A restless spirit intrudes on the characters in their everyday lives, or the characters enter the ghost's territory and are subject to its activity. Which of these methods of introducing the ghost is appropriate for your story says much about its particulars.

If the ghost intrudes on the everyday lives of the characters, the entity probably has a direct and personal connection to them. The nature of that bond and the methods by which the ghost makes its presence known determines the details of your story, but right from the start, a ghost that *seeks out* the characters is a proactive force. The ghost has a clear goal, even if that goal is short term. (Say, the spirits knows she wants to communicate with one of the characters, but nothing beyond that, and isn't sure how to go about it. See "Communication," above, for more.) You must decide what facet of a particular

character's history ties her to the ghost. A spirit doesn't call upon the aid of a character because the protagonist is "adventurous." The ghost needs to sense an intense personal bond to the character to seek her out specifically. This sort of story hook works best with players who take the time to roleplay through preludes, write histories of their characters, or who otherwise pay attention to the minor details to their characters' lives.

Ghosts who seek out particular people usually died as a result of another's actions, and learned the harsh truth before passing. They may have been murder victims, but even those who died in accidents can fixate on other people rather than circumstances if a victim knows that someone specific was to blame (or could help).

A ghost that haunts an area and who turns its attention on intruding characters is an entirely different beast. Such ghosts are typically shaped by the circumstances surrounding their death. Say a haunting ghost has a single, fixed anchor while a wide-ranging one has multiple or mobile anchors. Haunters are usually the product of a specific set of circumstances. Maybe someone dedicated himself to a workplace project or ailing loved one and died without seeing the job done or the family member recovered. These lingering spirits can remain in the area post mortem, unable or unwilling to leave (or unaware that they're dead and they still try to see the effort through). When intruders like the characters disrupt the area, the ghost responds with anything from curiosity to joy to frustration, and might express all of these emotions in the same way. From the characters' perspective, all sentiments manifest as terrifying or dangerous. And, of course, all this presumes that the ghost notices the characters at all. Some spirits simply repeat the same actions they did when they were alive, which results in objects being moved around, doors being locked and the living being horrified.

Victims of the Characters

While mortal characters probably don't kill people on a regular basis, if you run **Vampire: The Requiem** or another World of Darkness game in which players assume the roles of supernatural beings, someone's going to die by their hand sooner or later. Vampires and werewolves both suffer from murderous rage, and mages can lose control of their magic. Antagonists and innocent bystanders die easily.

The Storytelling system proposes the Morality trait as a mechanical "check and balance" for keeping characters from simply slaughtering anyone. But that system doesn't always resonate for (or matter to) players. Having a victim return from the grave as an angry and powerful ghost, however, might be exactly the object lesson needed to show a character that her actions do impact the world.

This type of spirit changes the themes of a ghost story slightly. If the character is the one responsible for the ghost's fate, the character must be brought to justice — or at least made to own up to what she did and make amends — in order for the ghost to pass. Players need to be mature enough to handle such a story. The difference between a ghost literally or figuratively saying "Look what happened to me" and "Look what *you* did to me" is considerable. Be sure your players are capable of appreciating that difference before you bring back one of their victims. Otherwise, what's the lesson learned?

Also, avoid important antagonists in an ongoing chronicle returning as ghosts. It feels cheap, especially if the players worked hard to bring the enemy down in the first place.

First Impressions

Most ghost stories begin with the protagonists noticing small, odd details. Tiny manifestations of the ghost's power that might or might not be evidence of otherworldly activity. A sudden cold shiver, a quick rush of movement down a hallway or a snatch of music. All of these are within the realm of the Ghost Sign Numen and might be a good start to a ghost story. The trick to using such subtle signs is that in a Storytelling game, the players know (even if their characters do not) that these little events are most likely evidence of the supernatural. Players react to these cues accordingly, because they react to anything to which you call special attention. If you seed such events into a different story, you can stretch this "buildup" phase for a while, disguising events of a future story in a current one, and piquing players' interest.

Alternatively, some ghosts aren't so subtle and make their presence known quickly. If the characters enter such an entity's haunt, the spirit might slam doors (Telekinesis), show them their own dead bodies in mirrors (Phantasm), or cause rats or other vermin to pour out from cracks and crevices (Animal Control).

Hooking the Characters

Why the characters get involved in a ghost story depends entirely on your players' creations. They might be devoted to investigating and uncovering evidence of the supernatural. They might be friends who have stumbled across the haunting and decided, for a variety of their own reasons, to do something about it. They might be workers in the same building who all share (or inexplicably develop) the Unseen Sense Merit (**World of Darkness Rulebook**, p. 109), and they realize that they all sense a presence in their midst. As Storyteller, you need to know what motivates the characters and you need to incorporate that motivation into your story, rather

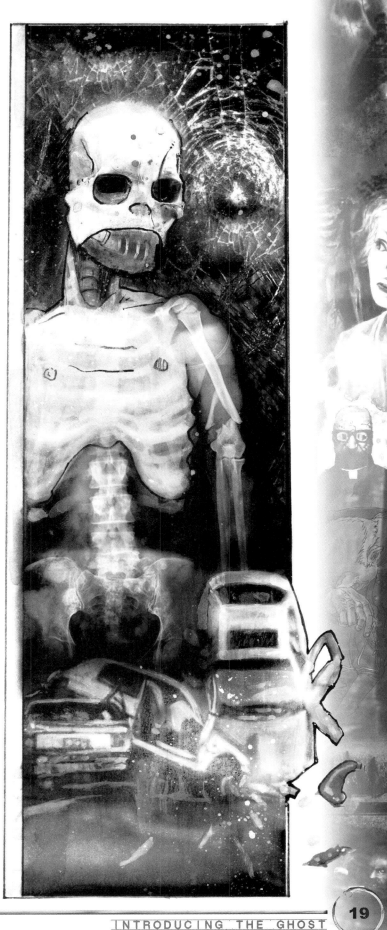

19

INTRODUCING THE GHOST

than design a scenario and try to push characters toward it. An important element of ghost stories is investigation. Before the characters can address the problem with any degree of certainty, they need to know with what (and whom) they deal. Players will pursue investigation with fervor if their characters care about the results.

Fear can be a powerful motivator to get characters to understand a ghost, but the disconnection between player and character is often sufficient that while a player intellectually knows that her character should be frightened, that fear doesn't necessarily influence the actions she declares. Put another way, characters in literature and film often take actions that make us yell, "Don't be an idiot," but that's because those characters behave according to identity and story, as opposed to us who have greater awareness. Players often regard roleplaying as a puzzle to be solved or a game to be won, meaning that only some address characters' debilitating emotions such as fear. Roleplaying moments of fear may not be as satisfying as portraying moments at which characters act from a position of strength. Fear can also seem mundane, and people roleplay to escape the mundane.

This isn't to say that fear can't motivate players in a ghost story, they just need to relate to it. Fortunately, the two fears that ghost stories most often play to — death and the unknown — resonate well with players. They don't want their characters to die or venture into a situation in which they have no control, so can make their characters apprehensive, scared or ready to flee — or curious, intrigued or enraged. When fear kicks in, the player's identity can impose itself, and so can the player's desire to preserve his character and solve the problems of the story.

If a ghost is intimately connected to one or more characters, the motive to lay her to rest is even stronger. The players feel as though they have a hand in creating the story. So, make sure you have a strong grasp of all characters and their histories, and encourage players to be as detailed as possible in conceptualizing their characters. That way they fully identify with their creations, can be sympathetic (or empathetic) for their characters' feelings, and fully capture the fear that a ghost story should inspire.

Investigation

Most ghost stories in roleplaying games require a great deal of investigation. It can be performed via library research, interviews with surviving family or associates, searching the ghost's haunting grounds, or even by conversations with the ghost through a medium. The style of investigation performed depends on the information the characters seek. Systems for these activities are covered in the **World of Darkness Rulebook**. How you approach them in a game session, however, determines the mood of the story.

Library research is rarely interesting to roleplay. It's best handled by letting players roll some dice, informing them how long the effort takes, and then providing the results. Consider, though, what might happen if the ghost realizes that characters do research on him. Is he flattered?

Angry? Violated? Does he understand at all? The ghost might try to help, but only succeeds in scaring the characters off. A library at night is a perfect scene for a spectral visitation. Shelves provide cover for a quick rush of movement, books can fall off shelves and land open on just the right pages, or books can flutter around the room like misshapen bats.

Interviews are tough on Storytellers because they require you to create a persona and keep it distinct from other supporting cast members. You can take inspiration from films and other media, of course, and emulate the performances of bereaved relatives, guilty spouses or amateur ghost-hunters. (Just don't cleave so close to actors' portrayals that players recognize what you're doing. That reminds everyone of the gaming experience.) When portraying the interviewee, consider both what she knows and what she's willing to share, depending on the methods the characters use (threats, bribes, appeals to good nature).

Physical investigation is probably the best way to establish the mood and danger of a ghost story. As soon as the characters come within a certain distance of the ghost's anchor, the spirit knows and probably watches. Whether it manifests depends on the ghost's identity and the characters' actions, but powerful spirits can cause "accidents" with Telekinesis, lure characters into dangerous situations with Phantasm, and otherwise use Numina to endanger — or aid — intruders. Consider, for instance, what would happen if two ghosts with conflicting agendas share an anchor, or if their anchors are close together. The characters might well be caught up in their conflict. The ghosts might try to lure the characters to their respective sides, each encouraging the living to sever the other's ties.

Finally, allowing a ghost to speak through a medium or by another means such as a Ouija board allows for slow revelation of information (perhaps one letter at a time), and the realization of encountering something quite beyond the realm of human comprehension. Another good method of ghost communication is automatic writing, by which the ghost possesses a host who writes the spirit's words. This host may be taken over completely and "disappears" behind the personality of the intruder, or the host could be completely unaware of his own possession. In the latter case, a writing hand moves as if of its own accord and conveys a message that the medium was never aware of. If you play the part of a genuine medium or have a friend "guest star" as the medium, play the scene by candlelight. The effect can be chillingly effective for players.

Resolution

When the characters feel they have collected enough information to do something about the ghost, your story enters the resolution phase. The characters might plan to destroy an anchor, help the ghost finish its earthly business, or even perform an exorcism to force the being out of the living world. No matter what, you must decide if the chosen course is going to work and what the ghost does about it.

If the ghost is destructive, expect players to take a violent route toward disposing of it. Burning down the house that anchors a poltergeist or smashing an urn that holds a deceiver's ashes can be extremely satisfying to players whose characters have been injured from beyond. Similarly, acquiring enchanted or blessed weapons and simply beating a ghost into oblivion can be entertaining, but the spirit might simply be able to jump to another anchor.

If the ghost wants to move on, whether consciously or unconsciously, it probably helps the characters in their efforts. But what if the ghost gets "cold feet" at the last minute? Or what if the spirit has simply been leading the characters on in order to position them in a way conducive to its own ends (see "Twist Endings")?

If the ghost is ignorant of its situation, it probably intuitively grasps what's happening as the characters take the final necessary steps — setting the fire or initiating the exorcism. What it chooses to do in the moment of revelation, when it finally realizes that it's dead again, depends on what you foresee as most satisfying for the story and on how the characters have conducted their investigation. If the ghost becomes aware moments before the characters destroy something precious to it (an anchor), it probably fights tooth and nail. If it realizes that they try to resolve its last remaining desires, it might watch passively or contribute directly.

The scene in which a ghost moves on to its final fate can be a horrifying revelation of hellfire and brimstone as a murderer is sucked into damnation, or a touching moment as a lost and confused soul finally finds his way "home." The last thing characters feel or see should sum up the story. A sense of peace might sweep over the area as all traces of the supernatural vanish. Or characters might feel an abrupt shift, as though the ghost is gone… but something else pays attention. The end of a ghost story is the most important time at which to remember that a spirit is all that remains of a human being, and there but for the grace of God go the characters.

Twist Endings

Ghost stories often rely on a twist at the end to elicit one final gasp from the audience. In campfire ghost stories, the storyteller jumps at a listener and says, "Boo!" Films such as *Sixth Sense* and *The Others* make audiences guess as to the true nature of the characters and their status as the restless dead. Twist endings are very much in-genre for ghost stories, but are somewhat difficult to pull off in Storytelling games. Players sometimes feel cheated if presented with information that their characters could or should have discovered, but didn't, just for the sake of a twist finalé. Likewise, since many players look at roleplaying games as problem-solving exercises (which they often are), they might foresee your intended twist before the critical moment. Finally, because the planned events of a story almost never coincide neatly with actual events, planning a twist ending that fits nicely with the rest of the chronicle is challenging.

An ideal overall approach is to know in advance what a "twist" could be. If the players anticipate it during the course of the story, allow it to proceed for maximum story value, as if that was the intended ending all along. The players don't know what's a twist ending and what's a simple resolution, so if they discover something through luck or cleverness, let them have their moment.

Another (and possibly the best) method of handling a twist ending is to literally make it up at the end of the game. Your players can't see it coming because you don't even know what it will be. That way you can make the twist fit the events that have transpired. If you think quickly, you can come up with a good twist that players might have figured out earlier had they thought about it. Okay, maybe this method doesn't "play fair," but who's going to tell?

Ghosts Summary

Ghost Traits

Ghosts have Attributes similar to living characters, but they are abbreviated to the three general categories of Power, Finesse and Resistance. Power represents a ghost's ability to affect its environment, from throwing objects to opening and slamming doors. Finesse represents a ghost's capability in interacting with or manipulating elements of its environment, from noticing the intrusions of trespassers into its "home" to terrifying someone with horrifying illusions. Resistance represents a ghost's ability to withstand forces that could banish or destroy it, from prayers to exorcisms to physical attacks with blessed objects. These Attributes can potentially range from 1 to 10, although only very old and powerful ghosts have traits higher than 5.

Ghosts do not have Skills or Merits unless they possess a living body (see "Numina," below). Nor do they have a Size trait in the conventional sense. A ghost is a being of ephemera, a sort of spiritual matter. As such, it has a "body" of sorts, but one that is insubstantial to material beings and things. For the purposes of forming this spiritual body, or Corpus, a ghost's Size is the same as it was at the time of death (5 for an adult human). Rather than Health, a ghost has Corpus dots that represent its spiritual essence. Corpus dots equals a ghost's Resistance + Size.

The only weapons with which a mortal can affect a ghost's Corpus are blessed or enchanted. Blessed items, bearing holy power, deliver aggravated damage to ghosts (see "Blessed Items," below). Some enchanted items (such as an ensorcelled baseball bat) might inflict bashing wounds, while others (a bewitched sword) could inflict lethal.

A ghost's Defense is applied against another ghost's assault. Its Defense trait is equal to its Power or Finesse, whichever is *higher*.

When ghosts or other spirits engage one another in combat, they deliver bashing damage (unless they have Numina that allow them to inflict lethal or aggravated damage). Roll Power + Finesse. Each success delivers one point of bashing damage to the target's Corpus. A ghost's Defense is applied against another ghost's assault.

Ghosts regenerate Corpus in the same amount of time that mortals heal damage (see p. 175). If a ghost suffers as many points of aggravated damage as it has Corpus dots, the ghost is destroyed.

Ghosts have other traits similar to a mortal's. A ghost's Initiative is equal to its Finesse + Resistance. Its Speed is equal to its Power + Finesse + 10 (species factor).

Ghosts have a Morality score and Virtues and Vices just like living characters do, reflecting spirits' sense of morality at the time of death. Ghosts are subject to de-generation just like mortals are (see Chapter 4: Advantages, p. 91), but unlike mortals, they cannot increase their Mortality scores. A ghost cannot grow or improve, only decline over the course of time.

Ghosts also possess a Willpower score (Power + Resistance) and Willpower points may be used for them just as they are for mortals. Ghosts regain Willpower by acting in accordance with their Virtues and Vices, just as living characters do. Additionally, they automatically regain one point of spent Willpower at the start of each day.

Finally, ghosts have Essence points that are spent to activate their Numina. Most ghosts can have up to 10 Essence points (truly old ghosts can have even more). Ghosts regain spent Essence at the rate of one per day when near their anchors. They can also regain Essence whenever they are remembered by the living, such as when someone lays flowers on their graves or — even more potent — if their ghostly form is identified by a living person. The Storyteller awards Essence whenever he thinks an appropriate instance of *momento mori* occurs.

The Nature of Ghosts

A ghost is an intangible spirit that exists in the physical world. A ghost with Finesse 1 or 2 is only aware of the area around its anchor (see below), while those with Finesse 3 or more can perceive the rest of their surroundings much as a mortal does.

Ghosts cannot be seen or felt by mortals unless a spirit makes a special effort to manifest (see below). Even when manifested, a ghost is an ethereal, insubstantial presence. Ghosts with a Power of 1 to 3 often appear as little more than an eerie, glowing mist or ball of light. Ghosts with a Power of 4 or 5 might seem as real and substantial as a living mortal — until someone tries to touch them. Ghosts pass effortlessly through solid objects, even when manifested. By the same token, they can't physically touch or manipulate physical objects unless they possess a specific power to do so (see "Numina"). They are immune to all types of mundane damage, and can see and hear clearly regardless of environmental conditions, whether in total darkness, fog or a raging storm.

Anchors

Ghosts linger in the physical world because something anchors them there, preventing them from continuing on to the spirit realm. Every ghost has at least one anchor rooting it to the physical world. Some powerful spirits may have more. The number and nature of a ghost's anchors depends on the individual and the circumstances surrounding its death. In most cases, an anchor is a physical place or object that held great emotional significance to the ghost during its mortal existence. An elderly woman who spent her last years largely confined to her bed might be anchored to the bedroom or to the bed itself. A man who carried a valuable pocket watch wherever he went might be a ghost anchored to the watch, haunting those who come to possess it. Occasionally, ghosts can be anchored to *people* rather than to objects. A father whose last thought was for the welfare of his children may be anchored to them, watching over them in death as he did in life. Or a woman murdered by a jilted lover may find her ghost anchored to him, sustained by a bitter desire for revenge.

Ghosts must remain close to their anchors at all times, whether they manifest or not. A ghost can travel up to 10 yards from its anchor per point of Power that it has. Thus, a ghost with 3 Power can travel up to 30 yards from its anchor. Ghosts anchored to a place instead of a person or object measure this distance from the spot where they died or from where a structure ends. A ghost with 3 Power whose anchor is a mansion can travel anywhere within the mansion, but only up to 30 yards away from the exterior of the building.

Anchors also make it easier for a ghost to manifest in the physical world. If a ghost is within one yard of its anchor it can manifest automatically with no roll required (see "Manifestations," below).

If a ghost has multiple anchors it can jump from one anchor to another with the expenditure of a single Willpower point, regardless of the distance between anchors. So, the father who lingers in the physical world to watch over his kids can jump from one child to another, even if they are on opposite sides of the world.

If a ghost's anchors are altered (subjected to sanctification or exorcism — see "Dealing with Ghosts") or destroyed, the ghost can no longer remain in the physical world. It passes on into the spirit realm and cannot return.

Manifestations

When a ghost wishes to interact with mortals or the physical world it must manifest, focusing its energies into a form just substantial enough to allow it a discernible presence. A ghostly manifestation doesn't necessarily have to be visible. A sentient ghost can choose to manifest invisibly if it wishes, but its presence still leaves traces that mortals can detect. Examples of invisible ghostly manifestation include cold spots, strange or intense odors and heightened magnetic fields.

Some areas are more conducive to supernatural energies than others. A graveyard is an extremely easy place for a ghost to manifest, while a laboratory often isn't. As a rule of thumb, locations where mortals frequently express powerful emotions — love, anger, sadness, fear — create conditions that allow a ghost easier access to the physical world. Sterile, emotionless places, or remote areas that have experienced little or no human emotion make it very difficult for a ghost to appear.

Curiously, the presence of mortals creates a cumulative effect that actually inhibits the manifestation of ghosts. This is apparently a phenomenon unique to the modern, scientific era, in which adults are conditioned to disbelieve instances of supernatural activity. The more people gathered in a particular location, the harder it is for a ghost to manifest.

Manifestation requires a successful Power + Finesse roll. Positive or negative modifiers may apply, depending on the location (see chart). If there is more than one mortal present, each person after the first imposes a -1 modifier to the roll. (This last penalty does not apply to other supernatural beings or creatures in the ghost's locale. Their numbers do not affect a ghost's ability to manifest.) If the roll succeeds, the ghost can manifest for the duration of the scene if it wishes. It can make itself visible or invisible at will, and can de-manifest at any time. If the roll fails, the ghost does not manifest and loses one Willpower point. The ghost can continue to attempt to manifest as long as it has at least one Willpower point remaining. If it exhausts all its Willpower it cannot attempt to manifest again until the following day.

Once a ghost has manifested it can attempt to interact with the physical world by communicating with any mortals present (see "Communication," below), or by drawing on its Numina.

Communication

Interaction with the living is difficult for ghosts, even under the best of conditions. Without the proper Numina, a manifested ghost has no voice. It can form words with its mouth and hope a mortal witness can read lips, or it can try to get its message across with gestures. Complicated gestures like sign language are very difficult for ghosts to perform, as they have a hard time translating their thoughts into physical motion. Make a Finesse roll for any such attempt with a -1 modifier for each decade that a ghost has been dead. If the roll fails, the spirit is simply unable to envision the right signs and gestures to get its point across. Simple gestures (motioning a mortal to follow, pointing to a hidden object) do not require a Finesse roll.

Ghosts with the proper Numina can communicate with mortals in a variety of ways, from speaking directly to writing on objects to imparting visions.

Types of Ghosts

Apparition

Background: Apparitions are the most common form of spirit, encountered in haunted places across the world. Typically the spirit of someone who met a sudden or violent death, or a lost soul that has become trapped in this world, an apparition has the power to terrify any mortals who encounter it.

Description: Apparitions can come in many forms, from shifting wisps of light to human forms nearly indistinguishable from the living. These spirits can bear telltale signs of death. The apparition of a murdered man might have bloodstains on his shirt. The victim of a plane crash may be burnt nearly beyond recognition.

Storytelling Hints: Apparitions are generally bound to their places of death, and may appear only when the time of their demise reoccurs (say, sundown each night). In many cases they don't interact with mortals at all, simply going through the motions of their previous existence, but some particularly angry ghosts vent their rage on the living if they can. In rare cases these spirits are capable of communicating with mortals, often trying to impart dire warnings or to prod an individual into solving the circumstances of their death.

Attributes: Power 2, Finesse 1, Resistance 2

Willpower: 4

Morality: 7

Virtue: Temperance

Vice: Envy

Initiative: 3

Defense: 2

Speed: 13 (species factor 10)

Size: 5

Corpus: 7

Numina: Choose one of Clairvoyance (dice pool 3), Magnetic Disruption (no roll required) or Terrify (dice pool 3)

Poltergeist

Background: The poltergeist, or "noisy ghost," is a spirit that makes its presence known by causing inexplicable sounds (footsteps, slamming doors) and by moving objects, sometimes violently. Plates fly across the room. Pens scrawl messages on notebooks or walls. In rare cases, mortal victims manifest bite marks or scratches all over their bodies. Sometimes these spirits are angry ghosts who have learned to use their powers to manipulate the physical world. Other times poltergeist activity seems to focus on an adolescent (usually a pre-teen or teenage girl) in a household, possibly suggesting a form of latent psychic power.

Description: Poltergeists are invisible entities that make their presence known by moving physical objects. Mortals occasionally witness glowing balls of light or glowing wisps of smoke, or more rarely see these beings on video recordings as fuzzy, humanoid shapes.

Storytelling Hints: Poltergeists can interact with the physical world only by acting on objects — almost always inanimate objects such as plates, glasses and furniture. Powerful poltergeists can affect living beings directly, punching or biting or hurling them across a room. These ghosts are capable of leaving messages written in a number of ways, but they are rarely interested in communication. Anger and violence are common hallmarks of the poltergeist, which can point researchers to signs of adolescent turmoil in the vicinity of the haunting.

Attributes: Power 3, Finesse 3, Resistance 2

Willpower: 5

Morality: 6

Virtue: Justice

Vice: Wrath

Initiative: 5

Defense: 3

Speed: 16 (species factor 10)

Size: 5

Corpus: 7

Numina: Ghost Sign (dice pool 6), Magnetic Disruption (no roll required) and Telekinesis (dice pool 6)

Page references in these summaries refer to the World of Darkness Rulebook

Deceiver

Background: A deceiver is a powerful, sentient spirit capable of terrifying (and even injuring) mortals by tricking them with potent illusions. These spirits can be the remnants of an older, more primitive time when human worship lent the beings greater power and insight into manipulating mortal thoughts. In rare cases, deceivers are the malevolent souls of powerful mortals bent on revenge for an injustice committed against them.

Description: Deceivers can assume any appearance they wish, taking the form of a mortal's loved one in one moment and appearing as a nightmarish monster the next. They typically prefer not to reveal themselves at all, relying on indirect illusions that range from the grossly obvious (blood running down walls) to the subtle (the victim fails to see the *Out of Order* sign as he steps into the elevator shaft).

Storytelling Hints: Deceivers are excellent antagonists for a classic ghost story, being able to create any image they wish in order to communicate with (or eliminate) their victims. Unlike apparitions, deceivers can communicate directly with mortals if they wish, through written messages or freakish illusions (a crosswalk sign flashes from "walk" to "run"), or simply by speaking through an illusory form. In many cases these ghosts are malicious entities, delighting in terrorizing or harming victims in retaliation for some past wrong. Others use their power to seek vengeance against specific enemies. The ghost of a boy murdered by local police might visit his own form of justice on those who killed him. Occasionally these spirits are benevolent entities, using their power to shield the innocent and coming to their aid with overt or subtle messages.

Attributes: Power 4, Finesse 4, Resistance 3
Willpower: 7
Morality: 4
Virtue: Fortitude
Vice: Envy
Initiative: 7
Defense: 4
Speed: 18 (species factor 10)
Size: 5
Corpus: 8
Numina: Ghost Sign (dice pool 8), Phantasm (dice pool 8) and Terrify (dice pool 8)

Skinrider

Background: Skinriders are rare and very powerful spirits that can possess the bodies of living people. These spirits are nearly always malevolent (some say demonic). They use their power to sate physical urges denied them by their intangible forms, or to inflict suffering on victims.

Description: Skinriders occasionally appear as glowing, insubstantial forms that flow like smoke over or into the bodies of their victims. Possession victims can show clear signs of being under supernatural control. Their eyes turn gray and milky or their skin takes on an unearthly pallor. Sometimes a ghost is powerful or subtle enough to operate without revealing itself, unless it is angered or frustrated.

Storytelling Hints: Skinriders are almost always evil spirits that force their will onto defenseless mortals to fulfill their desires. They enjoy taunting victims, and choose vessels who will suffer the greatest from the consequences of forced actions. A vengeful spirit could also attempt to possess a mortal body if the object of its revenge is nearby.

Attributes: Power 5, Finesse 4, Resistance 5
Willpower: 10
Morality: 3
Virtue: Justice
Vice: Wrath
Initiative: 9
Defense: 5
Speed: 19 (species factor 10)
Size: 5
Corpus: 10
Numina: Animal Control (dice pool 9), Compulsion (dice pool 9), Ghost Speech (dice pool 9), Possession (dice pool 9) and Terrify (dice pool 9)

Page references in these summaries refer to the World of Darkness Rulebook

Chapter 1: Dust to Dust

By Chuck Wendig

Summary

Sometimes, it's not just people who die, but places. When people die and leave unfinished business, sometimes a part of their souls linger behind as ghosts. From time to time, however, a place has a purpose too, and sometimes that purpose can't be realized because the place perishes before its time. Should that happen, part of the locale's spirit stays behind, much like a person's soul might, and the result is no different: a restless ghost.

This scenario is meant to take a handful of mortal, mundane characters (be they family members, vacationers or disparate individuals) and usher them through a horror story featuring one of America's ghost towns, a gutted mining center called Fort Assumption. This dead town isn't just abandoned, though. Its very spirit remains, lingering in madness and unresolved anger.

This story is meant to provide less of a linear plot laid out for you and more a toolbox of plot elements from which to create your own scenario. You're free to run with events as presented or you can change them to suit different ideas or the needs of particular players.

And I will show you something different from either

Your shadow at morning striding behind you

Or your shadow at evening rising to meet you;

I will show you fear in a handful of dust.

— T.S. Eliot, "The Wasteland"

Variant Locations

Fort Assumption is the default location for this story. It's a ghost town located somewhere in the American West. Where exactly the place is located is up to you. It could be a derelict setting in Colorado, Nevada, Texas or any other western location that feels appropriate and comfortable.

And yet, you're certainly free to think outside the box. The story could theoretically be told in any number of unexpected locations and still maintain its mood of both fearful alienation and loneliness. Ghost towns are more prevalent in the West, but can be found in every state and even in other countries. Eastern ghost towns are possible, perhaps created when a local mill went bust.

Actually, nothing says the setting has to be an abandoned town at all. It could be a single building (say, a forsaken factory, a deserted hotel or a condemned housing project). While the default setting is an out-of-the-way rural place, it's possible that you could set it in an urban location. Most major cities offer rundown, vacant sites, from fire-gutted warehouse districts to old industrial complexes. Any of these could be the location for such a "bad place" with its own lingering ghosts.

It's up to you to modify the details of this scenario to suit whatever location you choose. Provided the core elements are kept — that the characters are isolated in a "dead" place that somehow seems "alive" — the story can be told from practically any vantage point.

Motives

Players can create characters for this scenario based on any number of premises, some of which require the characters to know one another, some of which do not.

Players who want to create characters who are already familiar with each other have several options. This story requires characters to come across (and become trapped in) an abandoned ghost town. Several concepts play into such a scenario. Characters may be:

• Family members or friends traveling together on vacation. Perhaps they stray too far from the highway looking for gas or tourist attractions and come across the ghost town.

• A group of family members or friends moving cross-country. While it's possible that the group seeks tourist attractions off the beaten path, it's more likely that members are in search of gas, food or lodging.

• A group of reporters, journalists or other media figures who have come to produce a book, story or documentary based on America's ghost towns (Fort Assumption being one stop among many).

Alternately, you and the players may wish to run this game featuring a number of characters who have never met before. Such disparate groups are quite common to horror stories and fiction in general (see films such as *Identity* or *Twelve Angry Men*), and make for good conflict and tale resolution. Players have several character-creation options from which to choose:

• Travelers come separately to the town, drawn together with an eerie synchronicity and trapped within hours of each other. Possible lures are the enticement of a night's stay at a motel, a good meal or even a bizarre confluence of missed turns and deceptive highway markers.

• It's possible that the characters each look for someone (a friend, loved one or even an old enemy) who has gone missing — and their separate investigations lead them all to the ghost town.

• For increased creep factor, the characters go to sleep one night in their respective homes and wake up in the ghost town, completely unaware of where they are and how they got there. *Further* creep factor emerges later (probably by viewing graves at the cemetery). The characters are all descendents of people who died in the town almost a century ago.

Preliminary Events

Every story has build-up events that draw characters into a drama.

Getting There

The characters must get to Fort Assumption somehow. The general idea is that the town itself unconsciously draws them, hungry for the presence of living things. How this lure actually manifests is up to you. Most likely, characters come to town willingly. Vacationers could see a strange, rusty sign along the highway indicating "Just 17 mi. to Fort Assumption!" and may purposefully go there hoping for an obscure treat. More investigative characters (such as the aforementioned reporters or people look-

ing for missing loved ones) may come to town in an effort to uncover some kind of truth.

No matter the means, the town attracts the characters without them realizing what's happening, meaning that some may arrive at Fort Assumption quite accidentally. The town's dark power has surprising reach and could easily exert its will to (likely through the Phantasm Numen; **World of Darkness Rulebook**, p. 212) change road signs or highway markers to make characters *think* they're on the right track. In truth, they head down a dead-end strip of interstate that takes them right to Fort Assumption. If you don't want to invoke the town's trickery just yet, it's possible that characters simply make a mistake and arrive unintentionally, perhaps by taking a wrong turn.

While not a requirement, it's recommended that characters come to Fort Assumption during the day. The town may seem somewhat spooky and unsettling, but not overtly so. Having characters show up during daylight hours allows the story to build toward horror slowly. When the sun sets, the characters probably don't have much light by which to see. All the better for evoking a sense of isolation and helplessness.

Stranded

Once characters wind up in the ghost town, the plot requires that they be stranded. (The story isn't very scary if characters retain the option of simply getting in the car and driving away at any time.) How they become stranded is up to you. It could be the result of minor, mundane hazards. Say, the car is out of gas or a tire blows after driving over a sharp rock. Major events could also strand the characters. Anything from a bridge collapsing into a gorge to a bad sand or dust storm that keeps the group under cover.

The town itself also has the power to keep characters trapped. Use of the Magnetic Disruption Numen (**World of Darkness**, p. 211) causes automobiles to malfunction, and Phantasm may show characters (albeit falsely) that the bridge is out or that the aforementioned storm prevents anyone from leaving. Finally, town resident Donnie Pritchard (see p. 46) may try to keep characters around. He could shoot out tires, or for a more subtle threat might spread a bunch of nails or other sharp objects across the road to lance a car's tires.

Unless the nature of the stranding is extreme, characters may not want to leave town immediately. A ghost town could seem kind of cool for a little while, enough to warrant an hour or two of curious exploration. Places like the old church, post office and farmhouse might be fascinating for one or all of the characters.

Of course, whether immediately or eventually, some characters will want to leave town at any cost. Ultimately, they *can't* leave, but you walk a fine line in making that reality clear. You probably don't want to flat-out tell players that their characters can't leave — players are in control and should be allowed to make any and all attempts that they like. You may therefore want to make such efforts seem possible but undesirable. After all, walking out under the hot desert sun (or cold desert night) for a dozen or more miles is dangerous, especially when another car will *surely* come along sooner or later, right? (Wrong, but the characters don't know that.) Travelers may also have their own rations of food (or may find some in town, either old canned goods or soda bottles at the farmhouse, or Donnie's personal stash) that keep them comfortable enough to be resigned to wait for help to arrive *eventually*.

Or you may opt for more extreme measures to keep characters from escaping. Roads may double back on themselves or *seem* to lead away in a straight line when they somehow bring travelers right back to Fort Assumption. Or you could impose the physical barriers — dust storm, rainstorm, destroyed bridge — discussed above to keep characters trapped.

Or you may let characters leave. Allow them to walk away and get picked up 15 miles away by a trucker. You should introduce a reason for going back to Fort Assumption, though. A lost item of value, a family member left behind, or inescapable nightmares that seem to beckon characters to return to the place.

In the Beginning

The timetable for this scenario is flexible, depending primarily on when characters feel threatened or inquisitive enough to become proactive in dealing with the strange town of Fort Assumption. What follows are some ideas for small-yet-disturbing trigger events that lead into

the larger story. It's suggested that these episodes take place over the course of the first day, first night and second day, with the larger events (below) beginning at the start of the second night in town. If, however, you feel that characters need stronger motive to remain invested in the place, you can step up this escalation.

• Characters find signs of Donnie Pritchard's presence. They probably shouldn't actually *see* Donnie, but do find some indication of human presence. Characters may find his stash of food (and potentially a half-empty box of .30-30 ammunition) in one of the abandoned buildings. Or more subtle signs may turn up, such as footprints (leading them to wonder if the prints are very old or actually their own), or maybe a few globs of drying tobacco spit around town.

• During their first restless night, characters hear the distant squeals and grunts of a dozen or more hogs. The sounds come from the direction of the farmhouse and its wooden fencing out back. But when characters get close, the sounds stop and no animals can be found. (For added fear factor, if players make successful Wits + Composure rolls, characters spot shadows in the darkness moving as pigs might. Shedding any light on the subject immediately eliminates the silhouettes.) The pigs are the domain of the Pig Farmer (see p. 37).

• Characters are confronted by the presence of strange — but very *real* — animals. Perhaps after investigating one of the handful of still-standing structures in town, characters step back outside to be confronted by a few dozen big crows or vultures, all of which seem to be watch-

Jim Di Bartolo

ing their emergence from the building. The desert is also home to a number of coyotes, many of which prowl the perimeter of the town at night. Their eyes seem to glow an unnatural red. These coyotes do not attack characters yet, unless directly provoked. Other events might include a plague of flies that descends upon the town for five or 10 minutes, a similar plague of bats at night, or several rattlesnakes traveling together (which snakes generally don't do).

• At some point during the first 24 hours, characters hear children crying softly in the schoolhouse. Characters investigating the schoolhouse exterior may see a presence at one of the smashed windows, and it disappears quickly. (Ideally, only one character senses this presence and the rest are either unable or aren't present.) Inside the single-room schoolhouse, characters find no children, only empty and crumbling slate-topped desks. To intensify the creepiness of this situation, you may decide that someone has composed some poorly hand-written messages on one or more of the slate tops. Messages such as, "Welcome home" and "My children."

• Characters investigating the town are likely to come across the graveyard at the far end. The cemetery is raised on a small knoll of sand, scrub and sage. It bears 53 graves, each of which is nothing more than a big rock with a name and dates carved into its flattest surface. One grave at the far side of the hill differs from the rest. It has an actual headstone (albeit a small and crumbling one) and shows the name Esme Pritchard, with the dates 1890 – 1919. Successful Wits + Investigation rolls may allow characters to notice that the majority of graves (at least 80% of them) show 1919 as the date of death. Also, each grave marked "1919" (with the exception of Esme Pritchard's) has a word painted below the name and dates. It's either "Murder" or "Suicide." Counting these reveals 33 murders and seven suicides. Characters investigating the graveyard may also be subject to odd feelings, sensations that almost indicate a bad cold or sickness coming on. A character may be tight in the chest, become dizzy, start coughing or even exhibit a sudden fever or urge to vomit. These symptoms diminish about 20 to 30 minutes after leaving the graveyard, and are lingering spectral manifestations of the plague that once loomed over the town.

• Going to the sheriff's office could provide further clues as to what happened to the town. Upon first look, characters note the building is a combination small office with a desk and an old safe, what appears to be a dilapidated courtroom (seating no more than six or seven people, judge included), and two empty jail cells with rusted bars. You're encouraged to insert any details that make this place as spooky as possible, such as fingernail marks or handprints on the cell walls, the reflected face of "somebody" in one of the windows (that somebody being the ghost of Sheriff Pritchard), or just a general smell of rot and decay.

The significant clues found in this building aren't obvious, and are in fact underground. Under the sheriff's desk is a wooden trapdoor, concealed in shadow. If characters find this now, fine. If they don't, perhaps steer them toward it later through a vision or a Wits + Investigation roll made on their behalf. Physical clues indicating the presence of the door might include the silhouette of the trapdoor itself or a variance in the levels of dust and sand on the floor beneath the desk. (Alternatively, you may want to wait to reveal this room later, exposing the presence of the hole through an ongoing search or perhaps by having a character's ring/watch/coin drop and roll under the desk.)

The "room" below the trapdoor is hardly that. It's nothing more than a human-sized niche carved out of the ground, dug by past sheriffs as a bolt-hole in case criminals escaped or ran rampant. Within, characters find a human skeleton draped in unrecognizable garments. What *is* recognizable is the five-star badge pinned to its clothing. (This is the sheriff's skeleton.) In the right hand is a five-shot, .32-caliber, top-break revolver. The mouth of the skeleton hangs open and a hole extends from the top of its skull down through the jaw.

Tucked under the skeleton, in its left hand, is a book. The pages are weathered and decaying. Picking up the book looses the pages from their binding. It's a criminal log book, detailing the sparse crimes of Fort Assumption from the years 1910 to 1919. Up until the very end, the crimes were mundane (stealing a head-lamp, drunken assault, fraud). It's toward the end that the sheriff inserts personal notes and goes on briefly about that "rapist savage," and later about "the pox" that everyone seems to have. The sheriff's last scrawled words are something to the effect of, "That goddam savage cursed us all with this disease, even Esme. He'll make his peace in Hell, but now he's dragging us all down with him. I had to do what I had to do to make things right. Now I have to do one more thing. Lord rest our weary souls." (See below for the full story of Sheriff Pritchard.)

Buildings

Most ghost towns feature only a small number of extant structures, and Fort Assumption is no different. The town probably features five to 12 dilapidated buildings, with a number of other crumbled ruins around the circumference of the settlement. Most of these buildings line the remains of a single "main street." They include a church, schoolhouse and sheriff's office. Further outside of town is a single remaining farmhouse and at the opposite end is the graveyard. Also present are the faint remains of an old fort (hence the name of the town). Such a frontier fort was once walled with little more than wooden fenceposts. Need for it passed long ago and most of its materials were recycled to make the town itself. Any other buildings beyond these are up to you to include.

Nightmares

One final option that you may exercise to establish tension early on is to confront characters with bad dreams or waking visions. Note that such nightmares are not the basis of any mechanical system; they are not the domain of ghosts or ghost towns, but are purely a narrative tool that you may use to convey both cryptic hints about the problem at hand and to heighten characters' fear. Nightmare imagery can be inspired by any of the story hooks or plot details featured in this scenario. You're encouraged to come up with your visions, as long as they don't reveal any genuine facts or truths outright. Any pertinent details should be revealed through hints or be cloaked in metaphor. Some examples include:

• Townsfolk lynching a dark-skinned man (possibly a Native American). A thick knot of flies and maggots vomits from his mouth moments before he's dropped and his neck snaps.

• A dream filled with darkness and a cacophony of sounds ranging from hogs squealing, children screaming and people coughing violently.

• Fort Assumption is revealed as it once was, before time and death sank it into ruin. (Even here, the town shouldn't be vibrant, but already falling down, with a gray pall hanging over everything.) Nobody seems to be around and most doors of the town are marked with red X's.

• Staccato-burst images of several men, women and children being shot in the head. Like the roll of a snare drum, these images come hard and fast. You may want this nightmare to be silent or punctuated by out-of-synch gunshots.

What Does the Town Want?

Fort Assumption, as a ghost, is a character all its own. All characters want something. So what is it that the town wants?

It's important to remember that the town is not the specter of a human. Its soul is literally that of a place. While it does have moments of mortal consciousness due to the many people that lived there so many decades ago, it ultimately thinks more abstractly than a human being does. The town probably doesn't *know* what it wants, but that doesn't mean it doesn't have cravings and desires.

Assumption's yearning should be both horrific and sympathetic. Its base urge is to cause fear and death, because it understands these emotions best of all and can inspire them with ease. In fact, the town literally feeds off these emotions, gaining a single point of Essence when it successfully evokes fear in a living being. (See p. 44 for more information on this phenomenon.) Yet, the town causes fear and pain more as an instinct than as a concerted action.

What else does the town want? It wants either to be laid to rest or to be allowed to flourish once again. Neither of these feats is easy to accomplish and the town itself has little idea how to achieve them. For characters seeking to fulfill either, refer to "Putting Things Right."

Jim Di Bartolo

Outside Town

Characters are sure to wander. Whether they look for a viable exit or simply explore their surroundings (or the walls of their cage, depending on one's perspective), they are sure to wander outside of town. Obviously, characters can find anything that you want, but two places in particular are significant.

The first is the Babyhead Silver Mine, located next to a dried-up creek called Babyhead Creek. The mine entrance is a ramshackle lean-to of tin sheets and collapsing wooden beams. The door to the mine has a rusted lock on it — and that lock is broken and open. Entering the mine is hazardous. Not only is it utterly dark, but to descend one has to use either the hand-crank elevator (a claustrophobic, rusty cage that can hold only two to three people because there's a broken down, heavy mine cart aboard), or climb down the elevator shaft on a rotten wooden ladder. The mine itself is a tangle of unlit tunnels, pits, cave-ins and fractured cart track. (Most of these features are described on p. 41.) Characters may find — if they go as deep as the mine allows — a wall of tightly packed rocks that, if destroyed, gives way to a small niche where a skeleton remains and where veins of black rock striate the walls. Written spectrally in a dry, red-black substance on a nearby wall are the words, *"Here lies the bloody bones of the rapist Walking Cloud."* (See p. 39 for more information of Walking Clouds remains as an anchor for the town's spirit.)

The second thing characters might find about a mile outside of town is an Isuzu pick-up truck covered with a tarp and roughly hidden behind some trees and cacti. There's no license plate and no identification in the cab. The doors are unlocked, and the bed and passenger seat are filled with supplies. Such supplies include bulk foods that don't spoil in the heat, ammunition for a .30-30 rifle, a sleeping bag, a few changes of clothes for an adult male, some rope and various and sundry other goods. This is, of course, Donnie Pritchard's truck. He has the keys. The town lets him come and go, because he's sworn to serve it. Thus, he's able to go out into the world, get food and supplies, and return.

Characters may try to hotwire the truck (roll Wits + Crafts + any bonuses for tools used). If they get it running, it's likely that Fort Assumption itself or Donnie tries to stop them, likely using the methods outlined above to get characters there in the first place. (Donnie may shoot out the tires, for example, or the town may invoke a Phantasm to cause the characters to drive into and get stuck in a gully.) Even if characters don't face such opposition, driving through the desert isn't simple. The attempt requires a Wits + Drive roll, with a –3 penalty under such poor driving conditions.

The truck itself is far enough outside of town that characters may feel that continuing to walk may get them somewhere. They're in for a harsh lesson, though. Beyond the truck, there isn't much else besides rock, saguaro cacti and a lot of dirt and dust. Characters who try to walk *too* far out may invoke Intelligence + Survival rolls to find

their way back (or to find water or shelter). You may even need to resort to the Deprivation (**World of Darkness**, p. 175), Fatigue (p. 179) and/or Temperature Extremes (p. 181) rules.

Rising Action

At this point, which should be at least a full day after getting stranded in town, worse things happen as the characters' surroundings fully awaken to their presence. The town actively attempts to affect the newcomers, whether to communicate or harm them — or likely both. At this stage, characters should have little idea that the town itself is a presence. Instead, Fort Assumption makes its spirit known through "proxy ghosts" (see below). Characters are likely to assume that these are the problem, not the town itself.

Characters are also likely to want to get as far away from town as possible. Like before, don't stop them from making the attempt, but such efforts are extremely challenging. The same problems discussed previously apply, or you may wish to apply alternative ones. Perhaps traveling too far out of town means that those red-eyed coyotes attack, or the sun is so hot that characters get dizzy and their skin blisters.

Characters are likely to try all manner of tricks to stay safe and sane. Feel free to condone such efforts, but reward them with only limited results. Does a character have a cell phone and does it work? Probably, but only to a limited degree. Conversations are erratic and broken up, and any time a character tells someone her location, the other person claims he, "Couldn't make out the name." The radio in the characters' car might work, but again only sporadically. Same with any electronic device, really, even flashlights and GPS devices. What happens if a character with a high Crafts dots fixes a car? Let him. When driving away, the car breaks down again or weirder still, the highway leads right back to Fort Assumption. Most efforts should point to one fact: The group is undeniably stranded. If the characters are going to get out with their minds and bodies intact, they have to figure out what's going on and try to stop it.

Sheriff Pritchard's Ghost

After the first day, the town's only *human* ghost (i.e., not one of Fort Assumption's "proxy spirits") makes its presence known. It's the spirit of Sheriff Dyer Pritchard, the last surviving inhabitant of the town. That is, before he put a bullet through the roof of his mouth.

The sheriff's story is, for the most part, the town's story; both are inexorably tied.

Fort Assumption reached its height around the turn of the 20th century, which was to say it boasted around 200 people who worked a moderately successful mine (the Babyhead Silver Mine, about two miles south of town). Pritchard became sheriff at a relatively young age, about 22. Thereupon he met his bride to be, a 15-year-old named Esme. They had a child who would eventually leave town to work on the construction of oil wells a hundred miles away.

Over the next 20 years, the town underwent a steady decline. Any successes it won were short-lived as the silver veins dwindled. It didn't help that the town was subject to droughts and dust storms, either. The population fell to a quarter its original number and never recovered.

During the decline, few townsfolk were willing to work the mine, so foreigners were shipped in for a few weeks at a time, mostly Chinese immigrants and displaced Native Americans. One of these Indians was a Kiowa named Henry Walking Cloud, who soon developed a fleeting tryst with the sheriff's wife. Pritchard discovered Esme's infidelity, but was unable to accept her complicity in it, only that she had been "raped" by the "savage." Thus, Pritchard led Walking Cloud into the deepest part of the mine at gunpoint, pistol whipped him, and sealed the man up behind a makeshift wall of rock.

It was only a month later that an unusual outbreak of smallpox spread throughout Fort Assumption. Some escaped; most were afflicted. Curiously, Esme Pritchard caught the disease, but her husband did not. Some died by disease, but most died by the hand of Sheriff Pritchard. Unwilling to see his town suffer needlessly, and believing the pox to be a curse from the man he condemned (whether it actually was is up to you), Pritchard went around one night shooting the townsfolk. Some fought him and a few were able to escape his revolver. A few killed themselves. But most died from the sheriff's bullets.

Pritchard didn't shoot his wife, though. He choked her with his bare hands, believing it the most "loving" way he could send her to her maker. Not long afterward, the sheriff wrote his last journal entry, crawled into the bolt-hole under his desk, and shot himself.

The key thing to understand about Pritchard's living days is that he loved the town, loved the residents and refused to give up on them. Mind you, none of that stood in the way of being capable of tremendous hatred and jealousy. Enough so that he killed out of malice or "kindness."

What's important to remember now that Pritchard is dead is that his love for the town is similarly extinguished, having been replaced with a single-minded revulsion for Fort Assumption. His ghost isn't capable of much rational thought, and it regards the town as a harbor of sickness and death.

What does this mean for the characters? It's likely that Pritchard initially endeavors to scare them away. Of course, the characters are stranded and can't leave. Should they take a course of action that seems to aid the town in any way (such as attempting to rebuild or go into the mine to find Walking Cloud's bones), the sheriff's actions may become more pronounced, overtly attempting to harm. Other options include:

• The sheriff sees the characters as a chance to finally put the town to rest. He may attempt to affect them with his Numina (Compulsion or Ghost Sign) in hopes of having them destroy the remaining buildings. Or, he may be unwilling to take this step because the town itself

Jim Di Bartolo

serves as one of his anchors. He may even resort to a maddening practice such as encouraging characters to destroy the town, and then standing in their way and trying to harm them when they help.

• Anytime one of the town's "proxy ghosts" appears, the sheriff may not be far behind, as he potentially seeks to destroy these spectral puppets. This shouldn't play out as a visible battle of spirits; characters shouldn't ever bear witness to such obvious displays of supernatural combat. Such scenes should be played out subtly, with proxy spirits making cryptic comments such as, "He's coming for me!" or "He'll murder us all again!" before screaming in agony and dematerializing. After such an event, players might make successful Wits + Composure rolls for characters to glimpse the sheriff's face reflected momentarily in a nearby window, on the face of a wristwatch or in the lenses of a pair of sunglasses.

• Pritchard may try to turn characters against each other. He could choose one to turn against the others in a kind of replay (or mockery) of how he killed the remaining townsfolk. The sheriff is likely to choose what he perceives to be the weakest among the characters and focus on that individual to make her paranoid and fearful. Uses of Compulsion and Clairvoyance go a long way in that effort. Such use should brief, though. Overuse blunts the effect. Pritchard recognizes that subtlety is the key to breaking a character's will. Characters duly affected should be encouraged to play out a building paranoia. If a victim ignores or defies Pritchard's efforts, her player may have to spend Willpower points to represent such resilience.

How characters react to the sheriff's presence is up to them. If they wish to communicate, does he offer limited response? Or does he only threaten and attempt to harm them? If they in turn seek to destroy him, it probably requires some kind of assault on or alteration of his anchors. (These anchors and tips on their discovery are addressed on p. 39.)

Another important question is how does Sheriff Pritchard deal with his still-living descendent, Donnie? It could go one of two ways. The sheriff remains hidden from Donnie, recognizing that he's a blood relative and believing that any errors in judgment that Donnie makes are because of the town itself. Or, the sheriff actively opposes Donnie, seeing his kin's actions as unconscious betrayal and doing everything possible to undermine the living man's efforts (which may even mean helping the characters). The characters and players should motivate most story developments in town, but if events need a boost, a conflict between the two Pritchards could provide further mystery.

If by some means the characters deal with the sheriff early, somehow removing his influence or diminishing his presence, they can learn that there's more at work here than just Pritchard's restless spirit. He may go away, but the town intensifies any assault on the characters. Obviously, matters remain that need to be put to rest.

Holy Protection

This story is meant to expose ordinary folks to the ghostly side of the World of Darkness, providing them with little to no supernatural help. As vulnerable human beings, the characters are meant to triumph thanks to will and cunning, not thanks to magical weapons or *deus ex machina* ("help from above.")

That said, it's always possible that players could get in over their heads, or you intend to reveal to characters that while supernatural evil exists, so does supernatural good (albeit to a lesser degree). You may therefore want to arm characters with holy tools approximately halfway through the game. You have various options from which to choose. Perhaps the church offers a place of solace, where characters can't be touched or affected by any ghostly powers. Maybe characters discover some kind of abjuration or exorcism ritual in the church (hidden in a rotting hymnal or buried beneath a floorboard). It's even possible that such a ritual exists, because someone had to banish Henry Walking Cloud's spirit long ago and used these reverent tools to do so. Or perhaps the church is home to a cross or some other relic (femur bone of a Mexican nun?) that is capable of doing physical harm on the Corpus of ghosts or the town's proxies. See the **World of Darkness Rulebook**, p. 213, for rules on exorcising, abjuring and attacking ghosts with mystical weapons.

Donnie Pritchard

Donnie is a very real, very human presence in Fort Assumption. As an antagonist, he serves multiple purposes. Donnie puts a "human" face on what's happening, allowing characters to interpret the situation with him as a touchstone. Characters may initially assume that the source of seemingly supernatural events is actually nothing more than a mundane, demented prankster. (This "insight" shouldn't diminish characters' fear, though. Being caught in an abandoned town with a potential maniac is no more comforting than being caught with ghosts or monsters.) And yet, characters eventually encounter things that *cannot* be explained away through Donnie, forcing them to re-evaluate circumstances with Donnie as *part* of the supernatural.

Donnie's story is relatively straightforward. He's the blood relative — several generations removed — of Sheriff Pritchard and school marm Esme Pritchard. He's in his 30s and has lived a life fraught with dismal efforts and ill-founded plans. For the most part, he's a failure as a human being, desperate for some kind of purpose.

All his life, Donnie has experienced nightmares about Fort Assumption. He didn't realize early on just what he saw, he simply had visions of pain and suffering in some place out in the scrub lands. Every year the dreams got worse until they were unbearable and Donnie was hardly able to sleep more than an hour before waking in sweat-drenched sheets. Following clues and images put together from his visions, Donnie was able to get himself to Fort Assumption.

Once he was there, the town revealed itself to Donnie bit by bit, slowly chipping away at his already unsteady mind (see sidebar for the optional Numen Dement). While whittling away at Donnie's sanity, the town also used its powers to show him that he was "chosen" to help it. Donnie partly understood what he was to do, but helping the town was more than a one-man job. (After all, even he had come to realize that he lacked most of the salient capabilities required in life.) The town promised help.

Donnie has now lived in town for over a year. The place allows him to leave to get supplies, and he has been "planning" for the eventual visit of stranded individuals to put to work toward his mission. He's been establishing traps, finding good sniper spots (potentially granting him a bonus of +1 or +2 when firing his rifle), and getting very little sleep.

You get to decide just how deranged Donnie is. The default degree of his personal darkness is set pretty high, the assumption being that characters are not the first ones with whom he's dealt. The others didn't "make the grade," though, being killed and their bodies hidden around town (or left for the coyotes to pick apart). Characters can come across the bones or discarded gear of these victims. Other questions remain in regard to Donnie's evil. Did he rape any women lured to town in an effort to "repopulate?" Is he willing to do the same to the characters? Is he unwilling to take that extra step to serve the town in whatever inhuman capacity it demands? Or is there some part of him that remains sane and salvageable? The best way to gauge his state is to measure the players' characters. Would they be appalled by him? Intrigued? Could they sympathize?

Donnie can be used in a multitude of ways, depending on what you want to achieve.

• He may serve as only a distant participant in events, staying far enough away from the characters to be seen but still remain a mystery. (If they try to leave town, they spot him some 400 yards away in the heat haze. When they call to him, he runs. Or when they're investigating one of the buildings, they see him outside the window. When they try to find him, he's gone.)

• Donnie may remain distant, but set physical traps for the characters in an effort to "hobble" them and keep them in town. His tricks might include rusty coyote traps or maybe a pit-trap inside one of the buildings, concealed by a few weakened floorboards. His traps aren't meant to be lethal. Donnie doesn't want to kill the characters, only keep them local.

• Rather than set physical traps, Donnie may "test" the characters. Challenges would be moral or physical in nature. He's looking for "good, strong people" to help him fix and repopulate the town, the irony being that he himself is neither morally good nor physically strong. Moral tests might include leaving a bag of chips or a soda out in the open — only enough for one or two characters. Do the characters share or does one covertly or overtly take it all for himself? Or Donnie might steal something from one character while she's sleeping (usually something valuable like a food item, car keys or picture of a loved one) and put it somewhere so it appears that another character stole it. Physical tests could be anything from the aforementioned traps to putting heavy obstacles in the group's way. Characters who fail Donnie's tests may be silently marked for destruction. Characters who pass — those who are greedy, who survive, and who are strong — may be kidnapped at gunpoint in an attempt to employ them in a way that "best serves the town."

Again, much of this comes down to how much of a threat you intend Donnie to be. Characters may find hints of his horrific abuses before actually meeting him. They may discover the sexually abused and assaulted bodies of a family of three dropped down the mineshaft. It's even possible that Donnie keeps one or two other "guests" alive somewhere, whether in the mine or somewhere near his truck. Or Donnie's actions may make him an enemy of the sheriff, especially if the ghost views his descendant as a rapist, much like Walking Cloud was a "rapist."

• Donnie may not attempt any tests or traps, but simply steps out and tries to hold characters at gunpoint in hopes of having them do his bidding. He puts them to work fixing up the town or going to the mine to continue extracting silver. Donnie has practically no knowledge on the subjects of carpentry, repair or mining, which quickly becomes evident when he gives orders.

Any and all of these techniques can be used to establish Donnie as an antagonist. Characters can deal with him in any way they see fit, and shouldn't be restricted in doing so. Donnie isn't exactly sane, but nor is he an insurmountable foe. If he attempts to kidnap characters, they may gain the upper hand by jumping or outwitting him. That's fine, because they gain a source of information (albeit an unstable one) as a result. If he tries to run, rolls should be allowed for characters to catch him. If they overcome Donnie, the characters (and players) have to decide how far they're willing to go with him. Is threatening him acceptable? Beating? Torturing? Murdering?

Donnie doesn't know anything about the sheriff's ghost. It wasn't the sheriff who summoned him to Fort Assumption, but the town itself. In many ways, the crazed man is as subject to the town's mystery as the characters are, and he shouldn't have all the answers. Should the newcomers discover the connection between Donnie and the dead sheriff, they could leverage compliance or actions from the descendant. Donnie may not believe at first, but a convincing argument coupled with evidence (such as the items under the trapdoor in the sheriff's office) could break Donnie's will to resist.

How much does the man actually knows about the town's mysteries? He likely doesn't know local history, despite the dreams he's had. As mentioned, he probably doesn't know his own connection to the place, much less the truth about the crimes committed there. He stands to learn things from the characters, but by listening to him and to the descriptions of his insane dreams and experiences, characters may intuit what's really going on, and more importantly get insights into how to stop or free the town's spirit.

Optional Numen: Dement

You may decide that this Numen has been used to mold Donnie into an obsessive-compulsive sycophant of Fort Assumption. Alternatively, Donnie could have been sufficiently imbalance before, foregoing the need for this power.

This Numen assaults a person's mind with a cavalcade of nightmarish imagery, breaking down his sanity in the process. Such images are often personal and culled from a victim's own memory, although the user sometimes applies images from its own history or "memory" to decide such visions.

Use of Dement is a contested action, with opposing rolls being made reflexively. Spend one Essence and roll Power + Finesse versus the victim's Intelligence + Composure.

Roll Results

Dramatic Failure: The power can't be used against the same target again for a week. If a dramatic failure is rolled for the target, no contested rolls are allowed against other applications for a week.

Failure: The most or an equal number of successes are rolled for the target. The power has no effect on him, but successive attempts are possible.

Success: The most successes are rolled for the town or spirit. The victim gains a mild derangement of the Storyteller's choice (see **World of Darkness Rulebook**, p. 96) for a number of days equal to the successes rolled.

Exceptional Success: The most — five or more — successes are rolled for the town or spirit. A mild derangement is inflicted upon the victim *permanently*, or a severe one is imposed for a number of days equal to successes rolled. A permanent disability may be overcome only through prolonged treatment.

Suggested Equipment: Intended target already has a mild (+1) or severe (+2) derangement, target has a Morality of 5 or 6 (+1) or lower (+2)

Possible Penalties: Intended target currently under mental care (-3), target has the Meditative Mind Merit (-2)

Dement can be used successfully on a victim only once per week. Its range is variable, perhaps as far as a number of miles equal to its user's Power dots, or a distance determined by the Storyteller.

Fort Assumption

Remember that the town is a character unto itself, and that isn't a metaphor. It's literally the restless and angry spirit of a dead town, and it acts with its own bizarre motives. At this stage in the game, it's important to show the disconnection between what's really going on and the current "known" roster of antagonists, meaning that characters should begin to note that things simply don't add up. They may know about the sheriff's ghost and Donnie, yet other inexplicable events occur. Don't give away too much information, though. You may want to offer just enough clues to encourage characters to dig up the truth on their own, without being hand fed the reality. If they seem to flounder, they could be given a hint. If they make it through the whole game without ever knowing all the facts (which is unlikely), then so be it. No rule says characters have to be fully informed at some point. The less informed they are, the scarier the scenario is!

That said, here are a few ideas to help you present the town as an entity without ever coming out and telling the players.

• Donnie refers to the town as a "she." (He thinks of the spirit as a female presence, despite any conflicting evidence.) Unless pressed or threatened, he shouldn't come out and say that it's the *town* he talks about. Instead, have him speak in half-truths and cryptic phrases: "Who is she? *She's everywhere.*" Or, "She *is* this place. Can't you feel her?" Donnie should already appear unstable and characters may be dubious of any words that come out of his mouth. Essentially, have him make it clear that he serves some kind of higher power, one he personifies in his dialogue.

• While communications with the sheriff should be limited at best, they could still reveal the town as a separate presence. He may offer momentary "words of wisdom," either through a character's mouth or scrawled in the dust nearby where the characters sleep. Simple phrases such as "It watches us" or "It must die again" are enough to imply something larger and greater than what's already been experienced.

• The town is incapable of manifesting directly and as such never "appears" to characters as any kind of anthropomorphic spirit. That's not to say that characters don't have a glimpse of the ghostly nature of the place, though. The easiest way to make this happen is through "tricks" of the eye. (These tricks are actually not tricks at all, but indications of the truth.) Such glimpses manifest as parts of town that don't really exist anymore. A character may see a small farm a quarter-mile off in the distance. When she heads toward it, she blinks and it's gone. Or a character catches a sudden, half-second vision of the main road through town — except more buildings are standing, windows aren't shattered and doors aren't collapsing. Even weirder, let one character go into a building (a bar, house or shed) and see something strange like a message on a wall or fresh blood running across the floor. When he goes to get other characters, the building itself isn't even there anymore.

Close Encounters

Generally, the town relies on Donnie to achieve its goals. Most communication (at least initially) therefore comes from him in regard to "What needs to be done." If Donnie dies or is otherwise incapacitated, the town steps up contact, which is likely to be an incredibly frightening experience. (It's not necessary for Donnie to be taken out of commission for this to happen, either. You may want to "amp up" the fear factor and have the town act directly to communicate with the characters regardless of Donnie's presence.) You decide just how intense such an exchange is, but it's probably extreme and terrifying, and could get characters hurt. Options for direct contact include:

• The town expends a great deal of energy to have numerous proxy spirits (at least three, possibly as many as seven) overwhelm the characters. Proxies follow the general guidelines established for such a power (see p. 38) in that they are entities of the town and not actual ghosts. Thus, they act far stranger than most human spirits do, if that's even possible. It's recommended that proxy spirits appear as both pleading and hostile at the same time. They can approach characters, begging and praying in disjointed, broken words, but also attacking at the same time. Such an assault probably involves telekinetic tricks. Doors slam on characters as they pass through. Floorboards bend to trip them. Shards of glass from broken windows fly at their faces. No attacks should be lethal, as the town uses proxies to try to get help. But the town has little idea how to "ask" for help and hopes to damage characters into submission, instead.

• The town avoids a direct physical confrontation, so relies on a barrage of strange and scary images. (It may even try to trap characters in a single room to ensure that they get the message as clearly as possible.) Such images are up to your imagination, but could include a whole host of horrible things. A sudden glut of fat horseflies seems to come from one character's mouth and spell out words like "help," "die" or "disease" on a wall. Words and phrases seemingly written in blood draw across a floor. They start one at a time, but seconds later dozens of them appear at the same time. Characters hear a cacophony of almost indecipherable whispers. (You may ask players to make Wits + Composure rolls to see if characters understand any of them.) Any or all of these phenomena can happen individually or at one time. In a sense, the town simply reaches out to characters for help in saving it, but such communication comes across as stunted and terrifying and not very effective. You may also use the Dement Numen under these circumstances.

• The town communicates through nightmares when characters sleep. Any earlier nightmares (as mentioned in the previous section of this scenario) are comparatively sane and comforting compared to the head trips suffered now. These nightmares are horrifying and — while they last — seemingly inescapable. Characters may get more parts of the story (especially the history of the town, as described under the section detailing Sheriff Pritchard, above), though these parts should be conveyed through interpretive imagery or in disjointed flashes. One narrative trick is to stage a nightmare in which *all* characters participate, appearing together in a single dream. Such an event is likely to be hugely bizarre for characters, and they may even expect that they're not in a dream at all, but what happens is real. Nightmares or visions may also be used to inform characters of things they've missed (the location of the sheriff's body or Walking Cloud's bones, perhaps).

One important question is what if characters decide to jump the gun and destroy the town before much of the mystery is solved? At this stage of the story, the town still poses enough resistance to make such an act eminently difficult. Characters can be assaulted in some fashion by Donnie, the proxy spirits or by coyotes. Of course, if they succeed, they succeed. Don't deny them their victory artificially. At this point, you're encouraged to improvise. What if burning the town down doesn't dampen its spirit? What if the sheriff remains to be dealt with? Moreover, burning the town but leaving Donnie means he seeks revenge.

Proxy Ghosts

The town creates several spectral entities with limited consciousness to deal with the characters. These "ghosts" aren't really ghosts at all, but are beings of fractional consciousness summoned by the town (see the sidebar for more information on this Numen). Fort Assumption uses these proxies in a limited manner to frighten characters or to enact limited communication. These proxies can take on the form of any human that lived and died in Fort Assumption. Some of these individuals include:

The Pig Farmer: This old farmer is a rotund reflection of a man, with empty eyes and a slack-jawed mouth. He once raised dozens of hogs on his small farm (which still stands) not far from town. The proxy spirit doesn't say much, standing by (or mumbling incomprehensible

Jim Di Bartolo

words) and watching characters from a distance. He approaches only if the town needs to communicate something. Even then, such contact is made in his mumbling mush-mouth. No real meaning can be gleaned from him, as he doesn't have the Numina to speak properly or make signs. Typically, the Pig Farmer has the Animal Control and Phantasm Numina. He uses Phantasm to conjure up images of several hogs (usually decaying but eerily animated) that follow him around.

Schoolchildren: At the time of the town's ultimate demise — whether by smallpox or the hand of Sheriff Pritchard — seven children between the ages of five and 12 lived and went to school here. The town may manifest a proxy of any of these children, boys or girls. Such children are pale and sad-looking and may appear sick. Their eyes are wide and unblinking, their little hands curled into fists. The children tend to speak in nonsensical rhymes or cruel insults using the Ghost Speech Numen.

The Wailing Mother: This woman is the model of the legendary spirit *La Llorona*, a haggard and weeping mother crying for her lost or dead child. As a proxy spirit, she appears suddenly and without warning, her mouth frozen open in silent weeping and screaming. The town may use her to communicate using Ghost Sign. She also tends to appear with Magnetic Disruption active, causing phones, radios and even wristwatches to go crazy.

The Reverend: The Reverend is perhaps the most frightening of all the proxies created by the town. He is tall and thin (like Ichabod Crane might be), and has one withered polio-stricken arm. The town doesn't use the Reverend to communicate meaningfully with characters, projecting him only to frighten. The Reverend chases characters, yelling religious invective and threats of hellfire through constant use of Ghost Speech the Terrify Numina.

Numen: Proxy

This power allows the ghost town to create "proxy" spirits. These beings are not real ghosts, exactly, but nor are they illusions like those created with Phantasm. The proxies contain a fraction of consciousness and manifest as one of the people who died at the location. The image mimics a person's body and voice to a limited and imperfect degree. One of the town's Essence is spent. (No roll is required.) The result is a proxy ghost with four dots to be distributed between Power and Finesse. The proxy's Resistance is 4 (half that of the town, rounded up). A proxy ghost also has a Size of 5. You may add to any of these traits by spending one Essence per dot added. And you may spend two Essence to give a proxy any of the town's own Numina. Remaining traits can be determined as indicated on p. 22. The entity created persists for a single scene.

Proxy spirits are different from genuine ghosts in that they are just ephemeral simulacra of once-living mortals. They have no anchors. If capable of speech, they tend to communicate in stunted language, only half-comprehensible, and occasionally refer to themselves in the third person. (They also never claim to have names, only titles — a ghost town doesn't think of people as having individual identity and hence cannot translate that information over to proxy spirits.)

Harming proxy spirits is difficult. They can be banished through use of abjurations and exorcisms. They can also be harmed by blessed objects. The only other way to negatively affect a proxy is to harm or modify the anchor of the ghost town that created it — damaging such an anchor even slightly banishes all proxy spirits for a number of hours equal to (10 – the ghost town's Resistance), with a minimum of one hour.

When created, all proxy spirits count as "manifested." This is the manner in which a ghost town may accommodate a lack of its own manifestation ability. (See p. 23 for rules on manifestation.)

Putting Things Right

At some point, characters are going to get aggressive. With enough partial (or seemingly complete) information under their belts, and plenty of fear to make them desperate, characters are sure to try to find some way to solve the problems facing them. Essentially, they *have* to. The only way the town relinquishes its grip on them is for them to somehow "fix" the place, whether that means tearing it down board by board or giving into its alien demands.

Keep in mind that the solutions posited here are only the most obvious. Players are notorious for having their characters come up with methods that never occurred to you. Any such solutions should not only be allowed, but encouraged. And yet, such resolutions shouldn't be too simple; they should demand lots of work or danger. In the end, characters trying their own ways of doing things don't stand in the way of the game. They actually make it better and more memorable by personalizing events.

Resolving Anchors

The primary way of dealing with a ghost and diminishing its power is by resolving its anchors. Anchors are, of course, what tie a soul to the world, allowing it to linger beyond its intended time. Anchors are discussed fully on p. 22. Fort Assumption has three primary anchors.

Donnie Pritchard: Donnie has become one of the town's focal points relatively recently. In fact, his addition actually allowed the town to awaken fully as a spirit once again. When Donnie came to town, it regained sentience. Donnie serves as the town's "avatar," devoting enough to its service that he actually *worships* the place, uttering mumbled prayers up to it. Moreover, Donnie is a blood connection to the town proper. Where the sheriff once watched over it, now another of the Pritchard lineage takes his place.

Sheriff Pritchard: Dyer Pritchard remains an unwitting and unwilling anchor for Fort Assumption (and worse, the town is one of *his* anchors, forcing the two into a kind of grim spectral symbiosis). He watched over the flock, protected the town and was the one who helped to kill it by hanging Henry Walking Cloud and by murdering a number of townsfolk. The sheriff's very soul is bound to the spirit of the place.

Bones of Henry Walking Cloud: Whether Walking Cloud's curse was legitimate and brought smallpox to the already gasping town nobody can ever know. Henry's spirit passed on and does not linger, but his bones remain and they're a lynchpin between worlds. His osseous remnants carry a deep burden of tragedy and loss with them, emotions that resonate with the town's renewed purpose.

Finding these anchors is discussed throughout this chapter. Donnie either finds the characters himself or eventually becomes an obvious enough presence, allowing them to find him. The sheriff remains mostly unseen, but makes himself known in time. The bones, as previously noted, lay at the bottom of the mine. Characters may recognize Walking Cloud's remains either through relating them to a previous nightmare or perhaps they see the spectral, blood-scrawled message on the mine wall.

Once characters find the anchors, the next question is what to do about them. "Resolving" an anchor is a loosely defined term and it's meant to be that way. Anchor resolution primary involves dealing with or somehow making a kind of peace with each. It's also possible that the simple physical obliteration of anchors does the trick. In other words, characters who smash the bones, banish the sheriff (which likely involves resolving the majority of *his* anchors), and run off or kill Donnie Pritchard successfully release the town's spirit. Such resolution, however, requires not only significant effort, but a moral laxity allowing for potential murder. Killing Donnie and destroying the other anchors isn't impossible, but not all characters will be (or *should* be) willing to go quite so far. Other options must be allowed.

For example, you decide if Donnie can be brought back from the edge of sanity and given some semblance of reason. Characters may reveal the town's true history to him, which may rattle him free of his sycophancy (or it could deepen his insane resolve…). It's also possible that strong compassion in the face of suffering and danger could save him. If that happens, does the town's grip on him loosen and is Donnie no longer a viable anchor? Maybe to resolve the skeleton of Walking Cloud, characters can

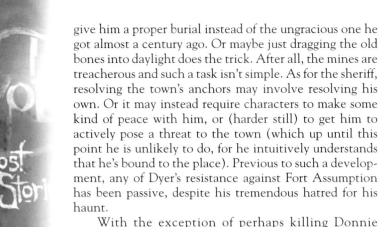

give him a proper burial instead of the ungracious one he got almost a century ago. Or maybe just dragging the old bones into daylight does the trick. After all, the mines are treacherous and such a task isn't simple. As for the sheriff, resolving the town's anchors may involve resolving his own. Or it may instead require characters to make some kind of peace with him, or (harder still) to get him to actively pose a threat to the town (which up until this point he is unlikely to do, for he intuitively understands that he's bound to the place). Previous to such a development, any of Dyer's resistance against Fort Assumption has been passive, despite his tremendous hatred for his haunt.

With the exception of perhaps killing Donnie Pritchard, resolving Fort Assumption's anchors shouldn't occur accidentally. Such tasks should require great effort and catharsis.

Variant Anchors

You are also encouraged to come up with your own anchors for the town, either to add to those above or to replace them. Maybe the cemetery on the hill counts as an anchor, because it holds all the old inhabitants. Characters can give them better headstones (ones without "murder" or "suicide" scrawled on them), or try to find desert flowers to put on each grave, or even dig up the graves to desecrate it. Maybe the silver mine itself is actually an anchor. After all, it was once the life's blood of the town. Characters could demolish the mine's entrance or actually pick for silver. Anything in town could be made an anchor with the right twist and infusion of history.

You may not have to come up with variant anchors; characters may do it under their own power. If the group decides that the sheriff's office is somehow a key part of the town's spirit, and they expend considerable effort to do something about it, make it an anchor. If characters are convinced that they're on the right track and they expend a lot of time and energy, assume they accomplish something. Allowing such independent thinking to go unrewarded helps no one.

Making new anchors apparent to characters is tricky. Certain narrative tricks (dreams, visions, foreshadowing) can be used to highlight them without beating characters over the head with their significance. For example, if one of your custom anchors is a desk in the schoolhouse, perhaps a different message appears scrawled on it every day. It's also possible that characters receive clues from Donnie, the sheriff or the gibbering proxy spirits. The best way to reveal anchors is to encourage characters to engage in a little deductive reasoning. Perhaps going near the anchor causes a flurry of spirit or proxy activity, or such an item is simply so strange and unique that it demands attention.

Destroying the Town

One means of settling the town may be its total physical destruction. Destroying the town doesn't mean dropping carpet bombs, but it does require a pretty wide radius of damage. Actually obliterating the standing buildings is

effective, but a small group of people tearing down entire buildings isn't a simple task. While the standing structures are certainly rotted and worn, destroying one isn't as easy as leaning on it. These buildings have withstood time, dust and decay.

So, how could characters conceivably destroy the place? Perhaps scattered around town are partially filled oil lamps, which can be used to burn the buildings. (It's recommended that characters have to find their own sources of flame, whether it's a finicky lighter that one of them carries, an old wooden match or two rocks struck together.) Characters may also be able to acquire makeshift tools from the mine, or fashion clubs out of fence posts. Hand-demolishing the town with such tools isn't a fast process, but it might do the trick if characters are diligent. Characters may come up with more creative ways of obliterating Fort Assumption. Provided such ideas aren't outlandish, let them try. Just remember that doing so requires concerted effort. (In rules terms, it might be an extended action that calls for Strength + Stamina rolls. A total of 25 successes is required, with each roll comprising a day. Teamwork rules apply.)

The town's spirit doesn't stand idly by as its "body" is destroyed. It interferes at every possible turn. Such activity is obvious enough to warrant the entity's undivided attention. (In contrast, other efforts to resolve anchors may be subtle enough that the town isn't completely aware of what's happening.) The town could send proxy spirits or red-eyed coyotes against the characters. It might use its various Numina (see below for more information), particularly Telekinesis. If Donnie remains alive and unhindered, he does his level best to stand in the way, likely taking sniper shots from across town with his .30-30. Finally, as much as the sheriff would like to see the town razed to the dusty ground, Fort Assumption is one of his anchors (as are some of the items in his tomb below the trapdoor). Survival instinct may compel this Pritchard to stop the invaders.

Characters hoping to destroy the town too early in the story likely meet even heavier resistance than they do toward the presupposed "end," when the town's mysteries are better understood and easier to solve.

Helping the Town

Not all characters may want to destroy the town. Some may be less destructive, and others may even want to help it. They have a few viable options, though they're sure to arrive at their own. Some of these options are actually ones demanded by Donnie, should he get the jump on characters and maintain an advantage over them.

• Characters with any degree of carpentry skill (or really, none at all) can set out to rebuild the town. Enough wood lies around from other collapsed buildings that could hypothetically be used to help patch and fix the structures that remain. If Donnie is around, he may offer a few rusty, almost-broken tools (alternately, aggressive characters with an edge over Donnie may find the tools and take them from him, or maybe even put *him* to work). Otherwise, characters have to improvise. Reconstruction calls for Intelligence + Crafts rolls as an extended action, with 40 total successes required. (Teamwork rules apply.) Each roll constitutes a full day's work. Characters without Crafts suffer the standard –3 penalty. Poor tools impose a –2 penalty. Dramatic failure means tools break or a worker suffers a rusty nail in the foot. Exceptional success on any given roll means characters perform exceedingly well that day and a +2 bonus is gained on the next roll (and only the next roll).

If Donnie is involved at this point, characters still aren't safe, even when they do his bidding or keep a close eye on him as their laborer. If a character slips up and breaks a tool, puts a board where Donnie doesn't want it (he has no talent at repair and knows next to nothing about what should or should not be done), or they afford their prisoner just a little too much latitude, he may snap. He's unlikely to kill a character, but he may attack and try to punish them for doing wrong by "her."

• The mine seemed to run dry decades ago, which is why the town began to fail in the early 1900s. The truth is that the townsfolk just didn't look hard enough and in fact were close to actually striking the mother lode. Characters may be able to find this seam, and doing so might invigorate the town. (Silver mining, while antiquated, is still done and could theoretically attract new people, which is partly what Fort Assumption *wants*.) Finding this silver, however, could be *incredibly* difficult. Depending on your plan, it could comprise a good portion of the whole

story. The mine is a complex of tunnels that reach 200 to 500 feet below the surface. Electricity no longer runs down there, so there's nothing but darkness down below. Characters who descend must bring their own flashlights, could get one or more from Donnie's truck, or could fashion torches or collect oil for lamps. Another option is that Donnie has a small generator on his truck outside of town, which may power *some* of the mine's lights.

With or without illumination, the mine is home to many dangers: collapsing tunnels, jagged rocks, explosions, natural gas and unstable ground that gives way to fissures. At the very end of these tunnels is the roughly sealed rock wall hiding Walking Cloud's skeleton. The wall just behind the skeleton is where a large stratum of silver (revealed as a network of black veins in the rock) is revealed. Characters could dig for it, be shown a small part in a dream, or notice the change in rock consistency when studying Walking Cloud's tomb. Finding the silver might be just what the town needs. If it is, it might be willing to let the characters leave.

• The town might also be willing to let them leave if characters swear to the spirit to bring new people back to "live" there. This can be something of a disturbing option, as characters essentially do the town's bidding and bring presumably innocent people (through friendliness or force) to this angry, confused place. Still, it could be viable. Letting characters leave town on this promise is a big step, and some characters may be encouraged to take advantage and renege on their end of the deal. That's fine,

Jim Di Bartolo

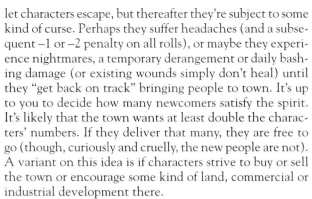

let characters escape, but thereafter they're subject to some kind of curse. Perhaps they suffer headaches (and a subsequent –1 or –2 penalty on all rolls), or maybe they experience nightmares, a temporary derangement or daily bashing damage (or existing wounds simply don't heal) until they "get back on track" bringing people to town. It's up to you to decide how many newcomers satisfy the spirit. It's likely that the town wants at least double the characters' numbers. If they deliver that many, they are free to go (though, curiously and cruelly, the new people are not). A variant on this idea is if characters strive to buy or sell the town or encourage some kind of land, commercial or industrial development there.

No matter what happens, any attempt to help the town meets with resistance from the sheriff. While the ruins remain his anchor, he certainly doesn't want to see the place thrive and be allowed to exert its alien will. Pritchard punishes the characters with unmitigated attacks and attempted torture to stop them from aiding and inciting the town's spirit.

Laying the Town to Rest

One thing to consider is exactly how to describe that final moment when the town is put to rest. Whether it involves burning or peacefully resolving Fort Assumption's anchors, putting the town at ease is a climactic moment and should deliver narrative punch. That doesn't mean the town needs to explode in white light while a chorus of angels croons, but it does mean that characters should get some indication that they've succeeded. Does the town let out an unearthly howl? For a bigger moment, consider a sudden thunderstorm. When a downpour falls in this dusty, dead place, it could be a "cleansing" moment. Or perhaps the mine collapses, pulling the town into its rocky embrace. Should a more subtle tactic be sought, maybe the town seems to exhibit a barely audible exhalation, a "last gasp" as the spirit shudders and dissipates. You must decide how to describe putting the town to rest, and how such an image best suits the mood and theme of your story.

Denouement

When all is said and done, the characters are left with a lot of emotional baggage, not to mention any potential wounds to the body and mind. The denouement of any scenario is less about plot resolution and more about character resolution. How do the players' characters deal with what they've seen and done? Before recent events, they may have been completely ordinary people, but they have now been confronted with the existence of ghosts and other unseen *things*. Do they draw any conclusions from the experience — conclusions that they can take with them into other World of Darkness stories? Some themes to explore along these lines are addressed below.

No personal developments or insights should be force-fed to players. Characters should come to their own conclusions about the truth they have uncovered.

Evil versus Instinct

After dealing with the town, Sheriff Pritchard and Donnie Pritchard, characters are likely to be left with complicated feelings about evil. Some characters certainly leave with a simplified, black-and-white outlook on the concept, believing that evil exists, *carte blanche* (they have seen proof!), and nothing can be done about it. Others may be less clear on the subject. Some may recognize that the "antagonists" of the story acted out of twisted self-interest and instinct. Sheriff Pritchard shot the other townsfolk because he thought they were sick and cursed; he did them a "favor." He seemed to identify the characters as intruders and trespassers. Any actions he took against them weren't spawned from direct cruelty, but from a demented defense mechanism.

Donnie Pritchard, on the other hand, was driven mad by his experiences with the town and served as its agent. Whether or not he was successful in his manipulation of the characters, they may be forced to ask "Is he evil?" "Were his actions and his insanity products of an evil demeanor or was he just another pawn?" If characters see him as evil, are they forced to believe that evil is almost strictly a human characteristic?

Then what about the town itself? It wasn't human. Its spirit may have reflected the mortals who once lived there, but that's it. It's an abstract entity, the soul of a place gone dead. Once again, the question of evil versus instinct rears its head. Did the town act on its urges and needs because of its nature, much like a lioness hunts a weak gazelle? Or was the town proof positive that, as Shirley Jackson wrote, some places are "born bad"?

Intestinal Fortitude

Characters in any horror story typically survive thanks to a combination of two factors: grim resolve in the face of fear, and the ability to think quickly and intelligently in dire situations. Characters who survive the ghost-town scenario almost certainly take stock of their abilities in such horrific situations. Was a character proactive enough to not only stand up against the horror but to find some kind of resolution? Or did a character coast on the brains and brawn of others, keeping his head low until the nightmare was over? The former may be ready (whether she believes it or not) for further "exposure" to other truths of the World of Darkness. The latter may recognize himself as weak and far too fallible for that sort of experience, deciding to live a distinctly sheltered and "safe" existence thereafter.

Furthermore, characters are forced to take stock of how far they were willing to go to survive and solve the mystery of the ghost town. When attacked by Donnie, did they revert to an almost *Lord of the Flies* mentality to bring him down and keep everyone safe? Or worse, did one character attempt to sacrifice another to keep *herself* safe? (Did any characters lose Morality and/or gain derangements in the course of the story for performing selfish or violent acts?) Characters willing to take extreme actions must examine their own morality, especially in comparison to so-called "monsters" like those encountered at Fort Assumption. Alternately, if characters were *unwilling* to go that far, do they now regret their morality and see such ethical reliance as a shortcoming?

Variations

Below are a few ways in which to change this scenario. Such changes are meant to be drastic, overhauling the entire mood and plot.

The Living Ghost Town

Instead of having the ghost town be abandoned, assume it's not a physical ghost town because *people still live there.* In fact, they're willing servants of the "bad place," acting as extensions of its urges. The town is likely more malicious than purely self-interested, as it willingly enslaves victims to do its bidding. The actual population is up to you. Perhaps the town merely seeks to recoup the number of inhabitants it once had before the sheriff shot everyone. It needs only a *few* more (i.e. the players' characters) to complete its collection. The town itself can be set anywhere, whether it's distant from other inhabited areas or is actually a suburb or housing development. The theme of this kind of piece is probably more *Stepford Wives* than *Identity*.

Contamination

Should you want to make it a reality of your chronicle that some places can be *made* evil, you can change the history of Fort Assumption by invoking a theme of contamination. You might put a factory (which we'll call Caltron) maybe a mile or two away from the dead place. Caltron opened in the 1950s and still operates. It hardly matters what the factory produces, only that its output is toxic and has irreparably damaged the very spirit of the town (and was probably responsible for the rash of cancer that killed most of the residents over 50 or 60 years ago). Helping the town may mean shutting the factory down, which is no small task. The mood of the story thus changes from the consequences of one man's actions to the effects of unsympathetic corporate policy. Variations on this variation might be that the ghost town is an experiment watched closely by Caltron executives, or that the town still creates proxies — except *these* proxies aren't ghosts, but shambling corpses!

Mableton

Instead of having a lone ghost town off in the middle of nowhere with the characters trapped inside, set the place only a few miles from an active and still-thriving town (which we'll call Mableton). Characters are no longer lost vacationers or wayward folks drawn together, but residents of Mableton who bear witness to the nearby ghost town

growing "hungry." The sister city's effects on Mableton are likely to be undeniable, and the characters must do something to save their own town and its 1000+ residents. This variant drastically changes the mood of the story. Characters are no longer trapped and alone, but are part of the organic whole of another town's population. They can go to the library to unearth history about their neighbor, and can interact with any number of locals who may help or stand in the way. This situation could demand more response than can be addressed in a short scenario. It could be the focus of a chronicle, with characters encouraged to create a network of allies and enemies in town, as well as having jobs and ordinary lives. All of which intermingles with the horror of the ghost town, making for a very different game.

Cast Members

The following are the character profiles for use in this story. You're are encouraged to modify them in any way to better suit your own mood, theme or plot.

Ghosts

This scenario really has only two genuine ghosts — the most obvious being that of Fort Assumption itself, the other being the restless spirit of Sheriff Dyer Pritchard. The proxy spirits created by the ghost town do not count as separate characters, being manifestations of Fort Assumption through the use of the Proxy Numen. See the **World of Darkness Rulebook** for full systems on ghosts and their Numina, pp. 208-216.

Fort Assumption

Background: Fort Assumption was founded in 1852 amidst the blowing dust and whispering sage, first as nothing more than a stopping point on the way to bigger and better places. It wasn't long before silver was discovered south of town and not long after that, the Babyhead Mine opened for business.

Over the next several decades, the town grew to boast a couple hundred people at its peak. When the mine supposedly dried out, so too did the willingness of the townsfolk to remain. Some stood fast, reluctant perhaps to uproot their entire lives, holding onto some kind of hometown pride. By the end, however, the population had dwindled to less than 50, with the mine's meager offerings worked by immigrants and Native Americans. After Sheriff Pritchard discovered his wife's infidelity (what he wrongly believed to be rape) and executed Henry Walking Cloud, the town suffered a mortal wound that was followed by a very real sickness. Smallpox came in the windblown nights of January 1919. By March, those who hadn't left were bedridden with disease. The sheriff, unable to abide such sorrow, went from house to house and shot those who had not died or killed themselves to escape his rampage. Come morning, he put a bullet in his own brain.

It was this tragedy that birthed the town's restless spirit. Assumption, it seemed, was unwilling to go gently into that good night. With the residual memories of all who ever lived there, an entity arose from the town's death and persisted in a bleak and restless "life" after death.

Description: For the most part, the town is a dry, dusty place of moldering floorboards and crumbling walls. Everything is cracked and earthen. Fort Assumption is dominated by rust-colored sand and stubborn desert weeds.

The town proper is little more than a single wagon-rutted street about half a city block long. Once upon a time, the buildings numbered a dozen or more, but many have collapsed. Left standing are the sheriff's office (and accompanying "courthouse"), the church, the schoolhouse and the cemetery at the end of the street. Some other structures might include the tavern, the mining office or a doctor's office.

Outside of town, marked barely by the memory of old roads, are various rancher homes and farmhouses. The only one standing strongly is the house of the old pig farmer, a man named Silas Brooker. The other homes and farms are in various states of ruin. Also outside of town is the ramshackle entrance to the Babyhead Mine, as well as Donnie Pritchard's pick-up truck.

The town has no electrical lights or plumbing. Sand gets in everything.

Storytelling Hints: The town isn't human, and as such doesn't act human. It's barely capable of thought, acting on some kind of foreign instinct. Any time it attempts to use human language (either through its proxies or its other Numina), it ultimately fails because it has little grasp of speech. Words are garbled in frightening, non-sensical chatter, whether scrawled on walls or whispered in one's ear. The town is slow to wake to the presence of intruders and only turns its attention to characters after a day or so has passed. Even then, the place may take longer to notice, unless newcomers perform extreme or dynamic actions. The town's initial reaction is to command attention and dominance by inspiring fear. It also hungers for such emotion. Fear and sadness are ultimately the last overwhelming feelings present in the town before it "died," and the spirit is most comfortable with such grim sentiment.

If an exceptional success is achieved on any roll made for the town to create fear, whether through its proxy spirits or the use of its other Numina, it regains a point of spent Essence. This is an optional rule. You may decide that it needn't come into play, and the town can use whatever Numina it has in any manner desired as if Essence were unlimited.

Attributes: Power 8, Finesse 3, Resistance 7
Willpower: 15
Essence: 15
Morality: n/a
Virtue: Fortitude
Vice: Envy
Initiative: 10
Defense: 8
Speed: n/a
Size: n/a
Corpus: n/a
Numina: Animal Control (dice pool 11), Ghost Sign (dice pool 11), Ghost Speech (dice pool 11), Magnetic Disruption, Phantasm (dice pool 11), Proxy (see sidebar on p. 38), Telekinesis (dice pool 11), Terrify (dice pool 11)

Ghost Towns

A ghost town is a very specific type of restless spirit. Obviously, it's not the ghost of a person at all, but literally the spirit of a place that has "died" in some fashion. It needn't be a town, despite the name, and could be a house, a factory or even a lonely stretch of country road.

When a place "dies," it's not necessarily death in the fashion one expects for a mortal. When a human dies, the body typically perishes. When a place dies, that may or may not be the case. While Fort Assumption is abandoned, a ghost town can just as easily be a place that's populated (though heavy populations make a spirit's existence all the more difficult — see "Manifestations" on p. 23). The requirement for a place's demise is some kind of trigger event, which is almost always some kind of tragedy. It could be anything from a workplace shooting to an earthquake to the murder of a town hero. No matter what, the event afflicts the setting's identity with an indelible mark. This scar actually *awakens* the region's spirit. Essentially, all human feelings about the tragedy coalesce to form the stuff of this entity, giving it a kind of instinctual sentience. It doesn't think like an individual human, but with a hive-mind of thoughts and emotions. As such, ghost towns rarely have complicated desires, focusing on simple urges (to be destroyed or to cause fear or suffering).

Ghost towns do not have a Morality score, as they are not human, despite the apparent commingling of mortal memories. Nor can they materialize in the rules sense. They do not have corporeal forms per se and can realize some kind of form only through the Proxy Numen.

Ghost towns can possess the Ghost Sign and Ghost Speech Numina, but such spirits are unlikely to use them to full effect. The spirit of a place has little understanding of human speech beyond a few words and phrases that were core to its identity at some point, such as a corrupt mayor's campaign slogan or a killer's farewell address to his victims. Use of expression Numina therefore produces a maddening jabber of ill communication.

Like the ghosts of humans, ghost towns have difficulty manifesting powers in the presence of numerous people. Every 20 people present within 500 yards of the town impose a −1 penalty to Power + Finesse (i.e., Numina) rolls made for the spirit.

Sheriff Dyer Pritchard

Background: It's hard to say whether Dyer Pritchard was ever a *good* man, but it can't be denied that he was a devoted one. His father was a Texas lawman, his mother a seamstress. He hoped one day to follow in his father's footsteps. He was offered the opportunity at an unusually young age, becoming sheriff of the flyspeck silver town of Fort Assumption in 1898. The job was hard at first (before then the town had known little law), but Pritchard made his means known, showing nary an ounce of mercy to criminals, and a world of mercy to those who respected the law. A prideful man, Pritchard chose one of the prettiest women in town, a miner's daughter named Esme. He took her as his wife and soon had a boy. Their son would later leave town (without his father's approval) to work on the burgeoning oil fields far west of Fort Assumption.

When Pritchard discovered that his wife had been cheating on him with one of the lowly "savages" forced to work the mines, he snapped. His pride discolored the truth and he decided, plain and simple, that such an animal could have his wife only by rape, which was a crime punishable by execution. Swift and painless or slow and tormenting didn't matter. Pritchard murdered the "offender," a Kiowa named Henry Walking Cloud, by walling him up deep in the Babyhead Mine. Not long after this brutal and unsanctioned act, an outbreak of smallpox swept through town. The sheriff, convinced that it was a curse levied by the Indian, couldn't stand to see the town suffer. Pride mixed with a vengeful urge and Pritchard met each sick, bedridden citizen with a bullet. Grief stricken by his "duty," he wrote a final journal entry, climbed into a holdout beneath his office, and shot himself.

He rose soon afterward as a broken soul, a ghost whose pride had been destroyed and was replaced with wrath.

Description: Sheriff Pritchard rarely manifests, but when he does, he appears as a tall, rail-thin man in a duster coat and a pair of crusty boots. He walks slowly, staring forward with unblinking, milky-white eyes. The hair on his head is mostly gone, while his face sports a patchy, uneven Vandyke.

Storytelling Hints: The sheriff is intense, driven by a burning hatred of the town and everything in it, which includes himself. And yet, he's conflicted. His instincts don't yet allow him to affect Fort Assumption overly negatively, for harming the town harms him; he clings to a strange sense of self-preservation, even in death. Never friendly, never funny, Pritchard takes on all tasks with a single-minded focus. Those who cross him are assumed to deserve punishment. Those who help him receive small mercy for as long as it's warranted.

Attributes: Power 4, Finesse 4, Resistance 3
Willpower: 7
Morality: 4
Virtue: Justice
Vice: Wrath
Initiative: 7
Defense: 4
Speed: 18 (species factor 10)
Size: 5
Corpus: 8
Numina: Clairvoyance (dice pool 8), Compulsion (dice pool 8), Ghost Sign (dice pool 8), Terrify (dice pool 8)

Jim Di Bartolo

Sheriff Pritchard's Anchors

The sheriff has two personal anchors, in addition to his overall bond to the town. The first anchor is the grave of his wife, Esme. Destroying or harming this anchor could be relatively simple — defacing it, demolishing it, digging up the woman's moldering remains. The second anchor is a bit trickier, as it lies beneath the sheriff's office, in the bolt-hole under his old desk. That anchor is his old five-shot revolver, used to murder a majority of the lingering townsfolk. Simply removing the revolver from the corpse's hand doesn't do the trick. It must be disassembled somehow (requiring an Intelligence + Crafts roll) or perhaps buried far out in the desert away from town.

Characters may learn of Pritchard's anchors by noting his presence around them or by simple deduction (after all, his gun and his wife's grave are obviously important items in the sheriff's history). Characters might also notice that the sheriff's holster is empty when he manifests, and that he tends to stare off toward the cemetery when he does appear.

Combatant (Live) Opponents

Provided you follow the basic outline provided in this scenario, the town features one other living human besides the characters.

Donnie Pritchard

Quote: "You just do what I say — you do what she says — and I won't have to put one of these bullets in you. Understand?"

Background: Donnie hasn't done much with his life worth talking about. While not every endeavor has failed, each has been mediocre. He didn't make it to college. He never had a real girlfriend. He never held a job for more than a year. He seemed fated for small things... or would have been if not for the dreams. They haunted him from youth, showing him horrific images and sights. The visions were so vivid that they seemed real, as if he could reach out and touch them, if only he could find them. So he set out in search of what haunted him, following strangely familiar signs and gut intuition until he made his way to the ruins of For Assumption. And then he was home. The place was in need of tending — service — and in return it fulfilled him. Finally, he was doing something worth doing, something that was worthwhile. Now he stops at nothing to see that the town gets what "she" wants.

Description: Donnie's appearance would be the pinnacle of average if he weren't so thin and unkempt. He stands about 5'10", has mousy brown hair and brown eyes, and unexceptional features. Time and his obsession have not been kind to him, though. Beyond his rail physique, the skin of his hands and face has become dry and cracked under the unyielding wind-blown dust. Donnie looks *haunted*.

Storytelling Hints: Where Donnie once believed he slept through life, Fort Assumption has since awakened him to his "true calling." He acts and speaks with manic intensity, and makes rash decisions and stammers words, belying a deep impatience or uncertainty. While he wants what he wants and is unwilling to listen to reason, he is also easily confused, which could be taken advantage of. Should Donnie feel threatened, he immediately reacts as if backed into a corner, countering with sudden vitriol and aggression.

Attributes: Intelligence 3, Wits 2, Resolve 3, Strength 2, Dexterity 3, Stamina 2, Presence 2, Manipulation 3, Composure 2

Skills: Athletics 1, Brawl 1, Drive 2, Firearms 2, Intimidation 1, Investigation 2, Persuasion 2, Stealth 1, Subterfuge 2, Survival 2, Weaponry 1

Merits: Danger Sense, Direction Sense, Fleet of Foot 2, Resources 1

Willpower: 5

Morality: 4

Virtue: Faith

Vice: Sloth

Initiative: 5

Defense: 2

Speed: 12

Derangement: Obsessive Compulsion (p. 98 of the **World of Darkness Rulebook**)

Weapons/Attacks:

Type	Damage	Size	Dice Pool
Hunting Knife	1 (L)	1	4

Type	Damage	Range	Shots	Dice Pool
Winchester Model 94† 30-30 (Rifle)	5	150/ 300/ 600	6+1	10

† This weapon requires two hands. If used one-handed, the Strength requirement (2) increases by one (to 3, which imposes a –1 penalty to shots).

Armor: None

Health: 7

Animals

Using Animal Control, the town is able to call to it countless types of desert creatures such as crows, vultures, rattlesnakes and scorpions. The only animals consistently summoned (especially against the characters) are coyotes, of which there are usually three.

Coyote

Description: These animals are rangy, thin and hungry looking. Their eyes glow a faint red when night falls.

The coyotes are unusually intelligent and cunning. They're cowardly creatures in general, though, and stay just far enough away from humans to keep them in sight (unless summoned for more nefarious purposes, when such cowardice is forgotten). These *canids* are not in any way enhanced by the town, meaning they have no supernatural abilities.

Attributes: Intelligence 1, Wits 4, Resolve 4, Strength 3, Dexterity 5, Stamina 2, Presence 4, Manipulation 1, Composure 3

Skills: Athletics (Running) 3, Brawl 2, Intimidation 3, Stealth 3, Survival (Tracking) 3

Willpower: 7

Initiative: 8

Defense: 5

Speed: 15 (species factor 7)

Size: 4

Weapons/Attacks:

Type	Damage	Dice Pool
Bite	2 (L)	7

Health: 6

Jim Di Bartolo

Chapter 2:
The Terrifying Tale of James Magnus

By Geoff Grabowski

He found that the Count was decidedly not a favorite. If his tenants came late to their work on the days which they owed to him as Lord of the Manor, they were set on the wooden horse, or flogged and branded in the manor-house yard. One or two cases there were of men who had occupied lands which encroached on the lord's domain, and whose houses had been mysteriously burnt on a winter's night, with the whole family inside. But what seemed to dwell on the innkeeper's mind most — for he returned to the subject more than once — was that the Count had been on the Black Pilgrimage, and had brought something or someone back with him.

— M. R. James, "Count Magnus"

Summary

James Magnus was a terrible man. Evil, greedy and cruel to those around him. After a life spent in the service of the black arts of torture and dark magic, he returned to his rural home Hampton County and purchased a large lot of land. For more than a decade thereafter he was locally famous as a villain and the terror of trespassers, neighboring landowners and those who had to do business with him. He killed his wife and himself in a murder-suicide about a dozen years ago, and dark rumors have lingered since. His foreign wife has been seen walking the roads late at night. Some say they have seen lights in the Magnus' abandoned house. A prominent local figure was found dead after establishing a hunting camp on the property, and while the death was by heart attack, those who discovered the body said the look on his face was one of unspeakable terror.

Though it has been on the block for a very long time, the Magnus estate has gone unsold, the house sitting vacant and the people of the local town being apprehensive of its very shadow. Magnus made quite an impression on Hampton County, and he will not be easily forgotten.

This is especially true, because the ghosts of Magnus and his wife still roam the house and grounds. So far they have had few victims, but they are quite potent when they exert themselves, and while they can be driven off, they are probably impossible to destroy completely without the utmost sacrifice from intruders.

Setting

This story takes place in a non-specific rural area called Hampton County. The region can be located anywhere that has enough tree cover to surround a small hub of settlement and commerce — basically a small town. Depending on what you desire, the county may be on the suburbanizing edge of an urban sprawl or far from any city. If the place is located near an urban area, events may be complicated by media coverage, so unless you're willing to improvise the consequences of a media circus, circumstances should probably be confined to a genuinely remote locale.

Inspiration

The following stories were all important to some extent in the development of this scenario. You may find the list illuminating; the story's intellectual forebears may provide insights into its intended structure and goals.

"Count Magnus", M.R. James — The greatest inspiration. M.R. James is the master of the "weird tale" ghost story. Anyone who wants to learn to evoke a frightening but not horrifying mood should start with James' works.

Blair Witch Project — Not for any specific element, but for the ability of the film to evoke the sense of panic over the fatally weird and inexplicable. Events clearly have some sort of significance to the being that stalks the protagonists, but they have no clue about its motives or methods. That is very much the feel intended for this story, assuming you want to capture it.

Salem's Lot, Stephen King — Not the actual tales of vampires, but the story of Hubie Marsden, the twisted, evil man who prepared the way for Barlow. Again, the protagonists have no real understanding of the situation, they simply know that the Marsden house is evil, while the reader knows that Hubie did something deliberately to taint the place.

The Shining, Stephen King — Possibly the definitive modern haunted house tale (others argue for *The Haunting of Hill House*, below) about a resort hotel that does little good for the broken family seeking to renew itself there. Well worth reading because of the shared thread of alcoholism and isolation.

The Haunting of Hill House, Shirley Jackson — The one that inspired King so much. Its brevity may reduce it to almost a skeleton, but it works well as a definitive tale.

Mood

The mood of this story varies, but generally involves a certain amount of stark terror. Characters may not possess any special abilities or weapons beyond carbines, hunting rifles or handguns (all of which are essentially useless against the ghosts of Magnus and his wife Aiesha). Characters may chase the ghosts off with gunfire, but do no permanent damage and just generate legal bills for themselves. The only permanent remedy to the ghosts requires all the determination characters can muster.

Protagonists' encounter with the ghosts is likely to be an extended cat-and-mouse game as the spirits torment the intruders, followed by a grisly or terrifying climax when the characters no longer entertain their "hosts." If you simply want to run the scenario as a sort of "weird tale" in which the characters have a brush with the supernatural, opening them to further contact in the future, then the ghosts' effects may be relatively minor. Characters may see some manifestation or experience a possession that causes them to do something dangerous or embarrassing. In the great scheme of existence, this isn't much, but it's enough to change someone's life and firmly convince her that there's an unseen world.

Or you may run this tale as a dangerous "victims" game, for pure horror and psychological thrills. The climax is bloody and violent, and the survivors (if any) are left without a doubt that the supernatural exists — it claimed one or more of their friends! You can exert a spectrum of intensity here. If the haunting is played at full strength, don't expect all or even most characters to survive. That may be fine for a one-shot story, but if you have a chronicle underway, you probably want characters to be able to resolve matters with their lives and some of their sanity intact. That means putting the solution to

the problem posed in characters' hands, and allowing them to try to execute it.

To complement the story's horror, gruesome or otherwise, another emotion is prevalent. This scenario is composed as a thriller, in which the characters' Vices and passions mix with those of the ghosts, leading to possession and possibly madness and death. The story can thus have a dark, Southern Gothic romance mood, fixating on the characters' passions and the self-destructive courses they

choose. The characters might be dysfunctional or in terrible trouble before they ever set foot on the Magnus property. This can therefore be a hijacking story; the emotions of the place overwhelm what good sense the intruders have and change their lives. Characters might be very hopeful and wholesome, or trying to lay personal ghosts to rest, only to encounter the opposition of the subtly destructive manor.

Whatever the story's mood, it's important that players work with it. A ghost story builds suspense in what have become familiar ways. Anyone taking part can predict what the source of the trouble is (ghosts). That means playing along and upholding character ignorance, not player omniscience. Players should agree to subvert their knowledge of the characters' context, letting the protagonists get deeper and deeper into danger, rather than immediately kicking and screaming against what is obviously a haunted house. Read *The Shining* and *The Haunting of Hill House*. They're stories about haunted houses, and about people who are haunted themselves. If players insist that their characters are of inviolate moral purity, unimpeachable character, or they constantly question every perception, your story won't be much fun.

This is a chance for players to act out their characters' shortcomings, fears and Vices. By cooperating, troupe members have a chance to shape the story and make it about their own creations rather than about events that transpire. If this is a prelude to a World of Darkness chronicle, it's an excellent chance for characters (and players) to make their entry into the unknown.

Avenues of Introduction

This story is something of a miniature setting for non-supernatural characters. Many different types of people can get involved in untangling the strange and terrible tale of James Magnus. They may end his ghostly existence, flee before his horrifying presence or die at the hands of his terrible evil.

• Characters may be locals who are youthful or simply brave and who wish to gain notoriety by "busting" the ghosts of the house. Or characters might be local game hunters determined to hunt on Magnus' property. In the latter case, you need to do one of two things. Extend the reach of the house such that it can haunt locals in their everyday lives, or draw the characters back again and again. It's probably easiest to extend the haunting. Rather than suffering flashes of the Magnus' memories in the house alone, the characters have them during the course of their normal lives, for they have caused something evil to stir and draw its attention.

• Character may be amateur spiritualists interested in studying the James Magnus story. The case is rather obscure, and inspires as much interest among true-crime buffs as spiritualists, because of the gruesome nature of the killings that occurred. There was some zine work on the story a few years ago, but none of it has made it online and the worldwide web is largely void of information on the subject. Characters presumably do preliminary investigations on site.

• Characters may be individuals from out of town who are attracted by the extremely attractive price of Magnus' house, or they seek to develop its real estate. A new family from far away is suckered into buying the haunted mansion, or a crew has to live on the grounds while the site is prepared for development, living in the house as a barracks. The house's price tag is a pittance, positively incredible for the acreage and basic structure, even given the dilapidated condition.

How to Cut the Sex Out

Unless this is being told as a strict monster-hunting story, there has to be some emotional component to the haunting. The text assumes a "red-hot thriller" sort of ghost story, and the emotional component is conveyed through erotic tension. Your group may not want to go that route, though. If the idea of describing physical sex during a flashback makes you or your players uneasy, don't abandon the passionate aspect of the story. Just leave out the sex.

By the end of their relationship, the Magnuses hated each other, having sex or not having sex. Just because you don't want to feature the carnal elements of their relationship doesn't mean you should excise the passion. That's what drives the story. The dead husband and wife can alternate between love and hate, as conveyed to the characters through spectral visions and through characters' possession, in the latter case characters acting out the couple's feelings.

General Progress of the Story

"The Terrifying Tale of James Magnus" assumes that events follow a relatively familiar haunted-house narrative. Individuals who are afflicted — by addictions, broken relationships, grief 0r defeats or deaths they cannot confront — arrive, and the house's troubled nature resonates with them. Their own dramas play out in tune with the place's evil. Did they bring the evil with them or did it await them all along? Who can say? The characters rise to overcome their own personal haunting, are destroyed or escape the house.

Events can be played along a spectrum that's blunt at one end. The house is obviously terrible, it destroys anyone who spends too much time near it, and characters are blind to the danger looming even while their players know all too well what's coming. At the other end of the spectrum, the story can start with an almost romantic or wistful overtone only to reveal more through conversations with townsfolk and characters' own experiences with the ghosts. As things progress, the characters gradually realize that sexy and intelligent world travelers James and Aiesha were in fact horrible individuals.

It might be best to err on the side of a gradual buildup. The haunted-house story is founded on perception, emotion and fear. Try your best to short-circuit situations that instantly lead to the end, such as destroying the place. Use the haunting as a blunt force if the characters are themselves hopelessly blunt — lighter-happy arsonists or determined bulldozer operators.

Distract characters from proactive efforts with the indulgence or rewards of the haunting. If the protagonists are resolved to level the house, it's time for the ghosts to exploit any crushes between characters that are laden with sexual tension. If the characters are workmen about to bulldoze the house, it's time for the carburetor on the earthmover to fail. "Oh no," you announce, "The guy at the parts place says a replacement won't be here for five days. Guess you'll just have to stay in the old mansion for a week on the company dime."

Regardless of pacing, the characters encounter increasingly powerful manifestations until the ghosts of Aiesha and James are roused sufficiently to possess intruders. At that point they're potent supernatural evils with harmful or murderous intent.

If characters are initially inquisitive or non-aggressive toward the house, matters intensify slowly. Characters experience occasional flashes of the ghosts' lives through use of Terrify, Phantasm or Compulsion. Tensions build over the course of hours, days or weeks as the characters live out their lives at the house, and the occupants are increasingly intruded upon by the desires of the restless dead.

In the playtest of the story, characters had flashbacks, but only the "audience" could see their content. Characters themselves had a sense of wrongness or a cold flash, but they weren't aware of what the Storyteller described to the players. (See the "You Can't See This" sidebar for an example.) Then, as the full evil of the residents emerged, characters became fully aware of flashes experienced, and of the things projecting them. Basically, run with visions and foreboding premonitions as long as players enjoy them. Once everyone has been sufficiently spooked and titillated, go to the climax.

If the game is a character study or serves as an initiation into the world of the unseen, the protagonists have a brush with the unnatural. It might be possession, ghostly manifestation or whatever seems appropriate to jolt the characters out of the ignorance they've always known. It may lead them to introspection about the truth of the world, leave them with emotional scars, or turn them loose to explore the reality they have just discovered.

If the story is told as a stand-alone game, roll out deadly horror as a shocking, unannounced change of pace at the climax. After raising expectations of an essentially psychological situation, James or Aiesha can possess a target and go on a murderous rampage.

What happens next is anyone's guess. The ghosts can be destroyed in theory, but the reality is that the characters may run and have little desire to return to the house. Perhaps they will develop greater power or understanding in the future and believe themselves able to confront the darkness of the Magnus House. Until then, the finale could well be a will-breaking, mind-shattering defeat for the characters.

You Can't See This

Miranda, the naïve young prize wife of down-and-out Mafioso Vic, inspects the bedroom on the first day in their new country mansion. She touches the bed and the Storyteller narrates a scene of torrid, kinky sex between the Magnuses. The players now know some of the themes and images that will appear throughout the story, while Miranda is left with nothing but the trademark, "I just felt something wrong about this," expression on her face.

Hampton County

The setting of this story is a dreary region called Hampton County. It's a rural administrative district with one major settlement: the county seat, Hampton, a tiny burg with a population of about 8,500. The rest of the county is home to a widely dispersed population of about the same number.

Once an agricultural land, most of the large farms in the area have closed down due to competition with agribusiness and importation, but the competition has yet to move in to snap up the fallow fields. The scenery is dominated by farm country slowly slipping back into wilderness. There are still feedlots and grain silos, but the farmers are fewer every year, and their children drift away to the city rather than spend their lives tilling the land for tiny profits and subsidy checks.

Hampton County's primary remaining employers are light industries. The area is home to a large subcontractor — Worth Industries — that provides enamel-covered metal letters to use on various sorts of outdoor signs. Worth, several small machine shops and the services that support them provide most jobs, but there still isn't enough work to go around. The residents slowly gray as the young move on; the population has drifted downward for the last several decades. While the city still has some "Main Street" style commerce, Wal-Mart and other big retailers have set up shop in neighboring towns and driven the small guy out of business.

Infrastructure

Hampton County has a reasonably modern infrastructure. A limited-access highway passes nearby and provides a small amount of business. Main roads are paved, as are routes to the houses of important political figures, but secondary roads are either gravel-covered or chipped and sealed. Bridges are in good repair and washouts are fixed promptly, although temporary repairs often linger for months or even years in isolated areas until budgets can accommodate permanent solutions.

Roads are lit only in Hampton proper. Unless you locate Hampton on the edge of a major urban sprawl, there isn't sufficient skyglow to allow dim, unaided vision at night, or to use early-generation nightvision devices on moonless or cloudy nights.

The only nearby accommodations are several "strip" motels. The employees are locals. Anyone staying at them is quickly noticed and talked about, especially if they act in a peculiar fashion or keep a shop full of electronic devices in their rooms. Suspicious individuals are likely to

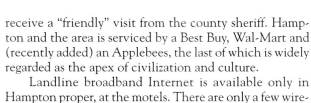

receive a "friendly" visit from the county sheriff. Hampton and the area is serviced by a Best Buy, Wal-Mart and (recently added) an Applebees, the last of which is widely regarded as the apex of civilization and culture.

Landline broadband Internet is available only in Hampton proper, at the motels. There are only a few wireless access points, none of which are not locked down. There is generally good analog cellphone coverage in the area, but no 3G coverage.

In general, the town has an excellent grapevine. Characters who are from out of town and can expect that everyone in the district interested in the latest news knows about everything they do in the public eye.

Official Reactions

Sheriff Withers is primarily interested in making sure the characters aren't in town to stir up trouble, say to contribute to the existing drunken resident problem or to find isolated spots to establish marijuana crops. If the characters are clearly well off (they wear business attire), he is extremely polite. Anyone who seems to present employment prospects is none-too-subtly courted.

And yet, Withers has no interest in characters trespassing or vandalizing the old Magnus place. Characters who run into the sheriff but who don't have a good excuse for going to (or being at) the Magnus house can expect (at best) a daylight tour, during which the sheriff tries to divine just what their interest is. The same treatment is extended to reporters and other individuals who are reputable but don't bring any money to the county. High-profile occultists or scene-makers find that the sheriff isn't worried about negative publicity for his county (the local ghost story has already driven property values down). There's no such thing as bad publicity when you're as small as Hampton. To his mind, the worst that can happen is the house turns into a tourist attraction.

What Withers does not want is unrewarding trouble. Characters who seem to be unsavory or cranks are told that the estate is private property and they're not welcome to go poking around. In this case, deputies stop by the house a few times each day as long as the characters are in town.

Characters who have bought the mansion or who attempt to develop the land can expect the utmost in cooperation. The police respond immediately to any problems at the house, unless the characters prove reckless or dangerous. Characters who can file convincing statute paperwork (Wits + Politics), or who can flatter the sheriff with promises of exposure in a book or documentary (Manipulation + Persuasion, and some convincing evidence of real intent) can gain access to department records of events at the house (Withers has been in office throughout).

Merwin Eberhardt, the attorney who works as DA for the county when it needs one, is unresponsive to inquiries or requests. He always seems "too busy." A successful Wits + Politics roll in a contested action against his Resolve + Politics (five dice) is required to get him to allow access to his records. Mr. Eberhardt doesn't personally know anything about the Magnus case. Furthermore, the former investigating attorney Jeremy Pritchard and secretary Wanda Paige are now both dead; the practice of Eberhardt and Pritchard has been reduced to merely Eberhardt. And yet, characters who do somehow gain access to Eberhardt's files find the handwritten speculation "Probably a spook?" (see below).

Protagonists who are actually from or who still live in the county are able to come and go from the Magnus house as they please. They're told to go home if they're caught messing around, and arrested and released the next day if caught trying to damage or destroy the place. In reality, everyone has expected the house to burn down for years, and most townsfolk would be glad to see it go. Unless the characters are caught red-handed or brag openly about their culpability in, say, arson, they're unlikely to go punished.

Emergency Services

Hampton County, including the town of Hampton, is patrolled by a local police department. There are 16 uniformed officers in the department (12 full time, four part time), four of whom are on duty in their cruisers on any given shift. In general, two stick close to town while two patrol the back roads. In town, police response time is under five minutes. In rural areas, response time is 15 to 30 minutes, depending on how close officers are. The department also employs four dispatchers and four additional civilian employees who work in the office during normal business hours. County sheriff is an elected office, currently held by Milt Withers, a crafty 45-year-old politician with no ambitions but to hold onto his job and keep his county safe. The normal run of crime is drunk driving enforcement, the occasional petty drug bust, and domestic violence. The sheriff's office is accustomed to this kind of day-to-day law enforcement. Sudden or incredible demands or bizarre crimes bring out the worst in their informality and close relationship with the community. That is, outsiders are automatically considered in the wrong, and the judgment of local officers is accepted without question.

Hampton County police officers are armed as detailed on p. 206 of the **World of Darkness Rulebook**. Each carries four spare magazines, a large can of OC spray and a baton. Their Remington 870s are racked in their cruisers, but they carry them on any call that looks like it might be dangerous.

Local police are moderately competent professionals used to handling situations on their own, but they call for backup when responding after dark or if a situation looks dicey. Remember that Hampton County is rural. Shots fired or fires burning do not draw police response unless there is some other good reason to believe that the situation requires attention. Characters who are arrested are held in the local jail, which has four cells, until they can be arraigned or at least until their bail is set at the start of business the next day. The county has three magistrates.

Any serious cases are sent to Canyon City, a larger town in the next county.

If events seem bigger than they can comfortably handle, local police request backup from the state police. State police officers are equipped similarly to local police, except they carry AR-15 type tactical carbines in their cruisers (use the stats for "assault rifle" on p. 169 of the **World of Darkness Rulebook**; capacity is 30 + 1 and the weapon cannot autofire). One or two state troopers may be cruising a highway near town, and a dozen officers and a helicopter arrive from the local barracks within an hour of a backup call.

Emergency medical services are provided by a volunteer ambulance team. There is one ambulance on duty at all times with two EMTs (there is a total staff of 10). There is a tiny hospital in Hampton, the Methodist Medical Center, that provides adequate basic care for normal injuries and illnesses. Any life-threatening injuries or exotic diseases are evacuated by air to larger urban medical centers (usually using the city hospital's helicopter, but occasionally by ambulance if the case is not urgent). The county coroner is Thom Wilson, a general practitioner who's competent enough to diagnose normal causes of death, but who lacks a sophisticated forensics lab. He can diagnose death by heart attack as natural causes (even if it occurs out of fear), for example. For suspicious cases or those involving violence or drugs, he calls on the state police forensics lab, which has excellent facilities.

Fire coverage is provided by a volunteer department with about 30 members, not all of whom respond to any given alarm. There is a pump truck, a ladder truck and a general-utility vehicle. Response time is about 10 minutes in town, 20 minutes outside it. Hampton proper has a pressurized water system (fire hydrants). Outside of town, fires that cannot be doused with the water in the pumper are contained and left to burn themselves out.

Other Local Notables

The following are other important individuals in town.

Betty Wilson — Coroner Thom Wilson's wife and receptionist.

Elmyra Withers — Milt Withers wife. Head of the Baptist Lady's League.

Shep Morton — Shep's brother Andy owned the town hardware store and was found dead of a heart attack after attempting to hunt on the Magnus estate. Shep can relate his brother's determination to put an end to the stories that had spread about Magnus' land, and he wound up dead. Andy Morton was a friend of Josh Tarkinton (see below). It was widely felt around town that Andy had gone out to avenge himself on the memory of the Magnuses. He confirmed their position as preeminent scary story, instead.

Terry "Brownie" Pandal — Owner of Pandal Contracting, the town's most respected contracting firm. His father was a doctor, and he likes to joke about how he couldn't bear to cut up meat like his old man did, so doctor and butcher were right out, but he's still in the family cutting trade. Terry is a rough-living, lifelong bachelor used to picking up any one of several nice girls from the local roadhouse when he wants sex.

Betty Nickles — The owner of the town lumber yard and remaining hardware store, who still holds on in the face of DIY home-improvement stores by dint of her connections with local contractors.

Hank Parsons — The cigar-smoking and offensive but amiable owner of the local feed lot. His shockingly young wife Betty is an inveterate gossip. Sons Bert and Franklin.

Maurice Willingham — A professional town manager happy to direct his little corner of nowhere. Wife Andrea; son Tom; daughters, Tamara and Angela.

Frank Hugh — Fire chief. Gay, not out and miserable. No partner.

Nathan Bedford Forrest Hugh — Hereditary owner of the local grocery store, currently withering under siege by Wal-Mart. About to be the town's next riches-to-rags story. Wife Marilyn-Eileen; sons Hank and Spike. His 22-year-old daughter Abileen is the town tramp and has quite a reputation.

Magnus' Story

James Magnus was born on a rural farmstead in Hampton County some 70 years ago to an alcoholic father and an abusive mother. A troubled child with a bullying nature, he was a constant truant and disciplinary problem who nevertheless performed well enough in school to skate by. He was, in fact, quite brilliant, and rather malevolent. While he was never caught, he was an inveterate torturer of small animals and an occasional arsonist.

He was drafted at age 18 and took well to the formality and discipline of army life. He rose quickly to the rank of sergeant, and his woodcraft and combat skills led him to a career in the Special Forces. His intelligence and a natural gift as a polyglot allowed him to quickly master a number of languages.

From the Special Forces, he drifted into various other forms of service, eventually being seconded to the CIA. By that time, he was already trained as an interrogator. He served as a technical advisor to Savak, the Shah of Iran's secret police, for several years. After that, he took a leave of absence and a long vacation with some locals with whom he'd fallen in. He and his "associates" traveled to northern Israel along Lebanese smuggling routes to Chorazin, where Magnus had learned one might gain long life, a loyal companion and the death of one's enemies by calling out certain praises to the "Prince of the Air."

What happened there is unrecorded. Perhaps Magnus made contact with the powers of darkness with the help of fellow devotees, or maybe he merely believed he had. Regardless, he returned from the north of the Sea of Galilee with a wife provided by his allies, a beautiful and silent Arab girl named Aiesha. Magnus already had a fearsome reputation prior to his trip abroad. When he returned, his reputation was doubled. He was a heartless master of the quick break that left a prisoner begging for his life, willing to reveal anything.

Magnus' technique was incredible and his new wife was his willing assistant. Indeed, she acted like a familiar in human form, always trailing just a few steps behind, always in his presence, even during interrogations. With her play-sexuality and her childish willingness to cause agony, Aiesha was quickly associated with the camel-footed demoness of the same name. Neither Magnus nor his wife did anything to discourage this supposition.

Magnus left Iran and the CIA and became a private contractor, working primarily in African security services. Still inseparable from his wife, he made occasional trips to Vietnam and Iran to help his Savak and CIA employers with difficult interrogations. Such contract work proved quite lucrative, both monetarily and in terms of political favors.

Eventually, Magnus saw the writing on the wall for his "regular" job in Africa and called in markers with the CIA. Normally the Company would have discouraged a free agent like him returning to the US, but Magnus was waved in as a retired friend of the agency, and shielded from any questions that might have come up about his associations with foreign governments.

Magnus returned to America and quietly arranged citizenship for his wife. Once arrived, he found his father dead from cirrhosis and his mother living in a skid-row slum. With his wife's help, he abducted and murdered his mother from her Massachusetts home. His motive was opaque. At some level he told himself he was covering his tracks, while another part of him wandered between a self-destructive desire to eliminate his own roots and a more "reasonable" desire to kill the woman who had been so abusive in his youth. After a few years of quiet life in Minot, ND, Magnus returned to his hometown.

Using his significant wealth, he bought his parents' former farmstead from its current owners. After snapping up a number of neighboring woodlots and properties to gain a sprawling estate, he had his parents' house demolished and a large, somewhat opulent mansion built on its foundation.

Why Magnus came back to his roots depends on your story needs. If there's no compelling reason, he was simply called home by the siren song of youthful memory, perhaps tinged by the ticking clock of a self-destructing agreement with dark powers. If you wish, however, he could have had a much more sinister motive. Perhaps he returned to dedicate himself, undisturbed, to his dark masters and lost his direction. Or perhaps his self-destruction was the intended result all along, whether he knew it or not.

Over the next several years, Magnus established a reputation among the Hampton locals for being a vicious, hateful man. A neighboring farmer who originally wasn't willing to sell his land was motivated to after his barn burned down. Magnus also patrolled his property with the help of a pack of Doberman Pinschers. Several individuals who hunted on his land without permission were attacked by the dogs. Indeed, Magnus claimed that one, a local favorite named Josh Tarkinton, had shot at him, and James killed the intruder with a rifle shot of his own. When Sheriff Withers arrived, Tarkinton's rifle was in the man's dead hands, complete with a shell fired. There was little doubt from the seeming circumstances that Tarkinton had tried to creep close to Magnus and assassinate the target as he left his own house. The district attorney chose not to prosecute Magnus, but there are still many notes about the matter in the DA's office files, including the hand-written speculation that the extremely shallow and exceedingly clean records of Magnus' life were falsified. "Probably a spook?" asks the note in an unknown hand.

The devil's luck that protected the veteran torturer hadn't failed, and Tarkinton's shot had missed. Yet there were signs of the paranoia that tore at Magnus' soul. It was revealed in the coroner's inquest that Magnus carried his rifle with him at all times when outdoors, and that he had for several years.

In the last few years of his life, after Tarkinton's murder, Magnus became more reclusive, coming to town only to purchase supplies and alcohol. Aiesha was never seen at all. It was assumed in town that she was a traditional Arabic wife, keeping to the home. This was to some extent true, though what none of the locals realized was that Aiesha and James' relationship had gone sour. Perhaps it had always been adversarial, or perhaps it turned that way only when the two had nothing but their own company on which to depend.

Whatever the case, the two came to hate one another, but their existence was so intertwined that there was no parting them. Love turned to hate without the ability to abide separate lives. Differences festered and swelled. They turned into shouting matches, screaming matches and then into physical abuse.

Finally, alcohol far outweighed any other supplies taken to the house, and the Magnuses became more and more erratic. Both were full-time alcoholics. When the postman finally realized that the couple hadn't emptied its post-office box in weeks, the sheriff was called. At the house, he discovered a scene of bloody murder. Aiesha had been killed with a hatchet, presumably as she fled down the front steps of the house. Magnus himself was found in the huge four-poster bed in the master bedroom, a .45 service pistol in one hand, a bottle of whiskey in the other, and his brains splattered all over the sheets. Magnus' dogs were found inside their cage in the cellar, where they had torn one another to pieces in a frenzy of cannibalistic hunger. The last dog had died days earlier, from infection of injuries sustained in the many battles fought to survive in the pen.

Discovering the Magnus Story

The couple's background is provided here mostly to give you an idea of what sort of people James and Aiesha were, and thus the nature of their ghosts. Characters with connections may be able to pull James' military service records, but doing so requires an Ally or Contact who's a high-ranking state or federal official of some sort. Research may also demand a trip to somewhere significantly bigger than Hampton, possibly Washington D.C.

Records show Magnus as having been drafted, voluntarily re-enlisting repeatedly, and being honorably discharged. He had top-secret clearance at the end of his career and was a trained linguist and interrogator. His files are very slim on details, but presumably characters can read between the lines. When an individual of his capabilities leaves the armed forces and drops out of sight for the better part of two decades, covert, internationally influential activities are a given.

Characters with very high-level access to CIA files can find out a fair amount, but it requires extensive research (–3 penalty). Nobody who worked with Magnus is still with the agency, and none of his commanders are still alive. Characters with access to African states or the Iranian secret police can probably learn the particular elements of his history relating to those places. Unless your troupe has created some really unusual characters, it's unlikely that characters have that sort of clout.

Almost a dozen years have passed since the Magnus' murder-suicide. The house has sat empty and in increasingly dilapidated condition ever since. A successful Intelligence + Investigation roll can track down a tiny note in the *Shawtok Valley Times*, a regional newspaper. (The effort requires a visit to the home of the elderly former editor and an afternoon rummaging through a large collec-

tion of poorly labeled diskettes.) There are notices of the Magnus' posthumous estate auction, stock and uninformative obits, and a very short piece on the murder that consists mostly of quotations from Sheriff Withers.

Stories circulate regularly around town about mysterious, often terrifying apparitions near or in the house. The most prevalent ones are common enough that they can be tracked down — not as friend-of-a-friend stories, but to actual individuals who can repeat their accounts. A successful Manipulation + Socialize roll can result in several accounts, and an exceptional success nets the characters a vivid description of the dogs (see below) and of Aiesha walking forest roads.

Witnesses include police deputies and other sober and reliable adults. The most common stories involve hearing the snarling and barking of Magnus' hounds in the woods around his mansion, seeing a woman walking the roads at night, and glimpses of lights in the area.

No one in town with the money has interest in buying the house. Any prospective out-of-town buyers have quickly fled, either turned off by the stories or by phenomena they claimed to have witnessed. Those who have spent even a night or two in the mansion have testified to bleeding walls, wracking sobs, the smell of alcohol, and awakening to the snarling and barking of dogs.

You may allow characters with high Occult (3+ dots) to know or discover the vulnerabilities of ghosts, or to discover them with an exceptional success while performing research — namely that spirits' manifestations are vulnerable to blessed weapons and rites (see the **World of**

Darkness Rulebook, pp. 212-214). Bare immersion in Occult (1 or 2 dots) might at least give characters some understanding of what goes on at the house, and whether it can be stopped or not. Meanwhile, most other characters who are devoid of any such knowledge are left to their own mundane means of coping.

Official Responses

Milt Withers was sheriff at the time of the Magnus murder- suicide and can provide his own rather harrowing account of the case. To elicit this revelation, characters have to convince Withers of their honesty or legitimacy in restoring the house or resolving matters there, by producing some sort of paperwork or a believable story to back up their claims, and perhaps with a successful Manipulation + Socialize or Persuasion roll at a −2 penalty based on Withers' reservations against opening up. Most successes inspire a sanitized version of events, while an exceptional success persuades him to recount the gruesome experience of finding the decayed bodies, and some other personal insights.

Withers knew that Magnus was some sort of criminal, but could never pin anything on him. He knew Josh Tarkinton was an excellent shot, and is fairly certain that he would never have missed Magnus if he'd been shooting at the old veteran. Yet, the circumstantial evidence to support Magnus' claim was there: a discharged rifle in the dead man's hands, a bullet hole in Magnus house, and a claim of self-defense.

Since Magnus' death, Withers has suspected that something inexplicable (if not "supernatural") as been at work at the mansion. He swears he's seen Aiesha walking the roads, and he's definitely seen the bobbing lights in the wood. Almost all the deputies have come to him with reports of seeing things near the estate, and he's filed it all away as just more "facts" about his jurisdiction.

Characters who persuade the sheriff to open up can count on him to overlook things they do to combat the ghosts, provided characters' activities are not shockingly criminal or would not implicate him as an accomplice. Obviously, Withers' understanding doesn't blanket all of the department's deputies and their response to, say, hacksaw murders. Yet, characters who come away from a brush with the house without committing homicide or maiming each other can expect any cases against them to be dropped, their paperwork lost and evidence mysteriously mislaid.

If deputies encounter characters in the throes of a supernatural sighting, the police are surprisingly understanding. They don't necessary treat the characters as madmen or women (even if characters are spotted running along the road in their underwear), but respond in a reassuring manner. Deputies' response is to calm characters down and to assure them that their eyes were deceived. Meanwhile, characters are driven to a diner to get some food or a hotel to get some clothes, and then deputies avoid the estate altogether for a few nights.

The Magnus House

The Magnus house proper is the central location of this story. While the ghosts who inhabit it are important, the house itself is the real central antagonist. The appearance of the supernatural is intermittent, but the house is always present.

Atmosphere

In general, the feel of the house is the same that its former inhabitants gave it. It was a retreat that became a fortress or prison for them, a retirement into an existence in which the couple had no victims but one another.

The house has the stale feeling of a place left undisturbed for too long. It has a sterile, almost authoritarian air. Even at their most positive, the Magnuses were splashes of color on their antiseptically well-kept home. They lived their lives as jailers, in jails, and in the end, they built a jail for themselves. When describing it, dwell on the institutional nature of various parts: the way the many doors on the living room balcony appear like a cellblock, the stark kitchen, the wire "cell" dog kennel in the basement, the house's Arabic-style internal courtyard and how it seems like a dusty prison exercise yard.

Don't beat the players over the head with these details, but point them out. "The kitchen is so big, you could feed an army." "The inner courtyard is big enough that men could do calisthenics in it." In a movie, there would be many long shots from ground level looking up the structure's walls to make it seem towering. You can play up the house's height, maybe by saying, "Standing at a spot where there are no windows to break up the surface, it's easy to see how incredibly huge the place is." There are bars across all the ground-floor windows, just waiting to be used in prison symbolism, as are the grimy parts of the basement and dog kennel.

At its most positive, the house can feel very much like a church or school. Much hay can be made of this if the characters are being fed a rosy line to start the story off. You can offer flashes of Magnus' halting attempts to teach Aiesha how to live like a "normal person," and then slowly reveal the fact that he believes her to be his possession through satanic pact and he barely knows how to live himself. Such flashes conveyed to the characters can seem to show a journey of self-discovery, until it becomes clear that what the couple discovered was that they were dysfunctional without a larger purpose to guide them.

In general, if the characters live in the mansion or simply sleep there for a few days, inquire about how they establish themselves, and how they decorate. Encourage them to develop a "feel" for how things look in the house. Do they seek a faux country manor? Is theirs a blue-collar life moved to a place far too large for their possessions? Or do they put on the ritz in a far-off location with the help of modern designers? Then you can cut between this feel and the antiseptic, institutional feel of the Magnuses to build symbolic strength between the characters tastes' and those of the previous residents, between the characters' minds and awareness and those of the previous residents, and finally between the characters' Vices and those of the previous residents.

Condition

Though left untended, the house is structurally sound. There's another 10 good years on the roof, so there are no leaks. The interior was stripped down to the bare walls and parquet floors; there are no furnishings. Various doors and windows have been broken in by trespassers, and there is a litter of old condoms, beer bottles and snack wrappers, but much less than one would expect for such an attractive location for teen drinking parties, drifters and squatters.

Windows: The windows are hung for modern multipane windows, but many are broken. All the ground-floor windows have ornamental but entirely functional iron bars over them that Magnus installed when he became nervous about the ghosts of his own past.

Television: The house has a satellite dish in the backyard. Innovative at the time, it is now huge and the service it used has long been discontinued. The dish is best torn out and replaced with a small, modern receiver, but it could be used as is.

Electricity: The mansion has a breaker box, not a fuse box, and a functional electrical system complete with grounding plugs and outlets that accommodates one-way plugs. Power is not currently connected.

Heating and Cooling: Gas for cooking and heating is provided by LP gas tanks, now long dry. There is no provision for central air conditioning, but heat is via forced air so AC could be added.

Water: Water is pumped from a well, through a vitrified diatomaceous earth filter, into a 10,000-liter cistern under the house. This is an unusual arrangement but leaves the house with a significant amount of water. Given the circumstances of the couple's death, the house wasn't mothballed properly, and the cistern now lies filled with 5,000 or so liters of putrid, stagnant water. In order for the house's water system to be used again, the cistern needs to be drained, cleaned and refilled over the course of at least a day's labor.

Telephone: The house is equipped with a modern touch-tone phone connection with modular wall jacks. There are no phones provided. The service is a pre-NID POTS bridge. The house is wired for a single line and the wire is intact from the pole up to the wall jacks. It just needs to be turned on at the switch in the CO.

Broadband: Lack of cable connection and distance from CO prohibits modern broadband data links. Characters seeking to install broadband connectivity are limited to 64 or 128 kb/sec ISDN connections, or a satellite link.

Manifestations of the Haunt

Each area of the house encourages various haunting phenomena that you can stage in your game, listed by each of the characters' senses. (After all, why should a ghost violate a living person's sight or hearing alone? What *tastes* could a ghost inspire?) These experiences are triggered by various uses of Ghost Sign, Phantasm and Terrify (see the **World of Darkness** Rulebook, pp. 211-212). Haunting phenomena may be occasional at first, but slowly gain frequency and intensity as time goes by.

Haunting events occur frequently after the ghosts manifest, and characters undergo flashbacks of the spirits' lives or are subject to possession. During these sessions characters can be made to repeat the activities that the ghosts carried out in life, whether they're shouting matches or more carnal pursuits. Events can occur at any time, but especially at night and during the winter, when the couple would have been cooped up indoors.

The following are general guidelines for how the haunting unfolds. "In the house" can include "on its grounds." Early in the haunting, only one sensation may be experienced at a time. As events progress, characters can be subject to more and more of these occult events at one time. When the ghosts use their Numina, the house as it is and the house as it was perceptually intermingle. Characters may seem to find themselves taking part in events of the past, or witnessing them.

Because the haunting of the house is so intense, each location is assigned a manifestation modifier (see **World of Darkness**, p. 210). This bonus or penalty represents the ease and degree of frequency of haunting events in the various rooms of the house. Some areas, such as the greenhouse, are never subject to haunting, while others have discernable effects on any character who spends so much as a few hours or days in them. Any rooms added by the Storyteller should be assigned a manifestation modifier as well, based on how much the Magnuses lived their lives there.

Hampton County as a whole is a stolid, conservative land, and can be assumed to have an overall −1 manifestation modifier. Of course, if the characters need to be dogged by the haunting, you can change this factor. Those under the house's influence might have a "personal aura" with a +1 manifestation modifier, for example.

James and Aiesha's dedication of the house as a black temple carved out a spiritual niche for them quite at odds with the local supernatural landscape. The ghosts can be abjured but not exorcised in the house or on its grounds. They can be affected as any spirit elsewhere in the county (see **World of Darkness**, pp. 212-214).

• Characters who attempt to damage the house may experience haunting phenomenon on the spot and, if working at night, may cause one or more of the ghosts to manifest automatically.

• Characters tend to experience phenomena during daylight hours only if they are alone, have the Unseen Sense Merit (attuned to ghosts), or if they already suffer altered perceptions. That is, if they're drunk, on drugs or crazed with grief, fear or anger. Remember, there is a penalty for manifesting in front of more than one onlooker.

• Characters who are in the house at night are very likely to experience a haunting event if they are alone, have the Unseen Sense Merit and/or experience altered perceptions of their own.

• Characters who are in the house at night and who demonstrate behavior like James and Aiesha Magnus are almost certain to experience haunting phenomena. Activities that resemble the couple's include alcoholism, isolation, suspicion of the outside world, psychological abuse, violence, black magic and kinky sex.

• The longer the characters are in the house, the more intense encounters are with the ghosts. After several days or weeks, events occur during the daytime and before multiple witnesses. Characters in the house feed and awaken the spirits as time goes by, so the activity they rouse grows increasingly extreme.

Mansion Locations

There's no specific map for the mansion. As with a haunted house in a horror movie, it's easiest for dramatic purposes to just let rooms be where they're needed. (And in a haunted house, rooms need not necessarily be where characters left them.) What's important is that the house is shaped like a "U" around an Arabic-style courtyard, with a large swimming pool located at the end of the yard. Otherwise, the house's features include the following.

Grounds

The grounds of the house are composed of several large farmsteads. Most were already partially wooded, and Magnus had the houses demolished and their sites planted with saplings when he bought them. The reforestation was unusual and extravagantly costly at the time, but decades later, those areas are covered with thick second-growth forest. A character must walk several miles to reach a neighboring structure. All inhabitants on the edges of Magnus' land can describe in detail haunting phenomena, mostly seeing or hearing dogs in the woods or seeing lights amid the trees.

Game is common on the grounds, because domestic dogs and cats rarely roam there.

Manifestation Modifier: +1

Haunting Phenomena

Visual: Bobbing witchlights in the forest. Very brief glimpses of dogs. A glimpse of Aiesha walking the road with a hatchet in her head (only near the woods). Discovery of animal remains mutilated by dog attack.

Smell: The smell of wood smoke or gun smoke, areas of inexplicable and repulsive scents (vomit, blood or rotting meat).

Aural: Sounds of someone attempting to move stealthily through the brush.

Tactile: Cold spots.

Taste: Sudden taste of whiskey.

Living Room

The house has a palatial living room, easily large enough to accommodate a regulation-sized tennis court. Even the largest selection of furniture becomes a collection of oddments in the vast space. If characters set up

some sort of conversation pit or other arrangement of furniture, they're surrounded by a huge dead zone that creates a blind spot from any angle.

This was the Magnus' "sitting room." They often passed the days here reading or otherwise amusing themselves in their respective chairs while they drank themselves into incoherence. The living room's most notable fixture is a line of five guest bedroom doors that open directly onto a second-floor balcony facing out over the main living area. This internal breezeway bears a notable resemblance to a block of cells in a prison, and the doors are prone to banging open unexpectedly.

Manifestation Modifier: +2

Haunting Phenomena

Visual: Reflection of Aiesha or James on the room's tremendous windows. They may seem to stalk a character or be involved in some intimate encounter.

Smell: The smell of alcohol, gun smoke or sex.

Aural: Clink of ice in a glass. Sound of a pistol slide being drawn.

Tactile: Brush of Aiesha or James' hand along a character's neck or arm, but no one there to perform it. Thrown objects and other poltergeist effects may also occur, an echo of arguments past.

Taste: Sudden taste of whiskey or sex.

Basement

The basement, while creepy, is not dank. There are no leaks in the foundation and no scuttling millipedes. It is cement-floored, with white walls and a number of small cubicles here and there to serve as storage, or a shower, or anything but the detention cells that observation suggests the spaces to be. While there are many opportunities for frightful encounters here, neither James nor Aiesha spent much time in the basement, so significantly few echoes of them linger. And yet, this area was the primary abode of the

dogs. Characters down here at night after the mansion has had enough time to awaken almost certainly get flashes of its canine aura, and smell or hear dogs. Even during the day, there seems to be a lingering dog-kennel aroma.

The basement has two main features. One is the six-foot-wide cistern that's some 20 feet deep, stretching down into the rock beneath the building. The cistern has a lip about one foot high and is uncovered. There are ladder rungs on the inside of the well that lead down to the bottom, but they are slippery with slime and are as likely to injure a character in a fall as help one escape.

When the house is first opened, the water here is black and rank, too shallow to safely jump into and too dark to see through. When the cistern is cleaned out and the water replaced, any character with a flashlight can easily see to the bottom.

A fall into the cistern inflicts two Health points of bashing damage, which can be reduced as normal with a Dexterity + Athletics roll (**World of Darkness**, p. 179).

The second feature is the chain-link-fence-enclosed dog kennel where the dogs died, tearing one another apart in the hungry dark. A pipe sticking out of a wall can be set to trickle fresh water, and there's a hose attached to an adjacent wall.

The basement also has a wine cellar. The cellar door opens from the outside only, and if it's propped open it has a tendency to slam shut without provocation. The cellar's contents were carried off by county employees who auctioned the house's contents, but a sweet scent still lingers.

Manifestation Modifier: +1

Haunting Phenomena

Visual: Breaker box trips and plunges the basement into darkness. Sight of dogs, either in their prime or at their end, when only one or two survived. Glint of light across the eyes of dogs in the darkness, but with no actual animals visible. Flashbacks of being the uncooperative hooker who was stuffed in the wine cellar until preparations were made for her "performance."

Smell: The smell of dog feces or urine. Strange, stagnant whiffs from the cistern. Smell of fear and urine from the wine cellar.

Aural: Growling, barking or whining of dogs. Sound of dog claws on the concrete floor or at the door of the wine cellar.

Tactile: Brush of dogs against legs or the feel of a dog rearing up to push its paws against a character's chest. A feeling of cold from the cistern. The sound of the dogs hurling themselves at the door of the wine cellar.

The sensation of being trapped like a kidnap victim. A character may "go along for the ride" with a hooker who is led out to the woods behind the house.

Taste: Sudden taste of blood, rotted meat, wine or stagnant water.

Library

The house's library is not huge, but it does have dedicated shelving. The shelves are now empty and the reading tables gone. The books were originally on history, military science, Arabic-language literature and black magic. This room was little inhabited. Many books were stored here, but the Magnuses normally read in the living room. The one thing that does linger strongly is the practice of magic. Any sort of Ouija board or reading or divinatory method used here produces results related to the haunting of the house. This is the residue of black magic in a house full of hate. Such efforts do not produce a meticulously spelled-out story of the haunting, but do result in bleeding tarot cards or smashed Ouija planchettes — testament to the anger and violence that occurred.

Manifestation Modifier: +2

Haunting Phenomena

Visual: Finding a single book in Arabic or that seems to be in Arabic, lying in the middle of the floor. Books spontaneously appearing on shelves where the shelves were empty before. Books stacked in towers. Books on the dark arts.

Smell: The scent of old paper.

Aural: The sound of books ruffling or fluttering. One of the Magnus' voices, quiet and incoherent, as if someone reads aloud and distractedly.

Tactile: Books on the shelves whip about in a poltergeist display. Pages turning on their own.

Taste: The sudden taste of mold or dust.

Master Bedroom

The master bedroom is where Aiesha and James spent much of their time. It is the scene of much sex, much hatred, and James' eventual suicide. It is the most strongly haunted area of the house, especially for individuals who have sex or who argue. It is a palatial bedroom with an equally huge attached bath and an in-floor tub, bidet and toilet. There's no kinky-sex act that characters can perform that doesn't echo a similar deed of the Magnuses. There's no quarrel they can have that does not echo some disagreement from the past.

Manifestation Modifier: +3

Haunting Phenomena

Visual: Hallucinations of domestic disputes, erotic encounters, and sleepless, angry brooding. Glimpses of James Magnus with his brains blown all over the sheets and his service .45 in his dead hand.

Smell: The smell of sex or liquor. The scent of blood or gun smoke.

Aural: The sounds of individuals enjoying rough sex. The garbled words of bitter bedtime quarrels.

Tactile: The feeling of hands on the body or of sexual intercourse. Hallucinations of the last seconds of James Magnus. Poltergeist effects are also possible in this room, as in the living room. Waking up soaked in sweat, blood or alcohol.

Taste: The tastes of blood, sex, whiskey or bile are all likely to wash across the tongue of individuals in the room.

Lesser Bedrooms

The house has seven small bedrooms (or more — whatever is necessary to accommodate the characters comfortably). Five of them line the balcony above the living room, lending it a "cellblock" appearance. The others are located elsewhere in the house.

The Magnuses used to pick up sex workers in a large city, bring them out for long weekends, and then dump them (*almost* always alive) back in the city when they were done. Those who never made it back were taken to the woods and disposed of. The couple put up their guests in these rooms. Characters who spend nights in these rooms are liable to meet the Magnuses in their dreams.

Manifestation Modifier: +1

Haunting Phenomena

Visual: Flashbacks of the Magnuses doing tag-team S&M on a prostitute. Flashbacks of their clinical cleanup of the room afterward.

Smell: Scent of sex, or smell of opium or hash given to "good" slaves, or odor of blood, fear or hot metal when things went sour with weekend guests.

Aural: Sounds of sex, sobbing or overheard arguments over how an overnight stay wasn't in the initial deal. Those who argued too much got a trip to the wine cellar and then an execution.

Tactile: Sharing the drug-withdrawal pangs of a hooker who spends a prolonged "visit" at the house.

Taste: Drugs, sex, blood, hunger, rubber from bite blocks or gags.

Kitchen

The kitchen is lavishly furnished with a stainless-steel island or prep table, a six-burner commercial stove, a small walk-in freezer, a large pantry and a commercial microwave. The kitchen equipment wasn't stripped out and hasn't been ruined by vagrants or teenage vandals, making the foundation for fine, restaurant-quality facilities.

In their dining as in many other aspects of their lives, the Magnuses appreciated the sensual. Both were excellent cooks, and the kitchen retains many generally positive impressions of the house. There are many memories of fine dinners and well-executed desserts to go with violent anger. Depending on your intentions, this may be an excellent place to introduce sensory flashes. It is possible to make the story initially seem like a Gothic-romance-through-the-ages, and then pull the rug out with the truth of the Magnus' lives and deaths.

Manifestation Modifier: +0

Haunting Phenomena

Visual: Fine foods and wines. Flashbacks of mutual love of fine food. Flashback of food-throwing alcoholic screaming matches.

Smell: All the flavors of the talented chef's palate. Spilled wine. Drunkenly cooked food burning.

Aural: The clatter of plates and crockery, the sounds of cooking, thrown and smashed plates.

Tactile: Cuddling while cooking. The feel of different foods in the mouth. Flying plates and glasses.

Taste: The many tastes of the kitchen, often heightened by the effects of a liberal dose of alcohol.

The Courtyard

The U-shaped manor surrounds an Arabic-style courtyard — a plaza with a fountain — with the open end completed by a swimming pool. Flowerbeds that once held shade-loving plants line the walls. They are now riotously overgrown. The fountain is decorated with a somewhat risqué and tacky statue of a satyr frolicking with a nymph. The fountain is dry.

Manifestation Modifier: –2

Haunting Phenomena

Visual: The fountain spraying blood (this never happened, it was just a frequent fantasy of Magnus'). The pool filling up with blood or wine. The illusion of motion from the fountain's statuary, which may play out skits or frighten the bejesus out of characters, but the figures don't attack.

Smell: The scent of jasmine and honeysuckle.

Aural: The sound of the fountain running.

Tactile: The remembered feeling of sore muscles while doing calisthenics in the courtyard.

Taste: Perceived water in the fountain tasting like blood or alcohol.

Swimming Pool

An Olympic-sized swimming pool is located behind the house, forming one of the "walls" of the courtyard. Sensual creatures that they were, the Magnuses loved to swim and exercise. The pool is currently filled with about five feet of water in the deep end, while the shallow end is high and dry. The surface of the water is slick with algae and pond growth.

Manifestation Modifier: −1

Haunting Phenomena

Visual: Sweaty swimming pool sex flashbacks. Memories of swimming like a seal.

Smell: The smell of sweat, chlorine and sunblock.

Aural: The sounds of swimming or of sex in the pool.

Tactile: Exercising characters may flash to the excellent physiques of the Magnuses and overperform to the point of injuring themselves.

Taste: Kisses and sex mixed with water.

Greenhouse

There's a greenhouse with a koi pond beyond the house. The greenhouse is excellent and, miraculously, only a few of the windows are broken. There is an internal sprinkler system and small shed full of garden tools. The pond is dried out, and all that remains of the plants are long stalks and aged leaves.

Manifestation Modifier: −2

Haunting Phenomena

Unless it's winter, the greenhouse is extremely hot, even at night. For characters to remain there for extended periods, players have to make a Stamina + Resolve roll every six hours, just as if characters had gone a six-hour period *past* the 24-hour exhaustion point (see "Fatigue," **World of Darkness Rulebook**, p. 179). This roll even applies to sleeping characters. Failing a roll means that a character can remain no longer and can't bring himself to return for a day. Note that according to the rules, p. 180, characters who are at a −1 penalty due to conditions are prone to mild hallucinations. While the characters may seek temporary sanctuary from the ghosts in the greenhouse (see its −2 manifestation modifier), staying too long is physically debilitating. The longest a character can remain in the greenhouse is a number of days equal to his Stamina or Resolve, whichever is lowest.

Concluding the Story

If this is being run as the initial story in a chronicle, the haunting is relatively easy to conclude. Events progress until the characters experience something that exceeds their determination to remain and you allow them to beat a retreat, suffering whatever injuries or emotional anguish is appropriate to impel them toward further conflicts with the hidden world. This is probably the place where cooperation between Storyteller and players is most important. The line at which the characters have seen enough, and been frightened enough, should be respected. If characters remain in the house beyond their will, it should be because they can't find an escape, not because you or other players insist that they stay. Characters who are ordinary people need to be eased into the truth of the supernatural. They can't be expected to immerse themselves in and deal with it bravely upon first contact.

Actually eliminating the ghosts is a challenge, and best undertaken by characters who have encountered the house (or one like it) before and have the occult resources necessary to best the place. The dogs can be destroyed simply by destruction of their anchor, the house. James and Aiesha are anchored to the land itself, not just the mansion. They continue to haunt the land after the destruction of their former home. Their dark ties also protect them from effective exorcism while in the house or on its lands. They are as vulnerable as any ghost, however, to blessed weapons and abjuration, regardless of where the ghosts are. Utterly clearing the land of trees or setting a forest fire could defeat the ghosts altogether. Otherwise, the couple's spirits are so tormented that actually putting them to rest really isn't possible. They have no intention of moving on and need to be forced.

Access to material about attacking and destroying ghosts is not presented here. It assumes the characters largely play the roles of victims. There are plenty of haunted-house stories in which the "winner" is the one lucky enough to get away merely maimed. If they don't know how to defeat ghosts, the characters probably just aim for survival. Don't be afraid to make it clear that character fatalities are possible. Players shouldn't be surprised when a character does something dumb (or smart!) and is hurt badly or even killed. If characters die, their players may help run the story by roleplaying the ghosts of their characters, now added to the spectral population of the house.

Ultimately, it's up to you if characters can be presumed to know cryptic and mystical information about ghosts, or can find it if they don't know it. They may recall it through a successful Intelligence + Occult roll, might find a book on ghosts in the town library, a grandmother's ghost might share secrets in a dream, or perhaps the characters find James' old book of black sorcery that fell down a heating vent. Such approaches are blunt, but it's not as if the characters are going to discover the means of eliminating the ghosts through trial and error.

Staying in the House

Why don't the characters just flee the house? The supernatural proves its existence! You might want to encourage characters to remain based on their identities, or there are other reasons why they might stay.

• **Fascination with the lives and pleasures of the Magnuses:** The ghosts prey on the Vices of the living, and were themselves slaves to self-indulgence. The house attempts to ensnare those within, and the players' characters may be sorely tempted by the blandishments of the haunting.

• **Physical constraints:** It might not be feasible for the characters to flee. Their vehicle may be disabled, there might be a terrible storm of some kind, or perhaps there's a big mean dog outside (it worked for Cujo). If they want to run off into the woods on foot, let them spend several gasping miles pursued by the dogs, Aiesha or dancing lights before they run into the yard again and find themselves back at square one.

• **Pride:** They got a great deal on this incredible property. Loss of assets or prestige is at risk. Or maybe the characters believe their own will can overcome the ghosts and the house can be claimed as their own.

The Ghosts

Three distinct ghosts haunt the Magnus mansion: James, Aiesha and the dogs. That's also a list of their descending power. The ghosts are not creatures of a normal day-to-day existence. They largely "sleep" and perceive their existence as a series of "hot" moments of activity when emotions and fear call them forth into wakefulness. They do not have the ability to think in linear time, and cannot concoct complex plans or conspiracies. Characters who are drunks, violent toward one another, who engage in kinky sex, and/or have unresolved emotional tensions (i.e., almost any derangement, mild or severe) are likely to interest and awaken the ghosts. The beings may thus seem to have "relationships" with such characters.

Generally, the more the ghosts awaken, the stronger their responses become, so they seem to "pay attention" to given individuals. In reality, passion breeds passion and people already under the ghosts' scrutiny are likely to be contacted and influenced, possibly encouraging the characters' own proclivities and desires all the more. The ghosts are what they are, and don't undergo major changes of heart about their behavior or decide they don't like one person in particular and single her out. They concentrate their power on intruders who are reminiscent of themselves in life, not on characters who intend to thwart the spirits.

The ghosts no longer have a relationship between them, either. One's interests do not necessarily draw the other. In some cases, certain behavior — sex, drinking, anger — may attract both ghosts, but there's no coordination between them. (And yet, a character having a vision or act of possession that involves sex with Aiesha might attract the spirit of an angry, jealous or participatory James.)

Don't bother to keep track of where the ghosts are at any given time. Just assume they have omniscience and omnipresence over the house and grounds. They are "present" for anything that attracts them, even if they are somewhere else at the same time. They cannot normally affect things off the grounds. They cannot usually sense things there, and don't care to. If the characters are locals, however, you may want to give the house power within county lines, or whatever other conceit makes it possible to harass the characters with flashbacks or forced parallels to the Magnus' lives.

There's no reason for the players to have any idea how many ghosts haunt the house, or to make it clear which ghost does what. There's no way to evade their spectral senses or to mark their location. The spirits are simply part of the house and land. Some players may expect just one ghost, and their characters may be confused by the various possessions and visions that occur, especially when such events seem to lack a coherent plan or motivation.

The Dogs

Background: Magnus kept a pack of very loyal, well-trained Doberman Pinschers as an "alarm system" and guard pack. The spirits are the residue of the horrifying death the hounds suffered by starvation and cannibalism in the basement kennel. The spirits are weak and cannot assume physical form, but can terrify and even manifest visually.

The dogs lurk mostly in the basement and rove the grounds at night. They cannot possess victims. They are destroyed if their anchor, the house, is destroyed. If the house remains, the dogs will be seen in the woods now and again for decades to come, gradually losing strength and direction until they are merely a phantom called up by bad luck or negative astrological conjunctions.

The dogs are vicious and would be terrible to face if they could make themselves wholly manifest. Reduced to phantasmal images and occasional glimpses, the spirits target individuals they may be able to frighten to death. They especially delight in terrifying individuals near the

Aïesha Magnus

Background: It's hard to know what Aiesha truly was. She remembered a childhood as a Bedouin, and then being taken away and educated, and sold to a distant cousin who, he told her family, wanted to make her his ornament. Yet the cousin seemed not to know much of her family, and showed no romantic intent toward her. He made it clear, however, that he held her for some greater power. She was schooled in the western arts and literature, and trained as a servant and handmaiden. To whom? She was never told. "One who has not yet appeared," he said.

That power, through its "cousin" servant, delivered Aiesha into the hands of James Magnus. She was a mere girl, given to Magnus in a ritual in a weedy field outside Chorazin. She was told to go with him and do as he wished under pain of strife for her family. Lacking any choice and merely a girl, she obeyed.

Aiesha was not necessarily a good person to begin with. Under Magnus' tutelage, her wickedness blossomed, fed a diet of self-indulgence and entitlement served to her by a white man twice her age and married to her in a black-magic ritual. He made no secret of the fact that he thought of her as his literal familiar, and she half-believed it.

Yet at the same time, Aiesha was never entirely comfortable with her bondage. At first, when Magnus was a well-paid interrogator, she found it acceptable. She could indulge herself as she wished and it pleased her to do so. When Magnus returned to America and turned in on himself, however, Aiesha was trapped in decay with him. Caged but knowing no other life, she taunted and badgered James until she finally provoked a murderous attack.

Aiesha's ghost, while able to manifest through the body of a possession victim, is much less powerful than

mouth of the cistern to make them fall in, or may chase characters into the wine cellar. When encountered in the woods, the spirits try to induce prey into a headlong flight, and herd victims toward cliffs, deadfalls and other dangerous spots.

Description: The dogs can choose from one of three appearances: a single, huge adult male; the same adult male when it was about to die from disease and injuries sustained in cannibal-starvation battles; and as an amorphous shadowy pack of indistinct hound-shadows with glowing green eyes. If favors the former two indoors and the last in the woods at night.

Roleplaying Hints: You're a vicious ghost-dog. Attack any who intrude on your territory.

Attributes: Power 3, Finesse 3, Resistance 3

Willpower: 6

Initiative: 6

Defense: 3

Speed: 16 (species factor 10)

Size: 4

Corpus: 7

Numina: Phantasm (dice pool 6), Terrify (dice pool 6)

Magnus'. She was in many ways a mere simulacrum of Magnus in life, and the ghost she leaves behind is a simple creature. It is filled with sexual hunger and hatred for its mate. It may attempt to seduce females, or possess them and use them to seduce or attack males.

Aiesha's ghost has two forms in which it can appear when using Phantasm or Compulsion: The woman in her mid 20s, at the height of her beauty, or still young and beautiful, but with a hatchet stuck in her head. When using Terrify, she appears as the hatchet-struck Aiesha. If necessary, she appears in transmogrified form (see below). If the disgusting monstrosity is injured, the host suffers organ damage and can die. (See the "Transmogrify Victim" sidebar.)

Description: In Aiesha's most horrifying manifestation, a possession victim is physically transformed. The host's pelvis and organs detach from the body, with arms and ribs seemingly left lying like bloodied, discarded husks. The creature attacks by grabbing with intestines and biting with its long-toothed mouth. The ghost can be defeated in this form by causing the host enough damage that it can no longer support life functions, at which point the possession victim resumes normal appearance and is dead, and survivors look guilty of a bizarre sexual murder. With her host destroyed, Aiesha is weakened and retreats for weeks or even months. (This is a personal result for her, not a strict reading of the Transmogrify Victim Numen.)

Even if the house is inhabited by very passionate individuals, Aiesha can manifest in any form only once a day.

Characters can spare the lives of friends by consenting to Aiesha's sexual advances in any form (she does not attack those who willingly submit). Those who can hide from her (a contested action involving Dexterity + Stealth or Survival against the ghost's eight dice) or run (Stamina + Athletics, again versus eight dice) can also wait out the 15 to 20 minutes that the manifestation lasts.

Storytelling Hints: Sate your desires — primarily sex, violence if you can fit it in. Aiesha's ghost focuses on gratification. It eventually kills, but it is a subtle shade that enjoys riding its victims. Her pornographic methods and vile denouement make her a nice shocker. Let your good judgement control your pacing. Keep titillating the characters with this sexy ghost until it gets old, and then progress to her murdered image, and then to her truly horrific one. At that last point, Aiesha takes what she wants and stalks anyone who doesn't provide it.

Attributes: Power 4, Finesse 4, Resistance 3

Willpower: 7

Morality: 3

Virtue: Hope

Vice: Lust

Initiative: 7

Defense: 4

Speed: 18 (species factor 10)

Size: 5

Corpus: 8

Attack:

Type	Damage	Dice Pool
Bite (Transmogrified)	3L	8

Numina: Compulsion (dice pool 8), Phantasm (dice pool 8), Possession (dice pool 8), Telekinesis (dice pool 8), Terrify (dice pool 8), Transmogrify Victim (dice pool 8)

Transmogrify Victim

Through use of this Numen, a ghost twists her victim into a terrible monstrosity made of human organs reshaped to perform roles that were never intended by nature. Spend one Essence and roll Power + Finesse against the host's Stamina in a contested action. If the most successes are rolled for the ghost, the victim's body is reshaped into a form that uses the ghost's Power, Finesse and Resistance instead of any traits the victim has, and which may have a number of grotesque physical attacks. When the transformation ends (after one scene or if the ghost terminates the effect prematurely), the host resumes normal shape and awakens. If the transmogrified being is killed, the host is slain. Any damage suffered by the host is retained after the host resumes normal form. If a possessed body is killed or knocked unconscious, the ghost is forced out and must transform another victim if it still wishes to act. (Note that if her host is destroyed, Aiesha is weakened and retreats for weeks or even months.)

Attacks using a blessed object against a ghost in possession of a transmogrified body damage the ghost's Corpus instead of its physical host.

James Magnus

Background: A product of his upbringing, James Magnus went out into the world and became rich performing malicious acts. He returned to his home with a wicked bride, and built the palatial house of his dreams. And thus he, his wife and their evil roosted until lack of company maddened them.

Magnus was always a marginal personality. The child of an abusive household, he never forgave humanity for his youth. He was a child-arsonist and animal-killer who later found military and political employment by perpetuating his talents. He had always been fascinated by black magic, and became involved with a circle of self-proclaimed "magi" in the Middle East. With their contrivance, he took leave and journeyed to the city of Chorazin, where he believed he sacrificed his soul to a dark spirit in exchange for long life, wealth and a loyal servant. A girl was procured for him, whom the magi said had been raised to serve him. Magnus took the girl and returned to his old ways, uncertain whether he'd been hoaxed, caught up in the delusions of a pack of madmen, or actually sold his soul.

Eventually, Magnus felt his age growing, his violent ambition lessening and an end looming for his political supporters. Thus, he decided to return home to America, where he "resolved" some lingering matters before building a suitable manor in which to live. It partook of far more than a farmboy's sensibilities, demonstrating a lifetime spent in exotic locales.

Once he and his servant-wife made their lair, their own ambitions and wickedness conspired to madden them with hate. They had no productive diversions and no feeling of social class or involvement, just a great deal of wealth, all the time in the world, and no one but each other. And so it was that Aiesha eventually provoked James into murdering her, and he took his own life.

If Magnus was a black magician of actual power or just someone who did horrible things and justified it as sorcery, only you can decide. He doesn't need to have been a warlock. Indeed, there's no reason why Aiesha can't have been the true source of any "power." It's possible that everything — including the murder-suicide — was a dark ritual of some sort, one that Magnus might not have known he performed. It may simply have served whatever forces that influenced his existence, or enabled Magnus' continued existence after death.

Description: As opposed to Aiesha's nightmarish physical form, Magnus simply performs spectacles and takes control of victims' bodies. He appears as himself while using Terrify, Phantasm or Compulsion, although his face is a mask

powers may not recognize when allies or friends are under the ghost's influence.

Storytelling Hints: Fuck them up and laugh. Magnus' ghost is more sadistic and less sensual than Aiesha's, and significantly less grotesque. He lashes out at intimate partners, friends and any available targets. Because the ghost displays only a vague semblance of Magnus when it possesses a victim, the spirit is dangerous; it can approach intended victims unawares.

When doing violence, James prefers knives and other cutting or stabbing instruments. Next, he favors firearms, and finally bare hands. He generally does not possess someone unless that subject is already armed and in a hostile mood.

Attributes: Power 4, Finesse 4, Resistance 4

Willpower: 8

Morality: 2

Virtue: Fortitude

Vice: Wrath

of hatred and anger familiar to any character who has a flashback or dream about the man. Anyone who has been the target of James' Numina (any of them) may recognize when another character is subject to Possession if a successful, reflexive Intelligence + Occult or Investigation roll is made. Mannerisms or flashes that are reminiscent of James' demeanor appear in the possession victim's behavior or manner. Characters who have yet to be the target of Magnus'

Initiative: 8

Defense: 4

Speed: 18 (species factor 10)

Size: 5

Corpus: 9

Numina: Compulsion (dice pool 8), Ghost Sign (dice pool 8), Phantasm (dice pool 8), Possession (dice pool 8), Terrify (dice pool 8)

Chapter 3: No Way Out

By Adam Tinworth

Summary

Suicide isn't always the way out that some people hope. Sometimes there really is no way out. In the World of Darkness, the crisis that drives someone to take his own life may leave him trapped in ghostly form, a mere echo of the passions, fear or pain that overwhelmed him in life. This story is based on such tragedy. David Richardson had lived a double life: two wives, two families, two sets of expenses. To make ends meet, he abused his position as financial director of a small manufacturing company. The well ran dry, however. Company auditors caught on to him and the financial demands of his families rose.

The players' characters, be they friends of either family, Richardson's fellow employees, suppliers or company clients, or representatives of the auditors or banks involved, enter the picture just as despair turns to frustration. Richardson takes his own life, but still lingers, watching the collapse of his families and company. His despair manifests as anger and he turns on everyone, blaming them for his own failure.

At its heart, "No Way Out" is a horror and detective story. Early on, characters become aware of the most significant haunting events only after they occur, and then through others' accounts. From such beginnings, the characters acquire an understanding of the man responsible for events, and potentially come to a seemingly impossible conclusion: The perpetrator is already dead.

The story presents a range of possible entry points. That makes it an ideal start for a chronicle, uniting characters from wildly disparate backgrounds with a common interest or bond. Final confrontation with Richardson's ghost opens the door for characters to seek more secret truths of the World of Darkness, first in search of a solution to their own problem and then to feed their own obsessions.

And yet, the story's loose structure makes it an interesting challenge for an experienced group, members of which have some awareness of the supernatural. Such characters may follow seemingly bizarre avenues to resolve Richardson's haunting, but their experiences here can drive them further beyond the world's veil of ignorance.

Possible Locations

"No Way Out" can take place in a number of places. The four main locations of the story — an accountant firm, an office/factory and two family homes — all easily fit in different districts of the same city. For the premise to make sense, however, the houses of the two families must be a significant distance apart. Preferably in altogether different communities. Richardson led his dual life for a decade, and that just wouldn't have been possible if elements of either part could have intruded on the other. Put the families too close together and you strain players' suspension of disbelief.

Life is unbearable, but death is not so pleasant, either.

– Russian Proverb

If you want to increase the challenge posed to characters, you can assign each of the story's four locales to distant towns or cities. The only real requirement is that the manufacturing plant be based in a community large enough to support the business and others like it, and the accountant firm must be in a large town. Branches in small communities wouldn't have the authority to deal with fraud on the scale of Richardson's crimes. The two family homes can be set in communities of any size.

Motives

There are a number of ways in which characters can get involved in this story. In fact, a combination of all of them might be possible as various protagonists are drawn together by common interest in a single set of circumstances.

Common Corporate Cause

Anyone who's an employee of Timmins Manufacturing Inc is in the line of fire. The ghost of David Richardson exacts revenge on his former employer; no one in the company is safe. The very first victim is an old board-level rival. Conceivably anyone who works for or deals with the company can be caught up in events, seeking to understand what's happening or just for personal protection.

Just Doing My Job

The employees of Timmins aren't the only ones in danger. The company's accountants Williams, Smith and Appiah unravel the financial red tape that Richardson used to cover up his fraud. He blames the accountant firm for his exposure and seeks revenge. Anyone at the accountant office, from employees, temps or even customers, could be caught in the haunting.

Guilty by Association

By the time of events described under "Rising Action" (see p. 78), Richardson's haunting has grown so aggressive that anybody belonging to any outfit that does business with Timmins might be caught up in circumstances. Suppliers, mailmen, couriers or customers might be victims of the ghost's desperate efforts. With the police struggling to find answers, characters' best means of protecting themselves is to discover who's responsible for themselves.

Friends of the Family

A number of Richardson's family members come under suspicion and police scrutiny, with all the neighborhood gossip and newspaper innuendo that comes with it. Characters who have no other links to the plot can be drawn in simply because of their concern for friends under fire. While the police seek obvious, simple, *mundane* solutions, characters can try to get to the truth of the matter, however unlikely it seems.

Richardsons All

A way to lure in characters in a very personal way is for them to be related to one of Richardson's families. They could be direct members, such as either of his wives or his eldest children, or close relatives such as siblings, parents, nephews or nieces. Personal, heartfelt involvement can truly motivate characters to act.

This approach does have significant impact on the direction of the story, though. The characters know early on — long before unattached investigators do — that events are caused by a dead man. And yet, discovery of Richardson's "other" family delivers far more personal shock, giving the final confrontation with the ghost added emotional weight.

I'm a Professional

The story involves a number of criminal acts that police need to investigate, some of which demand social services' attention. Journalists could also have a field day. It's possible that characters from these fields get drawn in as their initial assumptions about perpetrators collapse and unbelievable possibilities make increasing sense.

Just Plain Nosey

A final possibility is that protagonists have nothing at all to do with any of the people or companies involved in the story. This may be the case for characters who have developed an interest in the unusual and who sense that there's more going on than meets the eye. They can insinuate themselves into the situation. This is a challenging option, though, because few of the people involved willingly share information with nosey strangers. The characters may be stuck gathering evidence from a few peripheral contacts who are prepared to talk, at least until Richardson's actions escalate and his victims grow desperate for help.

Preliminary Events

The story of Richardson's double life started when he first slept with his mistress. For most other participants, the story only really began when Richardson lost control and others started to suffer. The same is true in his postmortem existence. That story began the moment he crossed the threshold between life and death. For the players' characters, events truly get underway when the ghost's powers grow to the point at which he lashes out.

Backstory

Twenty-five years ago, David Richardson and Molly Lambert were high-school sweethearts. Everyone assumed they'd marry soon after college. Everyone assumed right. David went on to a bright career in accounting and corporate finance, while Molly happily ran a small fashion boutique. Their respective businesses kept them busy, but they were happy. Fifteen years ago, the couple's happiness was cemented with the birth of David Junior. The Richardsons tried for a second child, but were never able to conceive again, and that disappointment weighed heavily on the couple, especially David, who looked forward to a large family.

With their businesses, a child, normal life, a pall of disappointment over it all, David and Molly found less and less time for each other. That was when David met Catriona Staples on a flight to a business meeting. They exchanged numbers, ostensibly to explore business opportunities, and agreed to meet again.

Romance blossomed between the two, developing into something deeper. Before he had the sense to get his life back on the straight and narrow, David found himself in love with two women and unable to choose between them. He lied to Catriona about his other family. He told her that he was married, but never talked about his son or the children he had failed to have. When Catriona got pregnant, he promised to support her. When she had a second child, he knew he was in too deep.

Richardson's final downfall started small, with the odd "loan" from company accounts. Over a period of years, his embezzlement developed into a complicated series of financial arrangements that, he assured the board, created financial efficiency.

A couple of months ago, David Richardson had two families to support, auditors on his tail, co-directors asking difficult questions, and no way of resolving his problems. Despairing, he left the office one day, drove randomly for a few hours, stopped at a café, wrote two notes, mailed them, and then drove his car into a wall, killing himself instantly.

But even then, there was no escape. He found himself trapped in the material world, anchored to his family homes, his workplace and to the accountant office that had been crucial to his unconventional lifestyle and undoing. He could only watch in horror as auditors and police worked together to expose his financial deals and then his double life. His anger grew until he found the strength to affect the living world. It started with petty acts of sabotage at the accountants' and factory, and with small interventions to help protect his families.

Now, with his twisted confidence, strength and anger at their height, Richardson is about to make his presence felt pervasively among the living, and people are going to suffer.

Previously

Richardson's spectral efforts have been small thus far. As the characters investigate intensifying matters, the people they meet may relate some of the following, initial encounters.

- A plague of computer failures at the accountant office and factory, which IT departments have yet to adequately explain.

- Computer failures at the family homes, whenever the children visit a site Richardson deems "inappropriate."

- Male visitors to the family houses tend to find that small items break around them inexplicably, as if the visitors are jinxed or just plain clumsy.

- Threatening messages appear inexplicably at the offices of both the accountants and manufacturer. Most are written in materials to hand: pencils arranged on a desk, fuzzy words appearing on security-camera footage, in dust on cabinets or machinery, and typed on computer screens. All the messages threaten revenge on the firms for an unstated injustice, but offer no further details.

The messages are taken seriously at Timmins, which has increased security for fear of sabotage by disgruntled staff or environmental activists. The accountant firm has largely treated the messages as annoying pranks that have led to nothing more than a few stiffly worded memos from a senior partner to the staff.

What Now?

The preliminary stage of the story is a rapid escalation of Richardson's willingness to inflict harm and then death. He goes from sabotage to an unintentional beating of a child to murder. The fact that this is an escalation of activity may not be readily apparent to characters, depending on how they get involved in the story. They may learn of the beating quite late, for example, if they get involved via corporate connections. Witnessing the progression really isn't important. The format of the story is a jigsaw puzzle of events that truly fall into place only near the end.

In the early stages, characters may investigate haunting events after they have happened (and they probably don't suspect a ghost just yet). As the protagonists build relationships with various people, they experience supernatural phenomena firsthand and can leap to conclusions from there.

Haunting

As Richardson's powers grow in strength, he lashes out at those whom he delusionally believes ruined him, and at those whom he perceives to threaten his families. These incidents mark the ghost's growing capability at affecting the material world, but only one of them could conceivably suggest any form of supernatural activity, and then only if a young, upset child's word is taken at face value.

The events below occur over a period of about two weeks, in the order listed. All of them are reported in local papers and news media, with the exception of the attack on Stacey Pringle, which is kept out of newspapers by the police and social services.

Taking Accountant

Chris Burnell, the primary auditor who investigated the Richardson fraud, had been having a lot of problems with his car. Sometimes it just wouldn't start at the end of a day's work. Sometimes the problem was obvious — a disconnected cable. Sometimes the problem was less apparent, but still the result of something being broken or missing. Burnell had changed mechanics several times, believing that sloppy workmanship was to blame. It wasn't. It was sabotage, performed by the ghost of the man he exposed.

Burnell lived a pretty safe life in the corporate-finance department of Williams, Smith and Appiah. The notion that he faced sabotage simply never crossed his mind until his brakes failed on the freeway, leading to a multi-vehicle pile up and Burnell's death. Investigation reveals the true nature of the car problems he had, which can be discovered in a number of ways.

• The characters are colleagues who get drawn into a police investigation about who would sabotage the car.

• The characters are employees of Timmins Manufacturing who read a news report about the accident and make the connection with the auditor who exposed Richardson.

• The characters are connected to either the Richardson or Staples families and recognize the auditor's name in a news report. The police might visit the families, as the Richardson case is one of the few leads authorities have in Burnell's "accident." In particular, David Junior falls under suspicion.

• If the characters have no direct connection to any of these sources, they can hear about the accident through the local news. Intentional sabotage of an accountant's car after a major fraud exposure is just too juicy for the media to pass up.

Significant information that the characters can discover includes the following. These insights can be gained from the contacts mentioned or through legwork, potentially with a successful Manipulation + Persuasion roll.

• Burnell's car had suffered a number of strange breakdowns in the past month (Burnell's colleagues or family) (1 or 2 successes)

• These breakdowns all occurred in the office garage (Burnell's colleagues, family, auto mechanics) (3 or 4 successes)

• The breakdowns could have been construed as consistent with stones or other minor debris hitting the car on the road, or with minor acts of sabotage. The frequency of problems suggested the latter (auto mechanics) (exceptional success; 5+)

Play Nice

Kids fight. It's inevitable. Best friends have a falling out. Tantrums erupt from what seem like trivial issues to adults. It's all part of childhood and is perfectly healthy — unless an overly protective and ghostly parent is involved.

When little Bethany Staples has a fight with her best friend Stacey Pringle, and Stacey raises a hand, daddy steps in to protect his daughter. As a restless spirit defined only by passion, Richardson can't control his temper. The result is a horrific incident in which Stacey is thrown against a wall, causing serious injury. Naturally, she cries out. Distraught, Richardson lashes out again while trying to placate the child, knocking her unconscious and traumatizing his daughter.

Nobody suspects the truth, of course. Stacey's injuries are too severe for Bethany to be the culprit, and the daughter's absolute silence when questioned leads investigators to conclude that she's either traumatized or covering up for a family member. Suspicion falls on mother Catriona, older sister Jenny, or on Catriona's new boyfriend of a few weeks, John Escott.

Characters can find out about the incident in a number of ways.

• They're friends of the family and are drawn in by concern.

• They're friends or colleagues of John's and hear about it from him.

• They work for Timmins and are informed by the pensions supervisor who has been keeping an eye on Richardson's "other family."

• They're neighbors of the Staples family and hear of the event either directly or through the neighborhood grapevine. Or the characters might be related to Stacey Pringle.

If the characters are drawn into the story through the accountant office or Richardson's first family, they aren't likely to hear about Stacey's accident until later, probably when they make contact with Catriona and the second family.

Significant information that the characters can discover includes the following, learned through a contact listed. Each discovery may require a successful Manipulation + Empathy roll.

• Bethany remains stubbornly silent (any neighbor or friend). Only characters who manage to win the girl's absolute trust — and that means winning Catriona's trust — might hear a quiet, whispered mention of a monster who hurt her friend.

• Police focus falls on the family; authorities make no significant inquires elsewhere (neighbors, friends, any police officer willing to talk about the investigation).

• Catriona and John were out of the house at the time, having lunch at a nearby diner. Staff and credit-card receipts support this alibi. Eight-year-old Jenny is too young to look after her little sister. Social workers investigate the family at this point (neighbors, friends, any police officer willing to talk about the investigation).

• Jenny was watching TV and heard nothing until a tearful Bethany came downstairs in search of help. Jenny is an initial suspect, but a medical report concludes that she's too weak to have inflicted such injuries on Stacey (police, medical examiners).

The result of all these seeming leads, alibis and discounted suspects is that no one seems responsible. And yet, the attack happened and Bethany isn't talking. Something disturbing appears to have occurred, but what and performed by whom? These questions go unanswered until the characters make their own, otherworldly discoveries.

An Industrial Accident

In modern industry, largely automated production facilities operate 24 hours a day, maximizing investment in premises and machinery. The Timmins company is no different. It's basically a large warehouse occupied by various pieces of machinery used to process and manufacture raw materials that come in through the combined delivery yard and loading bay at one side of the site. The result is various steel products that are shipped to other manufacturers. Despite Richardson's steady drain on corporate funds, the business is prosperous and the facility is generally clean, tidy and well maintained. The site manager adheres strictly (if unenthusiastically) to health and safety regulations. Sadly, no such regulations can protect against the actions of the restless dead.

Charles Segawa is chief operations officer of the firm. Up until a few years ago, he was a good friend of Richardson's. Their relationship turned strictly business, however, with Segawa's disgust for Richardson's double life, which offended the operations officer's strong religious convictions. Segawa was instrumental in the investigation that exposed Richardson's fraud, and David watched with growing anger as his former friend betrayed him to outside auditors.

Twice a week, Sagawa works late before meeting his family at church. He has fallen into the habit of taking a winding route through the warehouse gantries to the parking lot, keeping an eye on the machines. After all, it's his job to know how the manufacturing side of the business runs.

One Tuesday evening, about a week after the attack on Stacey Pringle, Sagawa's attention is drawn by an odd grinding sound coming from a machine on his walk. While looking over the balcony, he is shoved with unearthly force up and over the protective rail and falls into the processor beneath. He isn't killed immediately, but does die in the hospital two days later.

In his lucid moments, he swears to police, colleagues (and possibly the characters) that no one was on the catwalk with him. It's impossible to move quietly on the things, he states (and any coworker agrees). No one believes him, or at least accepts that he was alone, regardless of Sagawa's statements. The warehouse is entry-controlled, and logs suggest that no one out of the ordinary was among the machines at the time. Naturally, suspicion falls on someone inside the company, intensifying the search for a disgruntled employee or an ex-employee who's aided by a current one.

The characters can find out about Sagawa's accident and death by any of the following means.

• They are fellow employees of Timmins and can't help but hear (or see or be on the scene).

• The news spreads rapidly through the firm's suppliers, clients (including Williams Smith Appiah) and competitors.

• Word filters quickly to both of Richardson's families, through news reports if nothing else.

The characters can learn the following information about the accident through conversations with key people involved, primarily Molly Richardson, Frank Timmins or people who work at the plant, many of whom drink in the same nearby bar after work on Fridays. Each piece of in-

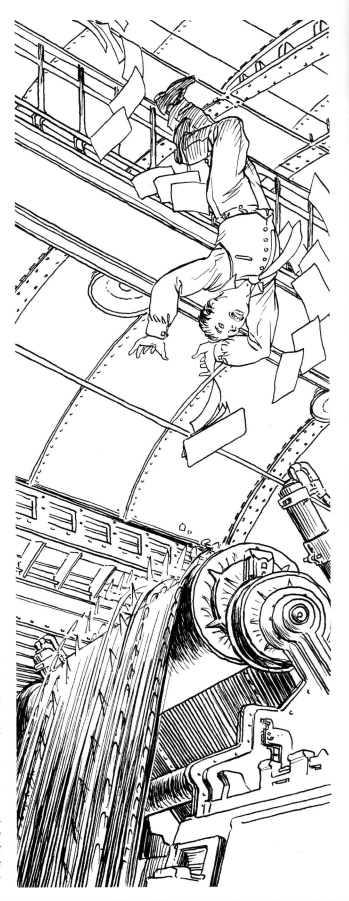

formation may require a successful Manipulation + Persuasion or Empathy roll to extract.

• Molly knows that her husband used to be friends with Sagawa, but had a falling out with him some time ago. She has no idea why. She does know, however, that Sagawa helped expose Richardson's fraud (Molly herself, her children, close family or friends).

• Sagawa was a man of habit, walking the same route on a regular basis (colleagues, particularly those who work on the manufacturing floor).

• Apart from his falling out with Richardson, Sagawa was generally popular, with no known enemies (colleagues, friends, family).

• The police have no clear leads, searching desperately for an explanation and considering corporate espionage (senior members of the company, police contacts, trusted clients).

Police Entanglements

Several of the key figures in this story come under police scrutiny at some point. All are innocent, of course, and there's not enough evidence against any of them to prosecute. Others have alibis. So how long should they stay under suspicion?

The story doesn't specify when police cease investigation of individuals, because those inquiries are a means of motivating characters who are close to or connected to suspects. Feel free to intensify police pressure to compel characters to help do something to clear suspects' names. Or, if characters leap in from the beginning, the police can look for leads elsewhere fairly quickly, letting initial suspects off the hook.

Catriona's boyfriend John Escott, for example, is largely free of suspicion once he's attacked himself (see p. 79). David Richardson Junior may remain under suspicion until the end of the story. The Staples family struggles to throw off both police and social-worker attention, and by the end of the story may be separated by government intervention.

As the characters get involved in events, they probably come under police scrutiny, particularly if they appear at one of the businesses or family homes and ask odd or meddling questions. There's probably nothing to link them to any crimes, so they'll be watched for any incriminating acts. Interfering in official investigations, tampering with evidence or simply getting a parking ticket could land characters in a police interrogation room or holding cell. Assuming there's no probable cause to hold characters, the police let them go after a few hours or overnight.

If any characters is a Timmins employee, he or she may be suspected of being the mysterious disgruntled employee. That could mean close-door meetings with company officials, close scrutiny in the workplace or even "working sabbaticals" during which a character is told to go home till matters blow over. (In other words, to discern whether problems continue in the character's absence.)

Investigation

Some of the initial information that characters can learn about prominent figures in this story is addressed above. As the protagonists investigate further, the most important things they can discover are links between what ostensibly seem to be unrelated events. How can a child's injury, a man's workplace death and automobile sabotage be related? There are a variety of ways in which characters can relate these "isolated" incidents.

The police investigate all three circumstances. For both police and characters, suspicion probably falls on people associated with David Richardson, not the man himself. After all, he's dead! Once anyone suspects a connection between Burnell and Segawa, scrutiny falls on the two families, or on business colleagues who might have been involved in Richardson's fraud.

Pure Research

Characters may research Richardson's fraud to learn that it was only sparingly reported in newspapers and the business press. No story ran in any media that directly associated his death with the investigation, and his suicide was not reported at all. Richardson just wasn't prominent enough in the business world to raise a stir. Divining all this information requires access to the websites of local papers (and at least two dots in Computer) or access to the local library (and successful Intelligence + Academics or Investigation rolls). Such research takes at least an afternoon.

While characters investigate, you may want to take the opportunity to throw them a number of false leads that can be pursued, as well. For example, a few years ago Timmins was fined a significant amount of money for breaching environmental regulations. The matter really wasn't as sinister as it sounds. The company had been reluctant (as many mid-sized businesses are) to approve an expenditure for expensive new machinery that met environmental standards, and it was caught in random checkups. The company then went through with the upgrades. Inevitably, such reparations never made the papers. The main source for information on this "scandal" would have been Charles Segawa, if he hadn't met an unfortunate end in one of those very environmentally friendly machines.

Company owner Frank Timmins is hazy on the details of the fine and upgrade. New financial director Martin Farrell (see p. 87), who has replaced Richardson, has studied the details but prefers not to talk to anyone about them if he can avoid it. He'd prefer not to contribute to any more company black marks. If anyone consults the firm's marketing department, members provide a press release that summarizes and resolves the issue.

If characters seize on this "environmental offense" and investigate the Timmins' accountant office, they can quickly persuade themselves of a full-blown conspiracy. Williams, Smith and Appiah also does contract work for an oil company that has been repeatedly fined for pollution at its refineries, and that company is involved in a class-action suit due to a high cancer rate among employees. The connection is purely coincidental, of course, but might be enough to send characters after any red herrings that you might like to offer.

Just be careful not to lead characters so far off track that they lose all connection to Richardson's ghost and his anchors. While seeming conspiracies involving environmental abuse look promising, they're ultimately dead ends.

Family

Of the two families, the Richardsons are probably the least promising for investigating characters. While Molly and David Junior are now aware that husband and father embezzled from his company, they weren't aware at the time and don't know how or why he did it. David Junior alone suspects his father of having an affair, but isn't fully aware that he maintained an entirely separate family.

If characters want to gather information from family members, they probably need to befriend them. That may be more a matter of roleplaying than dice rolls. Detailed descriptions of both mothers and Catriona's boyfriend are provided on pp. 87-89.

The Staples need friends badly. Catriona stands accused of being a bad mother, merely confirming the prejudices of many of her neighbors. Her boyfriend is equally shunned by neighbors. Both welcome friendly faces and voices.

Molly Richardson is least likely to be accessible, at least to a point. She's too proud (and naïve) to let her family name go besmirched. Yet, once her son falls under police suspicion for events following David Senior's suicide (the junior is suspected of a revenge spree), Molly seeks support. She accepts help to clear her son's name and to alleviate the shame leveled at her.

Woe betide any adult characters who try to befriend family children to get to know their mothers. The police watch both families and are likely to come down on any such behavior like a ton of bricks, especially after Stacey Pringle is hurt.

Investigating Richardson's family members requires establishing relationships with those people, whether friendly or aggressive. Wits + Empathy, or Presence or Manipulation + Intimidation rolls may net results. One success grants bare facts, three relate most of the information provided below, and five garner all of it. A character in a position of authority such as a high-ranking member of the Timmins company, a professional investigator or a policeman may call for Presence + Persuasion rolls, instead, and get a +1 to +3 bonus.

David Junior is the only Richardson who suspects anything about his father's secret life. A year or so ago, he poked around his father's papers while his parents were out. Some details on his father's credit-card statement didn't match up with his "business trips" and "working weekends." The boy doesn't know for sure, but he thinks his father was having an affair. David Junior is determined to avoid his father's name being dragged through the mud any further. His reticence does him no favors when it puts him on the police suspect list regarding Segawa and Burnell.

Molly Richardson reveals to sympathetic listeners that her son has been in trouble with the law several times over the last year. She fears he's going wild in his father's absence. He's taken to hanging out with a middle-class group of gang wannabes, which has lead to minor crimes. She's partly right in suspecting that the boy's associations are reason for police attention now.

Catriona Staples knows that David had a wife, but knows nothing about his son. She knows Molly's name and even where she works, but very little else. If characters conclude that Catriona has intentionally kept herself ignorant of David's full life, they're correct.

Bethany Staples hasn't told anyone that she had a fight with Stacey Pringle when the attack occurred. Partially because no one has asked, and partially because she feels guilty about it. If anyone thinks to ask if she's seen anything odd, she may admit to having seen someone over the past few months who reminded her of her father. She's most likely to confess this last point to a young, female character.

Jenny Staples knows nothing useful.

Business

Timmins is the characters' primary source of information on recent mysterious events. Company directors are aware of Richardson's double life, his fraud and of the corporate links to Burnell. The problem characters face is that company managers really, really don't want this information getting out. As a privately owned firm, Timmins has managed to downplay full details of Richardson's embezzlement, spinning it as the bookkeeping oversight of a trusted director who spiraled into depression and committed suicide.

Characters have two primary options in approaching the company for information. They could persuade managers to reveal the truth about Richardson and his activities. This tack is relatively easy if the characters are company employees or legitimate law-enforcement officials (a contested action involving Manipulation + Empathy, Persuasion or Socialize versus Resolve + Composure; +3 if a character is a cop). It's extremely difficult if the characters have no direct connections with the company (–3), and next to impossible if they're clients or journalists (–5). The company doesn't want details of Richardson's true activities reaching either of the last two groups, for fear of damaging its reputation. Threats might work (+1), but also result in characters being reported to the police. A more likely approach is to become friendly with company officials. In particular, CEO Frank Timmins' fondness for drinking might loosen his tongue (+2). His secretary Alyssa can be persuaded to reveal his favorite bar if asked by a character posing as a business partner or customer.

Alternatively, characters can break into the factory and office to access the files on the fraud investigation. Living security is lax (a couple of aging security guards who give up quickly if threatened, or who are avoided altogether as they sit chatting and drinking coffee). Electronic security is tight. An extended action involving Dexterity + Larceny rolls is required to bypass the several security doors between the outside world and the files the characters seek. Successful Intelligence + Investigation rolls allow characters to find the right paperwork. Should characters force their way in, police are probably on the scene before they have a chance to find out anything useful.

A computer-savvy character might be able to hack into the company's server and dig out the required files (**World of Darkness Rulebook**, p. 57). The firm's IT department isn't great, and automated security measures in place are rudimentary. A total of five successes is required to get in and find the desired information.

Accountants

Williams, Smith and Appiah may be a frustrating dead end for information-hunting characters. Chris Burnell was the only office member fully aware of the details of Richardson's dual life. Obviously, the characters aren't able to talk to him after his fatal accident, so that lead is closed.

Any senior member of the accountant office quickly makes the connection between Burnell and Charles Segawa. The Timmins case was the most serious fraud the office had ever dealt with, and all senior partners are conversant with the business end of its details. That sabotage occurred to one of them, and murder at a related company, all in regard to a single case is simply too coincidental. However, only characters with official relationships with either Timmins or the accountants stand much chance of learning the bookkeepers' suspicions. None of them want to be targeted next, and they know that a police investigation is underway. If something criminal is going on, the police are trusted to discover it.

Getting illicit access to Williams, Smith and Appiah records on the Timmins audit is significantly more difficult than obtaining the manufacturer's copies. The IT security on the accountants' files is extremely tight (a total of 12 successes is required to hack in, at a −2 penalty to Computer rolls). Physical security on the building is also strict. Even if one of the characters has professional burglary experience, she recognizes the place as a challenge: four different sets of extended Dexterity + Larceny rolls are called for, with 12 total successes required for each (see "Larceny," **World of Darkness**, p. 74). Occasional Dexterity + Stealth contested actions are also required to avoid security patrols (p. 75).

Making the Leap

David Richardson's biggest secret was (and is) his two families. He kept the secret for a de-cade by making sure that virtually no one knew the truth. Just to make things harder for the characters, the two people who did know or who discovered it — Burnell and Segawa — are dead by "accidental" means. So how can characters make the discovery?

Here are some options:

• **Catriona Staples** knows about Molly Richardson. If the characters know or contact Catriona, she may admit that David had a wife, and they may follow the lead to the truth about his legal family.

• **David Junior** suspects that his father was having an affair. The little information that he has — nights spent at hotels and purchases made in different towns than where David Senior was supposed to be — can prompt characters to look abroad for other women associated with the dead man.

• Either **Frank Timmins** and **Mark Farrell** (Richardson's replacement) could know about Richardson's "other" family. They might direct characters to either family, but only if characters persuade them that family problems are linked to corporate ones (successful Manipulation + Persuasion or Wits + Subterfuge rolls required). Deep down, neither man wants to see wives or children suffer so that the Timmins company can protect its name.

Rising Action

Richardson has killed. His blind frustration as a spirit now has a means by which to be vented. At first, he's placated, but frustration mounts again when suspicion for his crimes falls on both of his families. He makes some initial attempts to contact loved ones, but is unwittingly rebuked. A couple weeks after his fatal attack on Sagawa, Richardson is ready to strike again.

This is a point at which characters may get involved in the action directly. One or more of the events described below can happen in the characters' presence. They could have a chance to rescue the people threatened or potentially prevent deaths. Doing so brings the characters to Richardson's attention, if he hasn't become aware of them already (maybe they've visited his families). They become fair game for his outbursts thereafter.

Haunting

Events described below occur if the characters don't intervene or aren't yet fully involved in the story. Unlike the first round of developments, none of these is fixed; they can be altered if the characters do interfere. Intervention can provide characters with allies (if they stop the attacks on John Escott and Mark Farrell) and suggest that Richardson continues to linger (as seen by family members). No matter what, the ghost is all the more enraged by characters' disruptions.

A Face from the Past

At some point, events in one of Richards0n's families reach critical mass and the ghost feels compelled to reach out and "help."

• One or both families becomes fully aware of the other through the characters' actions. The protagonists may intentionally or inadvertently mention the other family. If the investigators have befriended both, maybe an unfortunately timed visit to a character's home occurs while a member of the other family is present. Richardson appears to either Catriona or Molly, as appropriate, in a desperate attempt to comfort her.

• David Junior is either arrested or brought in for questioning. Richardson appears to his son to explain or comfort him. Or if the younger David is held in custody, the ghost might appear to Molly to comfort her. If the characters have befriended Molly or David Junior, wife or son might tell them of the frightening visitation after a successful Manipulation + Empathy roll, or the characters could be on the scene when the ghost tries to make contact.

• Continued questioning by police or characters upsets Bethany to the point where Richardson tries to comfort her. If Catriona is preoccupied with trying to clear John's name (if he's been implicated in events), Bethany is all the more likely to be upset. A successful Manipulation + Empathy roll encourages Bethany to talk about her latest encounter with "daddy."

Of course, Richardson is utterly irrational in thinking that a visit from a ghost helps anyone. In each case, the reaction is the same: fear. David Junior, Molly or Catriona rationalizes the visitation away as a hallucination brought on by stress. Bethany might genuinely believe that the ghost is her father, but she remembers the attack on Stacey and cowers from him. Of course, such negative reactions infuriate the spirit all the more.

Love's Labors Lost

In the aftermath of the attack on Stacey Pringle, relations between Catriona and her new boyfriend John Escott are strained when he is suspected of the attack. Once the details become clear and his alibi is established, the couple tries to resume a normal relationship, but lives under a cloud of mystery and uncertainty.

Escott cares deeply for Catriona, and is far less selfish than Richardson was. He's also more practical. Catriona had been nagging Richardson to rewire her kitchen and dining room for months. In the aftermath of the attack on Stacey, Escott decides to cheer up his girlfriend by doing the job while she's out with Bethany. With Jenny's help, he gets access to the house and sets to work.

Richardson is furious. Already pushed into rage by rejection, Escott's "invasion" drives the ghost into a kill-

ing frenzy. Escott has Jenny throw the breaker between each stage of the project, so he can test it. Richardson interferes. Electrocution throws Escott across the kitchen. The skin on his hands is charred and his heart beats irregularly. He passes out almost immediately.

Jenny screams in terror, feeling responsible for the accident, and rushes to his aid. This reaction enrages Richardson further and he unleashes on his eldest daughter, tossing her around the room. When the ghost finally comes to his senses, he's horrified by his own actions and flees to one of his other anchors.

If the characters have befriended Escott or Catriona, Richardson might wait for an opportunity to attack the characters *and* Escott at one time. Maybe one of the characters helps Escott with the wiring. If events have developed to bring any male character closer to Catriona than Escott is, Richardson may attack the newcomer, instead.

Escott survives the assault, but refuses to have anything further to do with the Staples family unless a successful Manipulation + Empathy roll made by a player persuades him otherwise. Even if the characters succeed in keeping the couple together, the relationship is threatened by Escott's fear alone. That's good enough for Richardson and he moves on to his next target.

Death of a Director

Mark Farrell had nothing to do with Richardson's downfall. He didn't even work for Timmins at the time, but he's in the firing line nonetheless, simply because he replaced the dead man. Farrell is not as easy a target as others have been, however. He walks to work, doesn't go into the factory itself if he can avoid it, and has nothing more than a computer and cordless phone on his desk.

Richardson tries to use Farrell's computer to kill him by driving an electrical surge through the machine. He makes the attempt on two separate occasions, the first merely shorting out the computer, the second giving Farrell a mild shock and taking down the building's network. Farrell may not tell the characters about his experiences directly. An electrician is hired to check the wiring in his office. Characters may run into or hear about the electrician and make the connection to John Escott's "accident," or they may see that electrical outlets in Farrell's office are scorched (Wits + Composure, Computer or Crafts to notice). Everyone else chocks up the danger to a mundane problem in the building, but the characters may feel differently, especially when no one other than David Richardson's replacement suffers such dangers.

Unless the characters persuade Farrell that he should stay away from work or they interfere with him directly (say, by posing as utilities workers and claiming that he needs to remain home while work is done), Richardson tries to kill his replacement outright. The foyer of the Timmins building is decorated with relics from the company's early days under Frank Timmins' grandfather. As Farrell comes in one morning, Richardson causes a piece of steel art to fall on the man. Farrell doesn't die

immediately; swift intervention by the characters could save his life. Anything short of lifting the art and dragging Farrell out results in his death, however.

After that, the plant is under close investigation by police. Two fatal (or near-fatal) accidents are too much to overlook. Any characters who are employees or who were in the building at the time are probably under suspicion.

"Leave Me Alone"

At some point after the characters have visited at least three of Richardson's anchors (possibly multiple times), he appears before them. The characters may or may not have come to the conclusion that he is both responsible for events, and dead. The characters' frequent and widespread intrusion in his existence makes them a threat to him and his secret. If the characters have already exposed him as a bigamist and made his families aware of each other, he is absolutely hostile and tries to kill the intruders.

Richardson makes the attempt when the characters are alone, or largely alone, in or near one of his anchors. He starts writing messages to frighten them, or disrupts any equipment (mobile phones, cameras, recording equipment, laptops, PDAs) that they use. Messages are intended specifically for the characters, focusing on anything personal that the ghost may have learned about them during his observation. Maybe one of them has a secret, and it's revealed in words written in scuttling cockroaches across a wall. Or one character's betrayal of another is announced in the fog of a car windshield — "You did it" or "Betrayer."

Richardson warms up with these tactics as his anger comes to full intensity. He resorts to Telekinesis next, assaulting characters, suddenly turning a steering wheel, or breaking a railing against which one or more characters leans. Finally, he materializes his deathly image — face torn and bleeding, limbs twisted at sickening angles — to Terrify the characters and try to motivate them into rash acts or accidents.

Should the characters possess any means of hurting ghosts from other stories in your chronicle, and turn them on the materialized spirit, he immediately retreats to one of his other anchors. He does not appear before the characters again by choice, which may make the characters' subsequent efforts all the more challenging.

Pacing

There's potential for significant amounts of downtime to occur between the events of this story. It can be addressed in a couple ways.

The simplest is to step up the pace. Every time the characters run out of leads or pursuits (or just before they reach that point), kick off the next series of events.

Or you could interweave this story with the events of another. Real life rarely follows the structure of episodic TV, with one story concluding neatly before the next begins. Overlap phenomena, perhaps even in confusing or distracting ways. Events relevant to one story may seem relevant to another and be a red herring, or could simply keep characters from getting too involved in another scenario for the moment, allowing momentum to build in either while the protagonists are kept on their toes.

Indeed, whole other stories could be told between waves of Richardson's activity. The characters have a chance to deepen relationships with any of the people in this story, while continuing to deal with other issues. This approach allows some of the participants of this scenario to develop into supporting cast for your chronicle as a whole.

An overlapping approach to filling time has several advantages, not least of which is the fact that characters could come to each series of events with an expanded knowledge of the supernatural. Their experiences in another story may teach lessons about the hidden world, and they can be applied here. Overlapping stories also creates a realistic feel for the World of Darkness. Circumstances evolve in their own time, not according to the structure of game sessions.

Lashing Out

Richardson's post mortem existence merely perpetuates his anger. Police, former friends, coworkers and even strangers (the characters?) interfere in the double life he lived, and bring down the walls between the separate worlds he maintained. Restricted to his anchors as he is, he could unleash his wrath at home, but he instinctively resists a complete outburst against the ones he loves. Thus, he turns on his former workplace.

At a point of your choosing (perhaps after Farrell's accident, which might have failed to drive everyone away), Richardson goes utterly mad. He uses Terrify and Ghost Sign to cause chaos in the office, and turns Telekinesis on the manufacturing plant. Machines malfunction catastrophically, liquid metal pours across the floor and fires break out. The characters have a chance to rescue as many people as possible before the building is torn apart or too dangerous to be occupied.

The police and fire department are called, but people have trouble making cell calls. Phones malfunction thanks to the ghost's efforts. A call has to be made from a distance or from a landline in a nearby building. Emergency crews eventually arrive, but not soon enough to save the office and warehouse.

And yet, the building was one of Richardson's anchors. His anger overwhelms what survival instinct he has. The results of his tirade cause him to discorporate, and it's nearly a week before he reforms. This respite gives characters a chance to assemble the final pieces of the puzzle, and a clue to dealing with the ghost.

Characters can be on hand for the ghost's outburst by any number of means. Employees are present, of course. Clients or associated business people might have work matters that put them on the scene. Characters might have forged sufficiently close ties with an employee to be contacted whenever anything "weird" happens again. Or characters could simply keep a close eye on the company, expecting Richardson to reveal himself at some point.

The ghost's wrath narrows options for both him and the characters. All the accidents that have occurred at Timmins prove that the company was somehow important in whatever events transpired, mundane or supernatural. Now that the building is in ruins, only a few other locales remain that seem to draw strange events and ghostly attention.

Spectral Investigation

If they haven't before, players and characters may finally give credence to the idea of a ghost. (If Richardson has already appeared before the characters directly, there's little *other* explanation.) There literally seems to be no living explanation for all the accidents, or any earthly way for many of them to have occurred. Of course, the police never consider such "impossible" explanations. Anyone who suggests the supernatural gets a look as if she's insane. Some characters may also be so grounded in the material and conventional that notions of a ghost are outlandish to them, too. Those people might run down whatever other mundane explanations or options that could possibly remain.

Relocating

The characters may try to convince Richardson's families to go into hiding for their own protection, not to elude "ghosts" but to avoid harm from whoever is responsible. The families are uncooperative, however. The Staples can't move. They're under police and social services scrutiny. Any attempt to flee will bring the law down on them (and the characters). The Richardsons have little reason to believe that they're in serious or (indeed) any danger. Bizarre and shocking events have occurred to others, in other places, but nothing has happened at that family's home. It's also possible that David Junior is being held for questioning or is also being watched by police, so Molly refuses to go anywhere.

The families could be relocated forcibly, but characters who do so are kidnappers and subject to federal law. Police observation of the families soon generates a manhunt when they're discovered missing. Implications of these dangers, such as a TV report on a manhunt for a another kidnapper, might sway characters from such drastic measures.

Beyond the Grave?

The most likely alternative to Richardson being back as a ghost and seeking revenge is that he has faked his own death. Investigations at Timmins make him the most likely suspect as the "disgruntled employee." Indeed, he's perhaps the only person with any motive. At least one of his children confesses to seeing him at some point in the story, and he's the thread that links all attacks.

Should the characters be tactless enough to grill either family on the details of David's death, Molly and David Junior can name the hospital that took the body, where Richardson was declared dead. Catriona knows nothing pertinent on the handling of the corpse; she learned of the death later on and secondhand from Charles Segawa. Questioning either family very far on this issue seriously damages any relationships the characters have built, and the families are far less cooperative in future.

Richardson's death certificate is available from the local records office (characters with the Allies or Contacts Merits might be able to acquire a copy). The doctor who signed it works at the local hospital. He can be persuaded to meet characters if they make it clear that their investigation is an attempt to prevent other people from being hurt. The doctor confirms the details on the certificate and states that Richardson's wife (Molly), gave a positive ID, despite the deceased's injuries. Molly was asked to check the body for familiar marks. The doctor saw no need for dental identification or genetic testing in what seemed a clear-cut case.

Under no circumstances do the authorities sanction the exhumation of Richardson's body, unless characters can convince police that Richardson could have faked his own death. The characters need to build a convincing case, linking the living man to all attacks, and they probably need access to Timmins' files on the fraud. If they have all that "evidence," and a successful Manipulation + Persuasion roll is made, the police are sufficiently convinced.

An exhumation and autopsy confirms that Richardson is dead. The characters are thus forced to look for a new suspect or come to a more frightening conclusion: that Richardson is a spirit.

Hidden Accomplice

Characters may suspect that the killer and saboteur is actually a friend or colleague of Richardson's who uses the trappings of the dead man's passing to cover his own trail. It's a good explanation for most (but not all) recent events. If characters investigate Richardson's social life apart from his families, they can uncover the following facts. These "leads" can be pursued, but are ultimately pointless.

• Molly can give characters the name of David's best friend from school: Andy Dunn. Andy is also in finance, but currently works for a bank overseas. He can be contacted by phone; his name and contact information is listed on his employer's website. A call to any of the firm's branches is also routed to him thanks to a company-wide directory. Andy talks about Richardson freely, but sadly, saying that he's barely seen the man in the past 10 years. Richardson's death is news to Andy, and characters recognize that he's genuinely surprised at the loss with a successful Wits + Subterfuge roll.

• Neither Molly nor Catriona knows of any other close friends at all. In fact, when they socialized with David as couples, it was always with the woman's friends.

• Attempts to discover Richardson's hobbies turn up blanks. He just didn't seem to have any. He did go to a gym in the morning near the Richardson home, and any contacts at Timmins are able to give the gym's details (the company offers corporate memberships for staff). Gym employees vaguely recall Richardson, but say that he typically exercised on his own and seemed to appreciate the solitude.

• Inquires into Richardson's colleagues reveal that the only person he socialized with after his falling out with Segawa was Frank Timmins. Their friendship made it hard for the owner to even accept Richardson's fraud. Investigation exonerated Frank Timmins. He is innocent of any complicity, and falls back on the audit as proof. He learned of Richardson's double life only after the man's demise.

Eventually, the picture becomes clear. Richardson just didn't have much opportunity to maintain close friendships outside the workplace and his families. Trying to devote equal time to both families without betraying his secret demanded all of his freedom.

Putting Things Right

By now, the characters probably believe, perhaps beyond all reason, that David Richardson is behind events — and that he's dead. After coming to grips with that concept, what are they supposed to do next? If the characters have dealt with the supernatural before, they may have some idea of how to contend with him. Or if their previous experience was limited, they may know who to speak to or where to go to gather information on what to do next.

Characters who've had no previous experience with the otherworldly must ask themselves some life-shaking questions. If ghosts exist, what does it say about everything I believe? Have I been haunted before and never known? And where can I go or what can I do to resolve the ghost of this man?

Ultimately, how mortal, mundane characters come to grips and get a glimpse into the reality of ghosts is up to you and your chronicle. There's a variety of ways in which they could learn how to deal with spirits, as detailed in the **World of Darkness Rulebook**. They could search out someone they know or have heard of — a weird aunt, an occult author, a supposed psychic — who claims to have knowledge of the supernatural. Or they could research the supernatural online, at libraries or at arcane shops. Or they could go the classic route of seeking guidance and solace in religion. Whether priests believe in or scoff at characters' claims of ghosts, exorcists should not take responsibility for dealing with the spirit out of characters' hands. Maybe a priest had the faith to deal with such an entity *once*, but has lost it since, and gives the knowledge and tools to the characters for them to act on their own. Or a religious figure is sufficiently narrow minded that he refuses to intercede on behalf of characters of different faiths, but he does teach what needs to be done.

Destroying Anchors

Richardson is anchored to four buildings that were instrumental to his life and death: his two family homes, Timmins Manufacturing, and the accountant office that audited and exposed his embezzlement. With Timmins in ruins by the ghost's own spectral hand, that anchor has been severed. While the people who occupy his remaining anchors are the most important elements of them, he's tied to the physical locals as the foci for all those people's lives.

Characters leading, distracting or barring folks from the three sites don't affect Richardson's anchors. Nor does convincing them to relocate or move by some means. Harming or destroying the places does affect Richardson's bond to them, though.

Arson is certainly a choice, but the immorality of that course is unquestionable. Players undoubtedly face Morality rolls and characters may be psychologically scarred by their actions. Then there's the danger of people being hurt or killed in a fire, and the illegality of arson itself. Yes, characters could lure or drive everyone from a home or business (such as with a bomb scare) before it's put to the torch, but that doesn't undo all of the other problems inherent to the act of destruction.

Even if the buildings are somehow bought or acquired and the current occupants move out, the ghost remains. If characters can pull this acquisition off, whether legally and at considerable personal expense or through shady business dealings, they isolate the ghost and can challenge him directly. Indeed, a home or office effectively becomes a haunted house, where characters can perform whatever invocations they have learned, but where the spirit can also direct its powers against them without the potential risk of harming loved ones (again).

Letting Go

Perhaps the least morally offensive solution to the problem is to persuade Richardson to leave the world behind. "Least morally offensive" because no one necessarily gets hurt, and no property damage is done. But is this approach satisfying for characters — or even justifiable? There's no guarantee that Richardson will face any greater punishment for his crimes. (He may be a ghost, but not even he has any idea of what the afterlife entails. Indeed, the concept isn't important to him compared to the matters that keep him in the world.) It's possible that some kind of reward awaits Richardson, and he's a murderer! So can the characters let him get away potentially scot-free?

And how do they persuade Richardson to leave the world behind? One possibility is explaining that his separate families continued in blissful ignorance of each other until he interfered as a ghost. Official investigators into his death and crimes chose not to make his families known, minimizing the pain suffered after his demise. Richardson's haunting has let the secret out. If the characters can successfully argue that the ghost's craving for revenge endangers his true goal — protecting his families from each other — he may let go. (Roll Manipulation + Persuasion versus

Resistance in an extended-action argument that requires a total of 10 successes, and in which each roll represents five minutes of interaction.)

The characters may have also noticed that there are two facets to Richardson's behavior: attacking his business life and protecting his family life. The attacks on Catriona's boyfriend and Stacey Pringle obscure and emphasize this predilection. They obscure it by suggesting that he endangers family, but emphasize it by the fact that neither victim is family (family members get hurt "only" incidentally). Characters may therefore try to persuade the families to help get rid of the ghost by asking — or demanding — that he leaves.

It isn't terribly difficult to convince the families that there is a ghost. They've all heard of or been witness to inexplicable events. Characters simply being in either house may attract the spirit, or even motivate him to lash out at them before loved ones' eyes. Convincing family to ask or tell Richardson to leave is enough to force him on. One of his home-anchors may be resolved with each confrontation, or he may leave altogether if both families join together in the confrontation.

To Hell with You

If you need it, there's a third option. If the characters have any contact with Charles Segawa's family in the aftermath of his death, they learn about his church, the Blessed Evangelical Church of Jesus Christ. The church is in a low-class area of the city, one populated mainly by immigrants. Most of the congregation and care staff are people like the Segawas, who moved here, made homes and now seek to share their good fortune.

The characters find a friendly and surprisingly accepting ear in Father Paul Afoko. The priest tends toward Biblical literalism and genuinely believes in the existence of evil spirits and the Devil himself. He can perform (or teach the characters to perform) an exorcism as outlined in the **World Of Darkness Rulebook**, p. 214.

There are two challenges here. The first is finding Richardson. The characters may realize that he can be found in one of the family homes or at the accountant office. Ways to draw him out in those places might include:

• Appearing to threaten a family member
• Appearing to be romantically involved with Molly or Catriona
• Calling or challenging him

The second challenge is that Richardson has three remaining anchors and can escape to one when threatened. The characters may have to perform an exorcism at each in turn. Doing so depends on the relationships they build with the families and with Williams, Smith and Appiah. Being let into a home or building is one thing. Performing a noisy incantation is another. Perhaps characters have to break in at night, when the place is empty. And then there's the actual confrontation with Richardson himself. Sooner or later, he'll be cornered at a remaining anchor and will use all of his spectral capabilities to protect himself.

Final Impetus

It's possible that characters could decide that ghosts exist, that Richardson is one of them, and then they throw in the towel. After all, what could they possibly do to a ghost? Or why would they possibly want to face a ghost? The result could be characters who turn their backs on the whole affair. The results of the haunting don't go away, though. Once in a while, characters hear news reports or read newspaper articles about a strange event at Williams, Smith and Appiah. Or they spot a family member's name, be it the arrest of a rebellious David Junior or the suicide of Catriona. Can the characters live with the results of their inaction? That's for them to decide.

Denouement

Richardson is gone, driven from the world by spiritual force, manipulation, cunning or a heartfelt appeal. But what's left for the characters? What do they learn from the experience?

The Dead Are Tied to the Living

The most important and clear message is that ghosts exist and cannot leave their lives behind. Death's embrace does not necessarily heal all emotional scars.

Hopefully it's hard for characters to perceive Richardson as a mere supernatural *thing* that's completely divorced from the real world. His every action is inspired by relationships and feelings that anyone who's ever fallen in love or made a mistake can understand. Will the characters' eventual passing be any different? Can they learn from Richardson's lesson? If something horrifying happens to them or they change into something inhuman, will they be able to do better than he did?

Dealing with the Supernatural Raises the Stakes

If Richardson had decided not to kill himself, but to exact his revenge as a living man, he couldn't have done a fraction of the harm that he does as a ghost. Thus, the characters may feel a sense of responsibility for how they live their lives. If something goes wrong or grows out of proportion in life, it could have widespread repercussions if allowed to fester beyond the grave.

Death Is Not the End

Richardson sought to escape the problems he created for himself. It didn't work. He died, but he was tethered to the world by the very issues that motivated his suicide. Perhaps characters realize that they need to challenge life head-on rather than shy away from it. Maybe it inspires them to make peace with their world so as to not be eternally imprisoned by it. But when the World of Darkness is so harsh and bleak, can any peace or forgiveness be found?

Death Is a Mystery Even to the Dead

If the characters grasp the concept of ghostly anchors, Richardson's destruction of one of his own suggests that the restless aren't taught the "rules" of the afterlife. In fact, all he seemed to be aware of was his anchors themselves and the issues that kept him trapped. Are there even answers to the big questions, then? Is there a final reward, a heaven, a hell or a God?

Take All This with a Grain of Salt

The characters deal with a single ghost and a single set of circumstances. As far as they know, everything they see and learn might be applicable to Richardson alone. Experiences with the ghost put the characters in a dangerous position. If they try to draw too many general conclusions, a future encounter with another ghost or another kind of creature could get them killed (or worse). Of course, this is the kind of lesson that's really only learned in hindsight.

Variations

The story as presented may not suit every group of characters or players. Here are a few relatively simple variations on the main plot to help you customize it. The story is actually quite complex, involving four distinct and tenuously connected locations, and focusing on two distinct threads: Richardson's corporate and family life. It can take a while for characters and players to see the big picture. You could therefore focus on just one part of it.

A Family Affair

Are your players interested in intense stories about interpersonal relationships? Emphasize events surrounding the two families and their collision. Corporate elements could simply provide work colleagues or personal friends who know about both families or who can offer information on either.

Corporate Slave

Emphasizing the corporate world changes Richardson from a man who embezzled for his family to a self-interested criminal. You could add a different anchor in the form of the bank through which he laundered money, and retain a single family as a possible source of information. This approach reduces the emotional intensity of the story, which may be more comfortable for some groups.

Down and Dirty

The story as written is largely set in an affluent stratum of society. It would work just as well if Richardson was actually a criminal who embezzled from his gang boss. One of his families (probably the Staples) may be part of that world, while a "legitimate" family may be blissfully unaware of his other kin and his less-than-savory career.

A horror-detective story remains, but gains the possibility of more action and danger as characters have to work the seedy underbelly of the city to discover the truth of Richardson's life and death. It may also prove hard to solve the mystery, because the sort of violence and death already presented here is far more common among criminals and far less likely to attract public attention.

Cast Members

The Ghost

Background: David Richardson was born to a prosperous family, did as well as his parents expected in both school and sports, married a cheerleader, got a good job and settled down. That's the story most people know.

The secret truth is that Richardson's desire to please his parents developed into a desire to please everyone he loved, with unfortunate consequences when he fell in love with a second woman. He never made a conscious decision to have two families. Making a decision would have involved hurting someone, so he did nothing and was caught up in a web of emotional debt and financial obligation. Rather than escape it, he only got further entangled by embezzling and dedicating every available moment to his two families, leaving nothing for himself.

When it all became too much, he was rewarded with an afterlife bound to the very places he tried to escape. If it wasn't all his own fault, you could almost feel sorry for David Richardson.

Description: The ghost can look in death much as he did in life: handsome, but not remarkably so. His seeming age is reflected in a certain looseness in the jowls and broadening at the waist, with the haggard look he had in his last few years. His clothes appear to be expensive suits kept too long, and perpetually in slight disarray. When his rage rises, his appearance becomes that of the mangled corpse that was his mortal remains.

Storytelling Hints: The spirit of Richardson is wildly unpredictable. One minute he seems like a lovelorn teenager, obsessed with his families' happiness. The next, he's an engine of destruction, ready to hurt anyone whom he blames for his predicament. Anyone, that is, except for the true architect of his troubles, himself.

Attributes: Power 5, Finesse 3, Resistance 2
Willpower: 7
Morality: 3 (drops to 2 as the story progresses)
Virtue: Charity
Vice: Wrath
Initiative: 5
Defense: 5
Speed: 18 (species factor 10)
Size: 5
Corpus: 7
Numina: Ghost Sign (dice pool 8), Ghost Speech (dice pool 8), Magnetic Disruption, Telekinesis (dice pool 8), Terrify (dice pool 8)

Frank Timmins

Quote: "This is a family business and always has been. Our good name is what makes us stand out from the competition."

Background: William Timmins desperately wanted the family manufacturing business to remain just that, family. His son Malcolm had no interest in commerce, "throwing away" money on political campaigning. By contrast, William's grandson Frank was extremely keen to get into the family legacy, much to his father's disgust.

So, grandfather took grandson under wing, guided Frank to chief financial officer, and left the company to him when he died. Frank promoted his friend and deputy David Richardson to his old job and became CEO, rapidly modernizing the company and bringing in new blood such as Charles Segawa. In many ways, Frank was too good at recruiting. He got extremely competent people who could do their jobs without supervision, and created a contribution vacuum for himself.

In time, Frank became disinterested, complacent and then alcoholic, allowing Richardson to weave financial deceit. Frank's success as an employer wasn't matched in his personal life; he split with his wife five years ago.

Richardson's betrayal and death shocked Timmins out of his fog briefly, but old habits die hard.

Description: Frank is a friendly man in his mid-50s. He's beginning to show the puffiness in the face of someone who drinks too much, and his waistline suffers. He wears modern suits during the week, and slacks and blazer combinations on weekends. He never liked wearing ties and is almost never seen in one.

Storytelling Hints: Frank is affable and easygoing. His open nature betrays a lonely man who everybody likes but to whom no one is dedicated. At work, he's helpful but cautious, fearful of revealing how little he really knows about the business anymore. If caught in the bar at night, he's talkative and almost desperate to please.

Abilities:
Empathy (dice pool 4), **Socialize** (dice pool 5) — Frank is good with people, and a very good listener. The

fact that he doesn't make lasting friends is a sign of an innate character flaw rather than a lack of social skills. He's just a little too needy.

Intimidation (dice pool 3) — He can still be the boss when he absolutely needs to be.

Martin Farrell

Quote: "I'm sorry, but I can't disclose that information. Now, if you'll excuse me, I have work to do."

Background: Martin Farrell is a man on the up. He's in his early 40s and has worked his contacts from his days at a prestigious university to build his career. He was delighted when, just under a year ago, he was appointed chief financial officer of a manufacturing company that was in serious trouble thanks to his predecessor's fraud. Farrell has no intention of devoting his life to Timmins. He's out to make his reputation as a troubleshooter and then move on. In many ways, Richardson was a great boon to his self-motivated replacement, without the two ever meeting in the flesh.

Farrell leaves a simple, disciplined life. He's had relationships on and off throughout the years, but none that have lasted. He still nurtures the hope that he'll one day meet the woman who can hold his attention, but it hasn't happened yet. Maybe that's for the best. After all, career comes first.

Description: Farrell is tall and lean, with eyes slightly too large for his face. His body is reasonably well toned (he walks whenever he can), and he dresses in expensive but unassuming clothes. Labels are too vulgar for Farrell, but he does like to wear his wealth in a way that the trained eye can detect. He's been seen out of a suit at a company picnic, but his colleagues suspect he wears one on weekends, too.

Storytelling Hints: Farrell is reserved, professional and very slightly pompous. He has an annoying way of dismissing anything that he considers irrelevant, which

can make him frustrating to talk to. Farrell has never had to deal with a major crisis in life… until now… if he lives, anyway.

Abilities:

Academics (dice pool 5) — Farrell is the studious sort, with a good post-graduate degree in business.

Molly Richardson

Quote: "Look, that's in the past now. I'd rather not talk about it. Coffee?"

Background: Molly Richardson (maiden name Lambert) went to school with David Richardson, hung out with David Richardson, was a cheerleader for the sports team on which David Richardson played, and married David Richardson just a few years out of school. Even in the early years of their marriage, she was more comfortable with David than passionate about him, but couldn't imagine life without him.

For Molly, comfort was never really at stake. She had her business and David had his work. She suspected him of the odd dalliance, but she never made much of it, because she'd had one or two of her own. That had been going on since school, so why would either of them stop?

David's death came as a terrible shock. To this day, Molly has no clear idea why he was embezzling money, but grief has so clouded her mind that she hasn't really given the matter much thought. Instead, she's obsessed with the time she didn't spend with her husband, and with the parts of his life she didn't know. She now goes through the motions with her son and her own business; something vital has escaped her.

Description: Molly is average height and has always been thin, but now she's turned gaunt. She wears slightly too much makeup to compensate for her fading looks. Her clothes are a bit out of fashion, given that she lost interest a year ago. Her hands tend to flutter nervously and her eyes are restless.

Storytelling Hints: Molly wears the veneer of her former respectability over the insecurity and grief at her core. She pretends to be the woman she was, but without the man she had, she's lost. She comes across as calm and resolute, but her real self emerges over time. If she finds out about her husband's other family, she may break down completely.

Abilities:

Socialize (dice pool 4), Persuasion (dice pool 5) — Running a fashion boutique for over a decade has taught Molly some communication skills that she now uses to shore up her sense of self.

David Richardson Junior

Quote: "Yeah, what?"

Background: David Junior is a fit, athletic boy in his mid-teens. He resembles his father, to the point where photos of the two at the same age are only distinguishable by different haircuts and fashions. David Junior never got enough attention. His father was never around. In the year since his father's death, the boy has gotten into trouble at school and has been hanging around with a group of neglected suburban kids who play at being a gang. It's a classic plea for attention.

Storytelling Hints: David is a surly teenager with a chip on his shoulder, unresolved grief issues over his father's death, and familiarity with a handful of street terms learned on TV. Once trouble starts around him, the vulnerable child within comes out

Catriona Staples

Quote: "He loved me right up until the end. All he wanted was to protect his family. That's all I want to do, too."

Background: Catriona (never "Cat") had a difficult childhood. Her folks split up when she was eight, and she was shuttled among various aunts and uncles until she was old enough to get a job and a place of her own. She worked retail and did secretarial work before finally getting a low-level job and the promise of training at an accountant office. In short, she's done well for herself.

Catriona's upbringing taught her to be self-reliant, and she appreciates that quality. Part of her never really minded that her lover had a wife. She valued the free time it left her. It sometimes bothered her that David was picky about what dinner parties and functions he'd attend with her, but she figured the problems and benefits balanced out in the end. And David was a good father to the kids. When he was around, anyway.

David's death shocked Catriona, but not as much as she might have expected. She got on with things, held her kids when they cried, and resumed a lifestyle like she had known before. John was a surprise. She didn't expect to meet someone so soon. She certainly didn't expect to

fall for him. And she really didn't expect it to hurt so badly when everything got strange and the relationship floundered.

Description: Catriona is a striking woman, with angular and attractive features. Like Molly, she's tall and thin; there are physical similarities between the women. Catriona is in her mid-30s, but her looks suggest anything from mid-20s. She dresses smartly for work, but her casual clothes betray her humble origins.

Storytelling Hints: Anyone who assumes Catriona is a foolish, lovelorn mistress or even a white-trash goldbricker is in for a surprise. She's strong, assertive and can be vicious when she needs to be. Her manner sometimes suggests clinical detachment, except when she's with her children. She isn't desperately surprised or hurt to find out that David had another child.

Abilities:

Brawl (dice pool 4) — Catriona's not a fighter if she can avoid it, but she knows how to protect herself.

Intimidation (dice pool 5) — This is not a lady to cross.

Streetwise (dice pool 4) — Like Brawl, this is a remnant of Catriona's early life. She's lost her edge, but the basics are still there.

Bethany Staples

Quote: "Daddy's gone away, but sometimes I think he's still here."

Background: Bethany is tall for her age, with slightly curly, shoulder-length brown hair. She already dresses in a tomboy manner, to her mother's combined amusement and disgust. Bethany is the youngest of all of Richardson's kids. She alternates between bare memory of her father and claims to have seen him just recently. Catriona doesn't yet know what to make of these stories. No matter what,

Bethany has a loving sister and mother, and she rather likes Uncle John, her mother's new friend.

Storytelling Hints: Before the spectral attack on her best friend Stacey Pringle, Bethany is a bright, inquisitive child who is confident in dealing with others. After the attack, she is nervous and withdrawn, but displays an occasional flash of fortitude that's unusual in a young child.

Jenny Staples

Quote: "None of this makes sense. It's just stupid."

Background: Jenny's a pretty average looking eight-year-old, with shoulder-length hair and round glasses. She dresses in jeans and T-shirts most of the time, partially in imitation of John.

When her father died, Jenny was utterly devastated, but never really let it show. Her mother still worries about her seeming absence of grief, unaware that Jenny has cried on John's shoulder more than once and sworn him to secrecy. Jenny misses her father terribly, but does like John, and he's persuaded her that she must be strong for her little sister's sake.

Storytelling Hints: Jenny tries to be resolute, but she's too young to pull it off. She's easily frustrated and often on the edge of tears as a result.

John Escott

Quote: "Listen, I love Catriona and I love the girls. I'd never hurt them — or their friends."

Background: John Escott drifted from job to job for a decade. He always went home to visit his folks every Christmas, but otherwise had no real point of stability until he moved onto the same street as Catriona Staples and her family three years ago. He developed an instant dislike for Richardson and an equally instant attraction to Catriona.

Richardson's seeming lack of commitment to his family irritated John, as did his way of ignoring the neighbors. John didn't shed a tear when the man died. Instead, he was there for Catriona when she needed help, and he hoped that something would develop between them in time. He was surprised at how quickly it did. He moved fairly easily into the role of surrogate father. After all, he'd been around more than the girls' real father had.

At the beginning of this story, John thinks his life is finally coming together. He's in for a terrible shock.

Description: John is a short, stocky guy with a slight gut, balanced by a decent set of muscles. He has a ready smile and a surprisingly gentle look about him. He dresses casually pretty much at all times, and looks positively uncomfortable when forced into anything but his accustomed T-shirt and jeans.

Storytelling Hints: John is an affable and caring man who enjoys doing things more than talking about them. He gets fidgety when sitting still for long and occasionally loses the train of long conversations. Still, he's honest, genuinely tries to be helpful, and is fiercely protective of Catriona and the kids (until events become too bizarre and dangerous for even him).

Abilities:

Brawl (dice pool 4) — Escott's been in a few fights in his day and knows how to handle himself.

Crafts (dice pool 5) — Most of Escott's jobs have involved manual labor of one sort or another, although he's worked as an electrician in the last couple of years.

Chapter 4: Roots and Branches

By Rick Chillot

*Thomas Moth,
your children bleed,*

*Your wife was
stabbed by Henry
Creed,*

*All your silver, all
your gold,*

*Can't keep their
bones from growing
cold.*

*— Children's rhyme,
circa 1902*

Summary

There are all sorts of reasons why spirits don't move on to their final rest. Some are held back by unfinished business. Some don't realize that they've died. And some are trapped in the land of the living against their will, kept here by malevolent forces that they can't resist. In this story, characters delve into the past to understand angry ghosts that lash out against the living. Only then can they do what the ghosts can't do for themselves: cut the ties that keep the spirits from reaching their final destination.

This story is presented in three acts, each divided into individual scenes. But the story doesn't restrict characters to a single location — they're not trapped on a submarine full of Nazi ghosts, for example. For a full gaming experience, both you and the players should be prepared for characters to attend to the mundane details of life at various points. That doesn't mean roleplaying every hour of the day, but players should have a clear concept of where their characters live and work, and what they do in their off hours. As the story progresses, characters may need to arrange time off from work, explain their odd behavior to friends and family, or find time to catch up on their sleep after spending nights chasing spirits. Balancing the events of this story with the mundane events of life helps everyone create fully rounded characters, and allows you to have supernatural phenomena affect the protagonists when their guard is down. Ghosts don't just appear at night in haunted houses. They might appear in a mirror while someone is shaving at home, or make a spinach salad seem to turn into rotted meat during an important business lunch.

The open nature of this story also means that players may stray from the sequence of events presented. This chapter seeks to address possible courses of action, but players are always full of surprises. The best way to deal with this is to let characters follow the leads they concoct. They may waste their time, but you can drop hints that they're barking up the wrong tree, or that they should revisit an overlooked possibility. If characters consult with Contacts, Mentors or Allies, they may get advice that steers them back on track. Cast members presented here can also suggest that characters rethink their approach. Finally, be open to the possibility that players hit on something that's actually a pretty good idea. Reward their ingenuity by incorporating the concepts they create into the story, or allow their train of thought to actually bear fruit.

History

One summer night in 1900, wealthy industrialist Thomas Moth came home to find his wife Felicity and children Millicent and Edmond shot to death in their beds. The murderer was the estate's head gardener, Henry Creed, who was seen by Moth fleeing the grounds with a pistol in hand and blood spattered on his clothes. For the rest of his life, Thomas Moth was haunted by the loss of his family, and by the fact that Creed was never caught and punished for his brutal crime. Moth let his business sink slowly into bankruptcy, and spent his final years in an asylum as a mere shadow of his former self. The crime shocked the nation in its day, but in modern times it's been all but forgotten except by trivia and history buffs.

That's the official version. Once characters get involved in the story's modern developments, and become curious about Moth Park, they unearth that basic information by doing basic research on the park or on the life of Moth. But the truth of what happened that night has never been made public. First, it's not true that Henry Creed escaped. He was in fact chased down and apprehended by Moth and his servants on the very night of the murders. The reason Creed was never seen again is that Moth hanged him from the tallest tree.

But there's more. Thomas Moth didn't kill just Creed. He's also the one who killed Felicity, Millicent and Edmond. He shot them in a fit of rage when he discovered that Creed had been having an affair with his wife — and that the children were Creed's, not his own. With Creed gone, no one would suggest that a well-respected member of the community murdered his own wife and children. The few servants who knew the truth took the secret to the grave. Thomas Moth never confessed, though the guilt he felt ensured that his long life was miserable.

The story didn't end there, though. Moth's estate became a public park, and at its center was the ancient sycamore tree from which Henry Creed was hanged. The hanging tree was not ordinary, but a reservoir of great spiritual power. When that power was tainted by murder, it became poisoned and corrupt. The tree was transformed into a trap, a snare for souls that held fast to the ghosts of Creed, Felicity and the children. Every so often, the Murder Tree of Moth Park craves the taste of another murdered soul. It sends one of its ghosts to take the life of someone nearby, and that victim is trapped with the other spirits in the tangled branches.

Setting

Much of this story takes place in Moth Park, about 100 acres that can be set in any city. Once the site of Thomas Moth's estate, the park is now a boundary between the seedier side of town — warehouses, tenements, abandoned storefronts — and a more upscale, though past-its-prime neighborhood of brownstones, stores, offices and restaurants. The park is approximately rectangular in shape, with a bandshell/performance stage at the north end, a soccer field and softball diamond at the south, and a forested area in the center. It also holds two playgrounds (swing sets, slides, monkey bars), several fountains (most of which are nonfunctional), various statues, and a network of walking paths. Moth Park is popular with local residents as well as those who come into the area to work or visit. On a typical day, it's also a hangout for truant youths and burnouts, small-time drug dealers and the homeless. But it's fairly well policed and is generally considered safe, at least during the day.

The following are some features that characters encounter while exploring the park. Some play key roles and others are yours to use or ignore as you see fit. Feel free to add landmarks of your own to make the place fully suit the characters' hometown.

Bandshell: A performance stage with an overhead roof is located at the north end of the park. During concerts, additional folding chairs are placed for temporary seating. The roof has several severe leaks, making the stage unusable in inclement weather. Skateboarders often use the stage and stairways leading to it to practice their moves.

Sports Fields: A playing area for football or soccer, as well as a softball diamond, are located at the south end of the park. On most weekends in good weather, both areas are reserved for various amateur-league games. When not in use for organized sports, the fields are popular for pick-up games, kite flying, picnicking or just laying in the grass and watching the clouds go by. Characters are likely to encounter a wide cross section of people here: families, homeless, athletes and business people eating lunch. On the main path that leads to the sports fields is a marker that reads:

"When this land was bought from industrialist Thomas Moth, it included a large firing range. Shooting was one of Moth's favorite pastimes, second only to botany. When the Moth estate was converted into parkland, the range was turned into a playing field for organized sports."

Arboretum: The middle third of the park is covered with trees, providing shade and a pseudo-forested experience for those who walk the area's trails. There are several park benches and picnic sites among the trees. This area is home to the sycamore tree and the ghosts of Henry Creed and Moth's family. At the head of a trail that leads into the wooded area, a marker reads:

"When Thomas Moth donated his estate to the city, the land included several dozen trees that Moth had planted over the course of 20 years. An amateur botanist, Moth collected seeds and cuttings from all over the world with the intent of creating a vast arboretum that would be of interest to scientists and nature lovers alike. Unfortunately, he suffered a reversal of fortune before his dream could be fulfilled."

Sycamore Tree: The tree that ensnares the ghosts of Moth Park is a magnificent specimen. At nearly 150 feet tall, it's the largest tree in the park. Characters with Science 3+ or a Botany Specialty can tell that the tree is in extremely good health for its age. The only oddity about it is that one of its larger, lower limbs is completely without leaves. (This is in fact the limb from which Creed was hung). A talk with any parks employees reveals that they're aware of the anomaly, but it doesn't seem to affect the tree.

A post with a marker is set in the ground near the tree:

"American Sycamore (Planatus occidentalis): Perhaps the oldest tree in the park, this sycamore is said to have been present before Thomas Moth purchased this land and built his estate. Its true age is unknown."

Near the base of the tree, a valentine heart is carved into the bark. Inside the heart are the letters: "HC + FM."

Headless Statue: Located on the southern fringe of the arboretum is a larger-than-life statue of stained and corroded metal. Its most notable feature, aside from its age and dilapidated condition, is the fact that the figure's head is missing. The monument dates back to the earliest days of the park, and no one's sure who it represents. It appears to be a man dressed as a colonial American, but historians can't agree on whether it's one of the nation's founding fathers, someone involved in the city's early history, or even Thomas Moth himself in symbolic costume.

Doll Field: The southwestern section of the park was once used as a trash dump by a nearby factory that made children's dolls. Plastic body parts occasionally surface here after a rain. A bit of digging can unearth doll heads, legs and other pieces.

Park Gates: Moth Park is enclosed on all sides by a metal fence with a spiked top. The condition of the fence varies; many of the area's homeless know spots where there are loose bars, gaps or other ways through. The park can be entered through large metal gates located in the center of the north, east, west and southern borders. Other sections of the fence are equipped with hinges and locks and can be opened by police, fire officials or park employees. At each public entrance is an engraved plaque.

"Moth Park was originally the estate of Thomas Moth, a wealthy industrialist and philanthropist who made a fortune manufacturing nails, barrel staves, barbed wire and paper clips. He was a nature lover who maintained the grounds of his mansion as a well-landscaped oasis in the city. Moth was well liked by the community and admired for his generosity to charities, as well as for his business acumen. Shortly after the tragic death of his wife and children, the estate and mansion were sold to the city. Five years later, the grounds were converted to a park named in his honor."

Getting Started

The story requires that characters visit Moth Park, where they encounter the ghost of Lenore White, the Murder Tree's latest victim. The reasons for their presence aren't important. Visiting a park isn't that unusual for most people, so players may be satisfied if you begin simply by saying, "You're walking through the park one afternoon, and…." For Storytellers and players who need a more detailed setup, here are some possibilities.

• If the characters are already acquainted with each other, they might meet at the park for some type of group activity: jogging, walking, picnicking or just killing time at lunch.

• Characters might find themselves in the park for work-related reasons. A cop might patrol the area to fill in for a sick colleague. A journalist might meet a source for an interview. A college student or professor might collect insect species or plant samples. A musician might perform for tips or scout a location for a concert.

• Characters who don't live or work near the park might find themselves there because they're in the area on business, visiting a nearby relative or babysitting. Perhaps the car is in a nearby shop and a character takes a walk while waiting for it to be fixed. (She may later find that the repairs will take longer than expected, a good tactic to keep an out-of-town character in the area.)

If there's no credible reason for characters to be in the park, you can have them encounter Lenore elsewhere. The Murder Tree is her anchor, as it is for all its victims. But perhaps Lenore has a second anchor somewhere else, and can manifest near it. She might have a favorite coffee shop that's frequented by the characters, for example. If you go this route, create incidents similar to Lenore's appearances in the park (below). Have her drop hints that send the characters to the park (perhaps she even whispers "Moth Park").

Act 1

Cast: Lenore White. The latest victim of the Murder Tree.

Gray Pete/Peter Gray. (See his write-up on p. 109.)

Scene 1: Lost Lenore

The ghost of recently deceased Lenore White reaches out to whomever she can during her brief manifestations. In many ghost stories, small oddities early in a tale seem unremarkable until later events prove them to be significant. Lenore's first appearances aren't overtly supernatural. Most ordinary people might be puzzled by encounters with her, but don't do more than shrug. Of course, the players are well aware that they're involved in a story, and may be prone to reading significance into events that are even slightly unusual. Here are some ways to keep their first meeting with Lenore from setting off too many alarms too soon.

• **Mix and Match:** Consider running this first scene in the midst of another story. Perhaps as one scenario winds down, the characters meet Lenore in the park. They complete the first story, perhaps forgetting about the encounter with the strange woman, only to recognize its significance as events move on.

• **Distract Them:** Maybe Lenore isn't the only "eccentric" type in the park that day. The characters might also encounter a homeless stranger who follows them around. They might be the victims of an attempted mugging. They might reunite a lost child with her parents, or witness a performance artist juggle discarded bottles. The point is not to parade the characters from one encounter to the next, but to establish various interactions that downplay the significance of their run-in with Lenore.

• **Tone it Down:** If you really want Lenore to come in under the players' radar, make her first appearance more mundane than what's described here. Instead of a disheveled woman who stares at the characters from a distance, make her a slightly anxious passerby who bumps into a

93

SETTING | GETTING STARTED | ACT1 | SCENE1 LOST LENORE

character, excuses herself and keeps on walking. Perhaps she asks for directions to the park's exit or drops her umbrella, interacting with the characters just long enough for them to remember her later.

Aside from launching the story, sighting Lenore is a good opportunity for unconnected characters to meet. ("Excuse me, did you see that strange woman standing over there a second ago?") If having all the characters in the same area of the park at the same time doesn't work, have them encounter Lenore separately.

Meeting Lenore

Tell the characters that it's a cloudy but dry day, the first after several straight days of heavy rain.

Lenore appears to be a young woman dressed in a disheveled gray raincoat with a partly open umbrella. She holds her head at an angle, sometimes tilting it to one side so that her left ear almost touches her shoulder. Her dark hair hangs loose, and seems to be tangled with leaves and sticks. Her coat and hair look wet, despite the weather. Characters in the vicinity of the arboretum notice her standing several yards away, staring at them. Her lips move as if she's mumbling, but she makes no sound. Lenore's appearance is somewhat strange, given that it hasn't rained since the day before, but there's nothing to indicate that she's anything but flesh and blood (she's not transparent, for example). Once she's noticed, Lenore takes a few steps behind a clump of trees and disappears.

If the characters encounter Lenore separately, you can use these variations on her appearance to mix it up.

• She appears sitting on a playground roundabout. It rotates slowly, and when it comes around again, she's gone.

• A character walking through the arboretum sees her walking parallel to him several feet away. She passes behind a tree and doesn't emerge on the other side.

• She sits on a park bench. The view to her is blocked by a pretzel vendor pushing his cart, and then she's gone.

• A character sees Lenore standing near a pile of leaves and debris left by a park maintenance worker. A gust of wind blows leaves all around her (or blows dust into the character's eyes), after which she's gone.

This scene doesn't require characters to react to Lenore in any specific way. Those who look for her don't find her. If characters make a prolonged search, you can introduce them to some of the park landmarks or have them discover some items on the "Found Objects" list. You can also have characters meet each other, if they haven't already. If they question any park-goers or employees, no one else seems to have seen anybody meeting Lenore's description. (If you want to make the characters' lives difficult, have someone remember, after Lenore's body is discovered, that people asked about someone like her. Perhaps the police get a description of one or more characters, causing trouble for them if they're caught sneaking in or out of the park later.)

Found Objects

In horror stories, sometimes small details are the creepiest. Think of the fingernails embedded in the cistern wall in *Silence of the Lambs*. In a Storytelling game, creepy or off-kilter details not only establish mood, they keep players nervous and off balance. Surely some mundane object picked up off the ground doesn't have anything to do with the main story… but what if it does? Do characters dare ignore it? What does it mean? Here are some objects that characters might come across in the park or elsewhere. You don't want them tripping over these things, but use them judiciously and they may become the objects of characters' obsessions, wild theories or unlikely assumptions.

A teacup that, when turned over, is found to be covering a small, live frog (which quickly hops away).

A partly buried coffee can full of rusted bolts and screws.

A glove with a sixth finger sewn onto it.

A collar for a seemingly large dog with a tag that reads, "Richard."

A fragment of yellow, lined paper with these words written in longhand: "Razors. Tampons. Thread. Needles. Cough Syrup. Kerosene. Rope. Duct Tape." Each item except the fifth has a checkmark next to it.

A CD-ROM that, when read via computer, contains a single text file consisting of the word "sleep" repeated 4376 times.

A single crutch.

A beer bottle filled with live worms.

Two plastic picnic forks tied perpendicular to each other to form a cross.

A mannequin hand with the initials "M.D." written in ink on the wrist.

Scene 2: Haunted

This scene takes place the evening after the characters sight Lenore. The scene is most effective if characters drop their guard, pursuing mundane activities such as watching TV or grocery shopping. Ask in an offhand way what characters do for the rest of the day and night. Then have Lenore reach out to each with the following haunting.

The ghost is not completely aware of what's happened to her or where she is. She knows she needs help, and intuitively chooses the characters as the ones closest to her with the most potential, ability or willingness to respond to her pleas. Her visitations should be brief but disturbing, and in some cases may cause minor danger or a chance of slight injury. At least some characters should receive indication that it's not just Lenore who needs help (she says "Help us" rather than "Help me"), and something about a tree.

• A character who's driving looks in the rearview mirror and sees Lenore sitting in the back seat. She stares back, still tilting her head at that odd angle. The player must make a successful Dexterity + Drive roll for the character to avoid getting in a minor fender bender.

• A character is taking a shower when she's struck by the sudden, overwhelming odor of wet vegetation. The shower turns cold and the water sounds more like the downpour of a rainstorm than the output of a showerhead. The character feels wind and something like wet leaves slapping at her body. After shutting off the water and stumbling out of the shower, the character sees "MURDER TREE HELP US" written in the steam on the mirror. The words disappear after a few seconds.

• A character works on a crossword puzzle, writes an email, doodles or makes out checks and realizes that he's filled in all the squares, screen, page or checks with the words "LENORE HANGED MURDER HELP US TREE MOTH."

• A character dreams that Lenore is standing at the foot of his bed. She clutches at her throat and performs a choking pantomime. The character awakens to find a window open and a trail of wet leaves inside (and it's not raining outside).

• A character eats dinner when he feels a sudden tightness around his throat. The sensation feels like something constricting, not like an airway obstruction or choking on food. The player rolls Stamina + Composure. If the roll is successful, the constriction fades. If it fails, the character falters, falling to the floor and taking a point of bashing damage. The constriction diminishes just as the character is about lose consciousness, leaving no marks.

• A character talks on the phone when there's a burst of static. A woman's voice cuts in, saying, "The tree… please help us… the tree… please help us." Then the line goes dead or the signal is lost and the phone doesn't work again until the next morning.

• A character comes home to find her yard full of dozens of brownish, globe-like, one-inch-diameter fruits on thin stalks (some attached to zigzag-shaped twigs). Anyone with knowledge of trees recognizes them as the fruit of a sycamore tree. A little research online (no rolls necessary) turns up the same. For creepier effect, have the character find the fruit all over her bathroom floor. A successful Intelligence + Composure or Science roll reminds the character of where she's seen something similar of late: Moth Park.

After the characters have had a visit or two from Lenore, they may be motivated to return to Moth Park to better understand what's going on. In fact, they may want to go right away, in the dead of night. You can discourage this by having the weather turn bad (a dark, stormy night is perhaps not the best time for outdoor ghost hunting), or by having them warned off by a patrol car as they try to enter the park's locked gates. Or you could let them get to the park and move into a variation on the next scene. They arrive to find the park filled with police, media and a few homeless onlookers as Lenore's body is retrieved.

Scene 3: Of the Crime

The characters start their day to learn through a TV or radio news report that the body of a young woman has been found in Moth Park. She's been identified as Lenore White, a city resident who worked in a nearby office building. (You might add to the drama by having a character wake up to the TV or radio already on and tuned to the news.) The report states that a park worker found the body in a culvert in the arboretum early that morning. The police estimate that she died four days earlier. Her body had been covered by leaves, branches and other debris, possibly stirred up by the inclement weather. The cause of death has not been released, but police consider it a homicide.

Interaction

Characters may be moved to call the police or approach the authorities (possibly at the park) to share details of their encounters with the woman who might have been the victim. Doing so may provoke one of the following reactions.

• Those who claim to have seen a "ghost" or to have been contacted by the victim after her death are considered cranks. The characters are politely asked to move along, or they're thanked and then hung up on. Snickering, outright laughter or annoyed rebuff are also possibilities.

• Characters may claim to have seen Lenore in the park without mentioning any of the strange trappings of their sighting. That doesn't leave them with much more to say than, "I saw her the other day." Police take a statement; characters are asked to describe their encounter in as much detail as possible. The police know that Lenore died four days ago, and that it rained all that day. If characters say they saw Lenore just yesterday, the interview comes to an end. Otherwise, the authorities take characters' names and contact information, and thank them for their time, but are clearly unimpressed with what little information they have to offer.

Any characters who go to the park spot Lenore again, standing otherwise unnoticed among police, forensics specialists and media personnel. Once recognized by one or more characters, Lenore slowly points to the large sycamore tree that's a few yards away from the spot where her body was found. She then fades like a shadow caught in the sunrise. This encounter may also occur at any point when characters go to the park next, after investigators have left.

Gathering Information

Characters with the appropriate credentials or Merits (such as Contacts or Allies) can try to gather information from police or journalists. They can also talk to locals who hang around the park or who live or work nearby. Depending on whom they address, characters can try using various Social Skills such as Persuasion, Intimidation or Streetwise to gather information, or maybe a Wits + Manipulation roll is called for. Where appropriate, characters may gain a bonus by offering a bribe, from +1 (slipping $10 to the pretzel vendor) to +3 (buying dinner for the guy who spends all day fishing pennies out of the fountain). For the Attributes or abilities of these people, see "Antagonists," p. 201 of the **World of Darkness Rulebook**.

The police finish their work by noon, removing the crowd-control tape and leaving the scene. By early afternoon, most curiosity seekers are gone. If the characters approach the sycamore tree, a successful Wits + Composure roll inspires a sense of being watched. Characters who look up wonder momentarily if human faces look down from the tree, but the "faces" quickly prove to be the texture of the bark. Characters have this experience only once. It could occur any day they're present if the watched sensation has never come to pass before.

What the Authorities Know

Characters may ascertain a variety of information by talking to associates in law enforcement, the parks department or city hall. The police also know the basic facts of Lenore's life: her age, where she lived and where she worked.

The woman died of a broken neck. A rope mark around her neck suggests that she was strangled, but no fibers have been found on her skin or clothes, or at the scene. They could have been washed away by the rain. The position of the body wasn't consistent with a fall, the ground was soft, and there were no bruises or other indications of a fall. There were no other injuries or indications of sexual abuse.

Lenore's purse, containing identification, credit cards and cash was found near the body, ruling out robbery as a motive.

The police have no suspects. Interviews with family and friends turn up no disgruntled boyfriends, death threats or other indications that someone wished her ill. The police are well acquainted with the homeless who frequent the park; most of them are considered harmless. Others have already been questioned and ruled out as suspects.

Lenore was last seen at lunchtime by her coworkers on the day of her disappearance, which was a Friday. Lenore typically walked through the park on her break, even if the weather was bad. Her failure to return that afternoon was noticed by her supervisor, who called her apartment. He also left an angry message the following Monday (both messages remain on Lenore's answering machine).

What the Press Knows

Journalism contacts can provide the following information. You can also have journalists share the background information about Thomas Moth and the park provided at the beginning of this chapter.

Lenore died of a broken neck, and there are indications that she was strangled. (At police request, the media is holding this information back for a few days; it appears in later news reports.)

The police received an anonymous call from a self-proclaimed psychic who claimed that the killer was the park's headless statue come to life.

This isn't the first time that a body with a broken neck has been found in Moth Park. There have been seven others. The most recent was in 1952. Two others were found in 1931, another in 1920 and three in the years 1915 to 1918 (records aren't clear about the precise dates of these three).

A children's rhyme made the rounds of the city at the turn of the last century.

Thomas Moth, your children bleed,

Your wife was stabbed by Henry Creed,

All your silver, all your gold,

Can't keep their bones from growing cold.

The rhyme didn't have the staying power of, say, that about Lizzie Borden's 40 whacks, and fell out of use a few years after it emerged.

Characters who conduct their own research about the park may also learn any of this history with a successful extended action (Intelligence + Academics or Investigation + equipment; each roll represents a half-hour's work).

What Park Regulars Know

Here are some statements that characters might hear from locals — the homeless, vendors, or people who live or own businesses in nearby neighborhoods. Use them as the basis for interaction or conversations.

"I seen that poor girl here two or three times a week. Don't remember seein' her that day, though. It was rainin' so I stayed at the shelter."

"The cops think it was one of us did it. Now they're going to lock us all up."

"There's some places in this park I don't go even in the daytime. Them woods, they ain't right. Sometimes around sunset I see people looking at me from that big ol' tree."

"We just want to be left alone, we don't want to hurt nobody. Now the cops are goin' to throw us all out the park. What's so bad about sleepin' on a park bench? Who does that hurt?"

"That night I seen something strange. A tall man in a black coat walkin' with three big dogs followin' behind him."

"Some of those homeless people are pretty scary looking. I think they should round them up and lock them up. Make the park safe for decent people."

"You should look for Gray Pete. That guy knows everything that goes on around here, even if he is pretty weird."

What Friends and Colleagues Know

If the characters seek out friends or coworkers of Lenore, they find them understandably shaken up by her death. Those closest to her may be too upset to talk (−1 to −3 penalties if characters attempt to get information from them). Those willing to talk describe Lenore as bright and cheerful, an upbeat young woman who enjoyed life and rarely had a complaint. Her boss and coworkers say she was strong willed and not easily discouraged; the kind of person who kept trying until she overcame an obstacle. She was also great at recognizing and encouraging the strengths and capabilities of others. Lenore's parents and brother live out of state. They hold a small, private funeral in her hometown within a few days.

Ending the Scene

Let the characters take as much time as they like asking questions and investigating. Take this opportunity to feed players any information they may have missed (as long as characters ask the right questions). When the protagonists decide to leave the area, start the next scene by having Pete approach them.

Returning to the Park

At some point it's assumed that characters return to the park and look around or ask questions, which brings them to Gray Pete's attention. But what if characters aren't moved to investigate, they try to do all their sleuthing over the phone or Internet, or don't know what to do next (or don't want to do *anything*, clinging to their safe, mundane, ignorant worlds)? Here are some ideas for getting them on track.

• Make it part of their day. If one of the characters is a journalist, you might have an editor or supervisor assign her the Lenore White story. A private detective might be hired by nervous park officials to conduct a low-key investigation. An FBI agent or criminologist might be asked by a friend in the local police to visit the crime scene and offer advice. A landscaper, surveyor, garbage man, pest controller, dog walker or city worker might need to go to the park to do his job. Other characters might end up at the park for mundane reasons: to go jogging, to take the kids to the swings, or to do some painting, drawing or photography. Such characters might not be professionally interested in the crime, but can still find clues missed (or ignored) by the police.

• A voice of experience. Characters who consult Contacts or Mentors in law enforcement, journalism, private investigation or any other relevant field might be given fundamental advice: You can't find answers if you don't check out the scene yourself.

• Haunted again. Give a character another glimpse of Lenore, one that occurs at a critical moment and that distracts him enough to make a scene. Say, crossing against a red light; giving a loud, startled gasp in the middle of an important meeting at work; or gashing his neck while shaving. Perhaps the vision includes a glimpse of the sycamore tree.

Scene 4: Meeting Pete

After the characters have spent time talking to people in and around the park, or done some subtle or overt looking around, it's time for them to encounter Gray Pete. Unlike the rest of the park's regulars and visitors, Pete is well aware that Moth Park is home to some kind of unearthly presence. Intuition tells him that Lenore's death was not a mundane crime, but tied to the dark force that's associated with the sycamore.

You can have Pete seek the characters out after spotting them snooping around, or after hearing that people (not police or reporters) were asking questions about the woman. Alternately, you can have the characters come across Pete as they conduct their investigation. Pete's first reaction is to resent the characters' presence. He sees them as intruders trying to insinuate themselves into something better left alone. Even if he can't bring himself to confront the supernatural menace himself, Pete tries to keep others from endangering themselves.

To that end, he uses Subterfuge to try and convince the characters that he murdered Lenore. He claims that "voices" told him to do it, and if they don't stay away from the park they'll be next. He generally gives the impression that he's a deluded vagrant who may or may not be dangerous.

Pete's goal is to waste the characters' time and frustrate them, hopefully getting them to give up and go away. Failing that, he tries to Manipulate them into trying to turn him in to the police. He's already been questioned by the cops and they've accounted for his whereabouts on the day of the murder. So, Pete expects the characters to be made fools of, should they try to convince the authorities of his guilt. This, he reasons, will convince the characters that they're in over their heads.

Should a character see through Pete's act (with successful use of Empathy, for example) and call him on it, or prove persistent in the face of his ranting, Pete's next tactic is to frighten the group off. He warns them that the dead walk the park at night, that restless spirits take the lives of the unwary. Should the characters respond by sharing information about their own recent haunting, Pete calms down and questions them about their true motives for getting involved.

If Pete is convinced that the characters have a genuine interest in supernatural goings-on, or they feel the need to see things made right, he tells them to follow him if they want to learn more. He leads them to the sycamore tree. He tells the characters to look at the tree and asks if they see anything unusual. Characters who haven't been to the tree before may experience the illusion of faces in the bark now. If they examine the tree, they find the initials carved in the trunk. After giving the group a chance to relate any impressions, Pete points out the blackbirds sitting in the branches. He explains that from dawn to dusk, there are always 12 blackbirds — no more, no less. Then he adds that up until four days ago, the tree always held 11. After the characters have digested this information, Pete suggests that they return to the same spot after dark (when the park is closed) and they'll see who murdered Lenore White.

Characters who stick around to confirm Pete's observation about the tree recognize that it's more or less true. It's not always the same black birds, but whenever one flies away, another flies in to take its place within a few seconds. No other birds stay in the tree for more than a second or two before flying away again.

Once Pete has had his say, he refuses to speak with the characters any longer, acting as if he's never seen them before and replying to questions with Latin or Greek quotations. He walks away, and characters who follow find that he spends the rest of the day wandering the park seemingly at random, talking to anyone who crosses his path. If the characters don't try to avoid being seen (or if they do and Pete spots them), he finds a cop and says he's being pestered. Pete's on good terms with the regular patrolmen, so they encourage the characters to "move along" and leave the park.

Characters who stay in the park don't notice anything more that's unusual (aside from the matter of the birds in the sycamore tree) for the rest of the day. You might remind players that their characters may need to spend time attending to personal matters. Making up for lost time at work, for example. Wits + Stealth rolls may be made for characters who try to hide in the park until an after-hours meeting, to avoid being spotted by police patrols or park personnel.

Act 2

Cast: Everett Moth, last living descendant of the Moth family. (See his write-up on p. 109.)

Mrs. Delhaney, his nurse. For social interactions, give her intimidation (dice pool 5) and alertness to lies (dice pool 4).

Scene 1: Shadows

"After dark" is a vague time at which to rendezvous with Gray Pete. The characters need to decide when they intend to re-enter the park and seek Pete out by the sycamore tree. In his mind, "after dark" means anywhere from 10 pm till 2 am, but pretty much any time that coincides with the limits of characters' patience to wait any longer is ideal.

First, however, getting back into the park requires some planning on the characters' part. They need to bypass the gates or get over the fence. Picking a padlock requires a total of five successes in an extended Dexterity + Larceny action. Climbing the fence is an instant action, requiring one success for each person who tries to go over.

Once inside the park, the characters are subjected to discovery by police patrols. Since the murder, police have been driving through the park about once every hour. Unless the players state ahead of time that someone keeps an eye out for cops, rolls for surprise (Wits + Composure) need to be made shortly after entering the park. If a lookout is used, or someone makes a successful surprise roll and warns the others, they have three turns to take cover before a police cruiser approaches. Otherwise, consider them out in the open. Assign the cops a dice pool of 7 to spot characters in a contested action against Dexterity + Stealth. The police suffer a –1 penalty (their headlights and a spotlight cancels most but not all of the darkness), and additional modifiers if the characters find cover or have come prepared in dark clothing (another –1 penalty for the cops).

When the coast is clear, the characters can get to the arboretum without incident. The cops drive through regularly. If the characters don't take any subsequent precautions, follow the same procedure as above every hour. Cover provided by the arboretum automatically imposes a –4 penalty on police efforts to spot intruders. If characters use a lookout, she easily sees the patrol car's headlights in advance. Characters who actively take cover in the arboretum are automatically missed by patrols (but you don't have to tell players that). If the characters ask Pete's advice on getting in and out of the park, he gives them a route that imposes a further –1 penalty to police detection efforts.

Dealing with Police

Since the discovery of Lenore White's body, the police have stepped up patrols of Moth Park. The local force is understaffed and overextended, however, so it doesn't do the most efficient job of overseeing the place. A single patrol car makes a slow drive-through once an hour (plus the time it takes to unlock, open and lock the gates on the way in and out). Characters spotted in the park after hours are pursued on foot (in the arboretum) or by car (in open areas) if they run. Use the chase rules in the **World of Darkness Rulebook** (pp. 65 and 69). If characters are caught, they're taken to the station, booked for trespassing and possibly resisting arrest, and held in jail until late afternoon of the following day. They're given a steep fine, with the option to contest the charges in court at a later date. Characters who don't flee the scene are treated more leniently. They're kept overnight and then released with a warning. (Of course, characters with the appropriate Social Skills might be able to talk their way out of being arrested, or use connections or Allies to get themselves out of trouble.)

If characters are caught in the park a second time, they're interrogated by the detectives investigating Lenore White's murder. If characters convince detectives that they have an innocuous reason for breaking into the park, or sincerely believe that Lenore was killed by a ghost, the police let them off the hook, annoyed at the time waste of time. If the characters have alibis at the time of the murder, police free them but put them under surveillance (see "Shadowing," **World of Darkness**, p. 76). It's also possible that the local papers get wind of the characters' arrest and publicize the matter, leading to embarrassment and other social consequences.

A third or forth apprehension probably leads to more dire consequences for the characters, from damaging fines to incarceration to charges of interfering with a police investigation. Or if you'd like to cut the characters a break, you could decide that the police consider them a nuisance and give them a slap on the wrist. Or perhaps an officer has seen some strange things in the park and is sympathetic to any bizarre stories that characters tell.

Nighttime Encounter

When the characters meet Pete, he's either standing by the tree and staring into the cloudy night sky, or comes wandering up almost distractedly out of the bushes. At first he seems not to recognize them or remember why they're there. When the group reminds him, he snaps out of his seeming trance and asks if everyone still wants to proceed. If they agree, he announces that the killer will arrive momentarily. Then he crosses his arms and stares at the sky again. He continues to do so for several minutes, ignoring any questions or demands for results. You can stretch the meeting out as long as you like until it seems the characters are fed up. Then the cloud cover breaks and a bright moon is visible.

At that point, Pete announces, "The killer is here" and waits to see how the characters react. When asked what he's talking about, Pete points to the ground and says, "There."

The characters see that he's pointing to the shadow of the sycamore tree. He directs their attention to a strange shape in the tree's shadow. Close inspection reveals that it's the silhouette of a hanged man dangling from the dead limb, swinging slowly in the breeze. There's nothing actually in the tree to cast such a shadow. Successful Wits + Composure rolls allow characters to spot 11 human-shaped silhouettes in the shadows of the tree branches. Two are child-sized. Some hang limp and motionless like wet laundry. Others twitch and jerk like bugs caught in a web. If

characters don't spot the other shadows, Pete points them out.

Dog Attack

Pete doesn't know the identity of the hanged man. He can tell characters that there are spirits trapped in the tree, that he's heard them crying in the night. He believes the tree traps souls the way a spider catches flies. While the characters react to the sight of the shadows, a successful Wits + Composure roll allows a character to notice that the shadow of the hanged man raises one arm and points at the group. Shortly afterward, the characters are attacked by four stray dogs under the tree's control. Allow each player a reflexive surprise roll. Anyone who notices the pointing shadow gains a +1 bonus (which is conferred to the whole group if the spectacle is shared).

Characters who flee find that the dogs don't pursue them outside the arboretum. (Use the "Foot Chase" rules to determine if running characters make it to safe ground.) Characters can also climb trees (Strength + Athletics). The dogs harass any treed characters for a few minutes and then wander off as the Murder Tree's control fades. It's easy enough for characters to find a tree to climb, but any attempts to climb the sycamore fail automatically. Characters' hands slip or are cut repeatedly, as if beyond coincidence. If characters try to fight the dogs, the animals flee if their Health is reduced to 3 or less. After the dog attack, the shadow of the sycamore no longer displays

anything unusual. The dogs move on from any characters whose Health is reduced to zero.

Favors Returned

Pete runs off during the dog attack, using his knowledge of the park to find safety. He returns when the coast is clear, or if the characters pursue him, with no apologies for abandoning the group. He tells the characters that the souls in the tree are suffering. His eyes tear up as he adds that when he sleeps in the park, he dreams of them crying out for help. But the tree won't let them go, and it makes them kill when it's hungry for more. Pete cries as he says that he wants to help the souls, but he doesn't understand what he's supposed to do.

Then Pete collects himself and asks if the characters are willing to go further than they already have. Assuming the characters agree (if not, see "What If They Say No?"), Pete reaches deep into a pocket inside his ragged coat and gives the characters an object wrapped in newspaper and greasy fast-food wrappers. He tells them that this is all he could find out about the history of the tree, and maybe they can do better. He then turns and leaves, having nothing left to say. If interrupted, he forges ahead, claiming, "I've done my part." If he's followed, he walks to a distant bench, lies down and slips into a sleep from which nothing by physical harm rouses him.

Unwrapping the parcel, the characters find a plaque similar to the ones scattered throughout the park, but smaller, old, cracked and corroded. It reads:

"American Sycamore (Planatus occidentalis): Perhaps the oldest tree in the park, this sycamore is said to have been a favorite of Thomas Moth. He claimed it was already present when he purchased the land and built his estate, and he could often be seen walking or reclining under it as a reprieve from the demands of business. He said the tree put his mind at ease. Moth established several seedlings from the tree near his Columbus County summer home. The tree's age is unknown."

On the back is written in black permanent marker: "Too many words. Make sure the new one is shorter. H."

What If They Say No?

If the characters decide they want to walk away from events at this point — things are just too strange or they're scarred shitless — let them. At first, anyway. Then have Lenore continue to haunt them over the course of the next several days. Carefully timed appearances like those discussed previously could embarrass characters at work, cause them to loose sleep, interfere with social engagements or intimate moments, or cause harm or accidents. Even if the characters are actively involved in the story, you can use visits from Lenore to create a sense of urgency. The longer it takes them to put the spirits to rest, the more havoc they suffer in their daily lives. Indeed, the woman's visage may grow deathly as time passes, until characters are confronted with a maggot-ridden, decomposing corpse.

Scene 2: House of Moth

Following up on the clue from the old plaque, the characters undoubtedly look for Moth's summer home, which leads them to last surviving family member Everett Moth, and to more insights into the old sycamore tree. Here are some ways in which characters might pursue the matter.

• Those with the Occult Skill might know that many cultures regard trees as powerful spiritual forces. The history of an individual tree can be important in determining its spiritual identity and the proper way to deal with it.

• Searching the archives of the local paper for information about the tree (a successful Intelligence + Academics extended action that requires a total of six successes) turns up an article that discusses how Thomas Moth grew similar trees somewhere in Columbus County, and that some of them were still tended by a descendant as recently as five years ago.

• Questioning the city parks staff (perhaps with a successful Manipulation + Socialize roll) confirms that the tree predates the opening of the park, and that nobody knows by how much. A strange man used to come to the park once in a while and asked about the tree and its health. He spent hours at a time at it, inspecting it. He was supposedly a descendant of the Moth family, and seemed harmless. He hasn't been seen for years.

Just Visiting

Everett Moth's address is not listed in any directory. He lives on land that was once part of the Moth summer estate. Columbus County is a rural area about two hours' drive from the city. Characters who attempt to discern the location of the Moth summer estate through research (no penalties) can gain a general idea of where in Columbus County it was located. By driving through the area and questioning the locals, characters can also eventually be directed to Twelve Sighs Road, which winds through farm country. After about 20 minutes on that road, characters spot four huge sycamore trees growing across from a cornfield.

As they get closer, they see a dilapidated farmhouse with faded red siding located amid the trees. The house is clearly in bad shape, with a sagging roof, a partially collapsed porch and windows with spider webs of cracked glass. The lawn is overgrown and strewn with debris and trash bags. Characters with any Specialty relating to architecture or construction can tell that the house probably dates back to the 1940s, and is run down more from neglect than old age. The only other structure on the property is a large shed that's even more dilapidated than the house.

There's a gravel pad near the house with room for three or four cars. There's a single car parked in the he front yard; it's a relatively new economy model (this is the nurse's car). Once the characters approach on foot, they find that the ground is thick with twisted tree roots. Some have broken through the pavement of the walk that leads to the front porch. The porch is covered with broken branches, and a limb from the nearest tree seems to have grown right through the roof. The other three sycamores are located behind the house. They're so close that their branches hang right over the roof. It's as if the trees reach out for the house with giant hands.

A mailbox on a crooked post near the front porch is painted with the letters "E. Moth." A sign next to it directs visitors to use the side entrance. Upon knocking on the side door, the characters are greeted by Mrs. Delhaney, a big-boned woman dressed in a nurse's uniform. Without a hello, she crosses her arms and waits for the characters to say something. In response, she mutters something like, "The old fool said he'd have visitors today, damned if he wasn't right." She then turns and enters the house, leaving the door open, seemingly expecting the characters to follow.

Once everybody's in, they find themselves in a cramped hallway. Delhaney turns and gives a stern warning not to upset Mr. Moth. She glares at the characters, and then leads them into a sitting room where a frail-looking old man in a wheelchair seems to be waiting.

Everett's house is as broken-down inside as it is outside. The paint on the walls is cracked and peeling, and every corner is home to a spider web. The floorboards are worn and stained and covered with cheap rugs. The furniture looks like it was retrieved from the curb on trash day. Lamps and light fixtures are without shades. The house has a faint smell of manure, potpourri and boiled cabbage. The most unusual feature is what hangs on the walls: Every room and hallway is decorated with a multitude of religious icons. Most are Christian in origin: crucifixes, rosary beads, prayer cards, pictures of saints, even pages ripped from the Old and New Testament. But there are also Jewish items: Stars of David, mezuzahs, Torah quotations, and so forth. Careful observers (with Academics 1+) notice occasional Muslim, Buddhist, Hindu, Shinto and other religious iconography in the mix. These items seem to be tacked up in random locations. Many are askew and some are even upside-down.

Snooping

While some characters speak with Everett, others may excuse themselves to have a look around (on the pretense of using the bathroom, for example). Here's what they might find.

Thresholds: A thin line of some white, granular substance is laid across the floor of each doorway. A close look suggests that it's table salt, and a taste confirms it.

The Kitchen: Mrs. Delhaney is in here, using a blender and several vials of unknown substances to mix Everett's next "meal." She casts a suspicious eye on any character who hangs around her. A cursory glance reveals that all drawers and all but one of the cabinets have been nailed shut. A small table is littered with flowerpots, each containing nothing but soil.

If characters manage to charm Delhaney (all Social rolls are at −1 penalty because she's suspicious of any visitors), she can tell them that Everett suffers from diabetes and the aftereffects of a stroke. She's been caring for him for a year-and-a-half, but doesn't know much about his past. She regards him as extremely superstitious. At times he's made vague remarks to her about having, "Spent his life dealing with the forces of darkness," but she doesn't believe in any of that nonsense. Delhaney is convinced that Everett's mind is going. She knows that he's terrified of leaving the house, and won't even do so to sit outside. He apparently claims that the trees talk to him and if he gets near them, "They'll deafen him by reciting all his sins."

Hallway: The narrow hall that characters come though when they enter connects all first-floor rooms. The ceiling shows signs of water damage. There are several newspaper headlines, yellow with age, framed and hanging among the other items on the walls. If asked about these, Everett says he had forgotten that they were even

there. They meant something to him years ago, but now he doesn't care. They read:

LOCAL MAN HAUNTED BY FAMILY CURSE? Everett Moth's import business declared bankrupt, Moth family decline continues

THOMAS MOTH GRAVESTONE VANDALIZED "Murderer" found spray-painted on Moth's monument

POLICE ARREST "GHOST BUSTER" Local man arrested for trespassing, claims historic house haunted

CULT LEADER FOUND MURDERED Eccentric spiritualist and guru found stabbed to death in car

CAN TREES READ YOUR MIND? Scientists believe some trees act as resonators for human brainwaves

MUSEUM REPORTS RELICS MISSING Unknown parties steal ancient bones, scrolls

Front Room: This room includes the front door, which leads to the half-collapsed porch. The only furniture here is a card table and two folding chairs. There's a deck of cards on the table. If the cards are checked, characters see that that each has a sketch of a tree leaf drawn on the face in green ink.

On the floor under the table is a large jar filled with sycamore fruit.

One leg of the table is shorter than the others, and stands on a book to keep it level. It's a leather-covered scrapbook. Most of the pages are blank, but a few have papers pasted to them. They're fragments of larger pages, as if the parts of the articles that weren't glued down have since fallen away.

Clipping one: Part of a newspaper article

…some of his best ideas, Moth says. "Some days I just lie beneath the tree and daydream. And soon enough, a sort of voice comes into my head, saying, 'Thomas, here's what you should do.' And by George if it isn't good advice." One wonders what Moth's stockholders think of his unorthodox…

Clipping two: Part of a newspaper article

…seventy-five years since the awful murders of Felicity, Millicent and Edmond Moth by the family gardener Henry Creed. And still we do not know to where Creed fled, why he committed the crimes, or…

Clipping three: Part of a letter, handwritten with a fountain pen

…in the asylum for five years and he grows less and less coherent. Yesterday he said, "I saw them inside the heart and I knew." What heart, I asked, and he answered, "The tree heart. Bang, bang, bang. But if I…

If asked about the scrapbook, Everett simply says he's through with trying to make sense of the past, and tells the characters to put the book back where they found it.

Bathroom: There's a small bathroom on the first floor, containing a sink and toilet (no tub). The toilet has been outfitted with railings to make it accessible to Everett. The water from the sink is slightly muddy. The medicine cabinet is empty, but on the inside of the cabinet door is a yellow sticky note with the handwritten words, "I'M IN YOUR HOUSE." Everett refuses to comment on it.

Stairwell: The steps that lead upstairs are unusually steep and creek very loudly. The nurse hears and comes out of the kitchen, demanding to know where any climbing character is going. She's quick to point out the downstairs bathroom. Should characters manage to make it upstairs (perhaps by having one distract Delhaney while others sneak up), they find modest rooms but nothing of interest (unless you feel the need to drop clues that characters have overlooked).

Meeting Everett

When the characters enter the sitting room, Everett tries to rise, but gives up after pushing himself halfway out of his wheelchair. He nods, instead, and gestures for the visitors to sit on the tired-looking sofa and chairs across from him. He introduces himself as Everett Moth. Everett is a thin man dressed in pajamas and a robe. He's pale and his eyes are deep set and dark. On a small table next to his chair rests an oxygen tank and breathing mask, and various prescription pill bottles. From time to time, he takes a pill from one of the bottles and swallows it (without water).

Once introductions are complete, Everett begins. "They told me someone would come today, but they didn't say why." If asked who "they" are, he replies "The trees." Then he laughs halfheartedly and says he's joking. In truth Everett is haunted himself and suspects that the characters have come to discuss the trees or his family's past. If they don't get to the point, he simply blathers about the weather, the difficulties of being an old man in poor health, and the challenges of living in the country. If asked about himself, he says he's retired, that he suffers from a number of infirmities, and that he's just trying to live out his remaining days in peace. He doesn't answer any questions about the religious items on the walls, save to say that he's a collector.

If the characters try to tell Everett about their haunting, the murder in the park or the strange phenomena surrounding the sycamore tree, he professes disinterest in what they have to say. He calls it a lot of nonsense and demands that the characters stop wasting his time. He seems angry that such subjects are even brought up. In truth, he covers up for his longtime, secret fears. A successful Wits + Empathy roll suggests to a character that Everett hides his real feelings on these matters.

If asked about the trees growing around his house, or about the history of the sycamore in the park, Everett launches into a diatribe about his Great Uncle Thomas, who "cared more about trees than people." He says if Uncle Thomas hadn't wasted so much time growing trees, and attended to his business and family, maybe he would have left something to his descendants instead of "this wretched half-acre." Everett says that if he hadn't thrown away his uncle's family picture, he could have shown the characters where the man's priorities should have lain. (If characters haven't yet heard the story of Thomas Moth and the death of his family, you can have Everett relate the "public" version.)

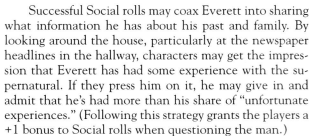

Successful Social rolls may coax Everett into sharing what information he has about his past and family. By looking around the house, particularly at the newspaper headlines in the hallway, characters may get the impression that Everett has had some experience with the supernatural. If they press him on it, he may give in and admit that he's had more than his share of "unfortunate experiences." (Following this strategy grants the players a +1 bonus to Social rolls when questioning the man.)

Characters may also try to leverage Everett's obvious distaste for his Great Uncle Thomas. If they encourage him to elaborate, he may be tempted to open up (+2 bonus to players' Social rolls).

Characters may try to elicit sympathy from Everett by describing the haunting they've experienced, sharing details even while Everett claims to be disinterested. Having suffered his own share of supernatural misery, the old man may identify with the characters and share what he knows (+2 bonus to players' Social rolls).

Everett knows the following.

• The sycamore in the park has been cursed since the days of Thomas Moth. Every generation of the family has known it, and some have searched for a way to put things right. Yet, the curse remains. The tree demands death.

• Thomas himself brought down the curse. He claimed as much on his deathbed, but no one knew exactly what he did. Everett tried to forget about any curse and live his life as he saw fit. When the tree killed in '52, he was a young man and was torn up with guilt. He used to visit the tree and beg it not to kill, but hasn't had the strength or will to go back in years. And how he's reduced to a feeble existence, with the "offspring of that accursed tree" reaching out to him, trying to claim him, too.

Beyond all this, Everett has little to offer characters. Indeed, he probably gets excited at some point and suffers a fit of shaking and choking. Nurse Delhaney rushes in to administer oxygen and sedatives, yelling at the characters to leave the old man alone. Trying to get to Everett after that is nigh impossible, with Delhaney running determined interference. The sedatives also make him groggy for several hours.

Scene 3: Buried Secrets

Eventually, the characters leave Everett's house. As the group approaches the car, someone notices that they're being watched. Across the road, Lenore stands in front of the cornfield, staring. When the characters spot her, she turns and walks into the corn.

At first she seems to have disappeared, but once the characters go after her, they spot her several yards ahead. Though she seems to be walking slowly, she always stays elusively ahead, no matter how quickly anyone pursues. When the chase is over, the characters are on the other side of the cornfield, where a dirt road runs between crops. Lenore is visible about 20 yards away, where two dirt roads cross. She stares longingly at the ground near where she stands, and fades away.

At the spot where she stood, the characters find a wooden platform about seven feet square, set into the ground in a concrete frame. It's hinged on one side and padlocked closed. If the lock is broken or picked, the platform can be lifted to reveal a circular hole six feet in diameter, bordered by a ring of large, flat stones. This is an old, hand-dug well, with a shaft so deep the bottom can't be seen — not even with a flashlight.

In all likelihood, the characters are compelled to get to the bottom of the well and discover what's down there that's so important to the woman who haunts them. There are a few different ways in which this scene could develop.

Characters might knock on Everett's door to see if he has any tools or equipment that they can use. Delhaney answers and says Everett is sleeping and can't be disturbed for the rest of the day. The characters can try to convince her that Everett would want to help them, as long as they come up with some explanation for why they need the tools (possibilities include helping someone whose car is stuck, or moving a tree limb that's fallen across the road). If one of the characters was successful at getting the nurse to share information earlier, there's no penalty to any Social rolls now. Otherwise, she's suspicious and rolls suffer a –1 penalty. If the group wins her over, Delhaney points to the shed for whatever's needed.

In the shed, characters find three, 100-foot lengths of rope, a pair of working flashlights, blankets, a basic tool box (hammer, screwdrivers, pliers, nails), three buckets, some scrap wood, several flower pots and gardening tools (trowel, rake, clippers, tongs.)

Of course, characters could always sneak into the shed and get what they need without permission. It's your call if the nurse spots them and confronts them or calls the local sheriff.

If the characters leave their car in Everett's driveway and don't explain their lingering presence to Delhaney, she waits for Everett to recover from his drug-induced sleep and asks him if he has any idea why the car is still there. That occurs four or five hours after the group leaves Everett's house. He tells the nurse not to bother about it. Whether she heeds him or calls the sheriff depends on how polite or rude the characters have been, and on how difficult you want to make things for the players.

Characters' attempts to call in help at the well via cell phone are foiled by a lack of signal.

The characters might try to find a hardware store and purchase equipment there. The closest store is 30 minutes away. It offers rope, flashlights and the usual hardware items, but no sport-climbing equipment.

The characters might want to return home to equip themselves and then return the next day (or the same day if it's early enough to get back before dark, or they don't mind risking their necks after sundown). If they park on Everett's property, Delhaney may call the sheriff's office or Everett may tell her to let them be.

Finding the well again after leaving the area requires a successful Intelligence + Composure roll. Success indicates that the well is found within 10 minutes. Failure

indicates a half-hour of searching before it's located. Assign a –1 penalty if characters don't park within sight of Everett's house. At night, the roll is at -2 and failure means an hour or more of searching. If the characters leave someone behind or put up some kind of marker, they're able to find the well without difficulty.

The well is 90 feet deep and wide enough for one person to descend at a time. Dropping a rope to the bottom establishes that it's dry. Attempts to lower someone require a total of three Strength + Athletics + equipment rolls. There is no equipment bonus for using Everett's gear. Teamwork rules apply if multiple people work up above. A failed roll means the rope slips and a single Dexterity + Athletics roll can be made to catch it. See the falling rules (**World of Darkness Rulebook**, p. 179) if anyone plummets to the bottom. Follow the same procedure on the way back up. Characters can also choose to climb up or down under their own power, in which case standard climbing rules apply (p. 64).

The bottom is layered with dry leaves, sticks and twigs. A flat, rectangular object leans against the wall, its bottom third buried in detritus. It's a large oil painting in an ornately carved (and fractured) wooden frame. It's hard to make out any details in the darkness of the well, but a flashlight reveals some kind of group portrait. The canvas bears scrapes and small holes, but is otherwise in fairly good shape, the painting having faced downward for who knows how long.

Retrieval

The portrait is about four feet by five feet. It can be raised to the surface by tying ropes around it. A character could also tie it to her back while being pulled up or climbing (–1 penalty in either case).

The painting is coated by a thin layer of dirt and dust, but it's easy to see that it depicts a man, a woman and two children. All are dressed in late 19th century clothes. The man is jowly and broad, with bright blond hair and a thick mustache. He stands in the center of the portrait, holding a large garden spade in one hand and a potted tree sapling in the other. The woman stands slightly behind him, her hands clasped in front of her waist. She's thin, also blond, and stares solemnly at the viewer. The dark-haired children are on either side: a boy holding the woman's hand, and a girl peeking out from behind the man. Characters who've researched Thomas Moth recognize this as a portrait of him, his wife Felicity, and his children Millicent and Edmond.

Anyone who looks at the painting for several seconds witnesses a horrifying spectacle. Moth seems to transform into a bloated, dark-haired man (Henry Creed) who's strangled by a hangman's noose. Meanwhile, Felicity, Millicent and Edmond all appear to be rotted corpses, and the frame of the painting seems to transform into living tree branch. The "altered" portrait looks like it was painted in the same style as the original, and then reverts to normal. Even in their grotesque states, the children bear more resemblance to the hanged man than they do to Thomas

Moth. After being witnessed once, the painting never changes before anyone's eyes again.

If the characters return to Everett's house to ask about the painting, Delhaney refuses to let them in. She does agree to take a message to Everett, though. He replies to any questions that he threw the painting out years ago because he couldn't bear to look at it any longer.

If the characters take it home and have it examined (or use their own Academic, Science or Crafts Skills to do so), they find that it dates back to the turn of the 20th century. The painting is not particularly valuable or unusual, especially in its current condition, but the city's historical commission or the park would certainly appreciate its donation.

Act 3

At this point, the characters probably attempt to put the ghosts of Moth Park to rest. They may approach their task in a variety of ways, and possibly hit a few dead ends before finding a rewarding course. Rather than a sequence of scenes, this act is a collection of story elements that can be combined or overlapped as needed, depending on the choices players make. If characters take their time to decide their next move, haunting by Lenore and perhaps even by Creed, Felicity, Millicent or Edmond may make characters' lives and sanity increasingly tenuous.

Trial by Fire

Characters may hope that destroying the sycamore will release the souls trapped in it. The most obvious method is to burn or cut the tree down, but execution of it poses significant challenges. Attempts to burn it certainly attract the authorities, who may put the fire out long before the tree is consumed. And then there's a danger that the fire spreads throughout the park, or beyond, endangering countless lives (including fire fighter and rescue workers').

Characters with any dots in Occult may recognize that there's another problem with this approach. If ghosts of people appear to exist, then the spirits of objects — or at least the tree — might also exist. If any part of the tree is left, even its stump, the spirit may linger, or the spirit could remain even if the tree is obliterated.

If the characters come up with a plan to destroy the tree, and manage to execute it without getting caught, allow them to enjoy a few ghost-free days. Then have Lenore return — perhaps along with the angry ghost of a firefighter killed when the blaze spread out of control. A midnight visit to the park reveals that the charred stump of the sycamore casts the shadow of a full tree, complete with silhouettes of the trapped spirits.

Exorcism

A spiritual banning (as described in the **World of Darkness Rulebook**, p. 214) might be used to release the spirits that are bound to the tree. Characters with Occult or Academic Skill can attempt to locate a ritual for abjuring spirits or dispelling an evil curse. The search involves an extended action, requiring a total of 10 successes and a day of research for each roll made. Access to specialized archives or libraries can add bonuses to the rolls.

The characters may lack the resources or understanding to find an exorcism ritual on their own. Or (for a more challenging conclusion), you could decide that the necessary rituals are too difficult for the inexperienced characters to perform. In either case, the characters may need the help of Gray Pete. You could steer them in his direction by having them come across his name while researching occult solutions. Perhaps they find a book on spiritual possession written 15 years ago, and notice that the picture of the author, Father Peter Gray, looks familiar. Or maybe while flipping through old newspapers to research the history of the park, characters spot the man's picture in an article about "visiting professor, Father Peter Gray."

If the characters tell Pete what they learned from their visit with Everett, he realizes that an exorcism ritual may free the trapped spirits. (Or maybe he's already come to that conclusion). But Pete is not the man he used to be. Even though he wants to help, he no longer has the faith — in God or himself — that once empowered him. The characters have to restore his conviction. Doing so might take prolonged roleplaying sessions, even overlapped with other stories, in which the characters try to appeal to Pete's sense of duty as a priest, or to his obvious concern for the souls who wander the park — living and dead. Or maybe they inspire him by demonstrating their own determination to free the spirits, whatever it takes. He may be moved if he witnesses the characters try to keep the park safe, perhaps by standing watch over the tree night after night, patrolling during the day, or returning again and again after being arrested for trespassing.

Dark Deeds

Everett Moth is the last descendant of the man whose actions cursed the tree. Would Everett's death — ending of the Moth family line — put the curse to rest? If the characters contemplate this possibility, and they don't wait for Everett's illness to do the job for them, you can preempt his murder by having the characters find Everett's house abandoned. He fled, unable to face the family curse and the trees encroaching upon him. Or, if you let the characters kill Everett, they may find that the tree goes unaffected and they've committed a heinous act for nothing. Perhaps even more disturbing, you could let the murder actually release the trapped souls and end the curse. That resolution suggests that one evil act can be undone by another evil act. What will the characters feel compelled to do if they ever run afoul of the unknown again?

In any case, there are consequences to killing Everett Moth. An ongoing police investigation might plague the characters in future stories, causing them to take increasingly drastic steps to cover up their crime. The ghost of Everett Moth could haunt the characters, ideally after things have settled down, they've done a "good deed," and they think they've gotten away with murder. And, of course, murderers are subject to Morality rolls and possibly derangement.

Final Stand

Whether the characters perform a ritual on their own or with Pete, the rite needs to be performed in the tree's presence between midnight and dawn. It requires all characters to participate, with one of them designated as the leader or primary actor (**World of Darkness Rulebook**, "Teamwork," p. 134 and "Exorcisms," p. 214). If Pete participates, he can be leader. The ritual is not difficult to set up. Four candles are placed at the four cardinal points, and contributors join hands to form a circle around the leader, who reads aloud with the others repeating. Remember that if the characters are in the park for more than an hour, they have to avoid police patrols. Someone could even lead the police on a wild-goose chase to distract them.

The ritual seems to have no effect after about 30 minutes of performance (don't make contested rolls yet). Finally, the characters are swept by a cold wind as a sudden storm blows in (despite the season), stirring the tree's branches and sending leaves and twigs flying.

The tree's first defense is to send a pack of four dogs at the group, using Phantasm to make it seem that many more animals attack. As before, the dogs flee once their Health is reduced to 3 or less. If the characters withstand this effort, the tree manifests the spirit forms of Henry Creed, Felicity, Millicent and Edmond. Each uses Teleki-

nesis as a direct attack, though their effects are perceived differently (see the write-up for the tree and its spirits on p. 108). The tree's final defense is the Terrify Numen, making it appear leafless and white-barked, with corpses impaled on its branches and blood running down its trunk.

During any conflict, the storm persists and pelts the area, though the candles do not go out. The ritual continues as long as the leader stands his ground, remains conscious and does nothing but perform the exorcism. If the characters can maintain a tight defense, the tree's attacks may be unable to reach the leader. Characters who confront the dogs or spirits, and who aren't frightened away, can still contribute to the rite. Should the leader go down, another can pick up any manuscript used and continue (just remember to apply any penalties if the new leader lacks the ideal Skills or Morality).

If the characters are forced to flee, because the ritual fails or the attacks drive them away, they're free to try again on another night. The tree and its ghosts regain any spent Essence and Willpower by the next night. You might also want the tree to be so angered that it commits another murder on an innocent park-goer. If this occurs, the police shut down the park. They maintain constant patrols, day and night, for weeks. Meanwhile, characters waiting for the heat to cool are haunted by yet another spirit.

If the tree's Willpower is exhausted, lightning flashes and splits the sycamore in two. The dead limb from which Henry Creed hung falls to the ground, smoking. To onlookers' amazement, slightly luminous shapes rise from the center of the split tree, one for each soul trapped in it.

A.H.

The storm recedes as quickly as it arose, and a palpable calm settles. When the clouds part, the felled tree casts an ordinary shadow and no birds perch in its branches.

Aftermath

This scenario leaves some loose ends dangling that can inspire future stories.

Gray Pete: If the characters convince Pete to help them, it might be his first step back to his old life. Perhaps he disappears for awhile and then returns in priest's vestments to recruit the characters as his allies against other supernatural dangers. Is he overconfident now, pushing the characters into jeopardy that they're not capable of handling? Or maybe the ordeal overwhelms him with old memories, motivating him to retreat further into vagrancy and madness. Does he seek revenge against the characters? Does he snap and take his anger out on innocents? Can the characters heal Pete's soul?

The Sycamore Tree: The tree (if it still stands) no longer shows signs of being haunted. But what about its "offspring" in the country? Thomas Moth planted those with seeds from the cursed tree. Do they carry its taint? They certainly seemed to have intentions for Everett Moth, or was that just a trick of the characters' collective imagination? If Everett disappears, have the trees finally claimed him? What harm — if any — can the remaining four sycamores cause?

Cast

The Murder Tree

Background: No one knows the age of the sycamore at the center of Moth Park. Its roots sink deep into the earth, and its history may stretch back for centuries. Perhaps it's always been a great reservoir of spiritual power, or maybe that power was awakened by some knowledgeable shaman in ages past. In any case, the murders committed by Thomas Moth tainted that power, turning the tree into a supernatural predator. When it thirsts for blood rises, the Murder Tree takes the life of whomever happens to be near, and then adds a soul to its tormented collection.

Description: The sycamore appears as a towering, lush, healthy tree, except for the bare branch from which its first victim was hung. Near the base of the tree, the initials "HC + FM" have been carved, offering a clue to the events that poisoned the sycamore's spiritual energy: Henry Creed + Felicity Moth.

Storytelling Hints: The tree is not sentient, but can control the spirits that it has ensnared. It uses them to claim more victims or to protect itself. It also uses its Numina for defense, acting simply but brutally.

Attributes: Power 5, Finesse 4, Resistance 4
Willpower: 9 (automatically replenished each night)
Essence: 12 (automatically replenished each night)
Morality: 3
Virtue: Justice
Vice: Wrath
Initiative: 8
Defense: n/a
Speed: n/a
Size: 20
Corpus: 24
Numina: Animal Control (dice pool 9), Phantasm, (dice pool 9), Telekinesis (dice pool 9), Terrify (dice pool 9)

Controlled Spirits

When the tree is threatened or hungry for a new soul, it uses the ghosts of its past victims as weapons. The tree tends to use its oldest spirits for these purposes; Henry Creed is usually enough, but it may also manifest Felicity, Millicent and/or Edmond (or others if your story requires it). They use the Telekinesis Numen as a direct attack, which is experienced differently, depending on the ghost. Henry seems to strangle victims with a hangman's rope. Felicity seems to attack with a kitchen knife. Millicent wields a pair of scissors, and Edmond bites with needle-like teeth. The spirits remain silent and blank-faced when attacking. They keep fighting until they're out of Essence, at which point they sink into the ground amid the tree's roots. Damage done to the spirits does not affect the tree. Nor does the spirits' expenditure of Essence draw on that of the tree. Spirits can appear and range inside the park's arboretum, but not beyond.

Attributes: Power 3, Finesse 3, Resistance 2
Willpower: 5
Essence: 6
Morality: 3
Virtue: Temperance
Vice: Wrath
Initiative: 5
Defense: 3
Speed: 16 (species factor 10)
Size: 5
Corpus: 7
Numina: Telekinesis (dice pool 6)

Gray Pete

Quote: "If God knew what the hell He was doing, would people be sleeping in dumpsters? *Quod erat demonstrandum.*"

Background: Peter Gray was an excellent educator, a brilliant scholar and a gifted priest. But his dedication and faith were slowly eroded by exposure to the dark secrets, evil forces and shadowy adversaries he encountered as he carried his church's standard on various battlefields. At some point, the struggle against the darkness became more than his mind could bear, and he fled the priesthood and his old life. Now he lives as a homeless vagrant, keeping his past concealed from those around him, and sometimes from himself.

Description: Peter is a broad-shouldered man in his late 40s, but his prematurely gray hair and beard and stooped posture make him seem older. He dresses in the nondescript uniform of the homeless: tattered coat, torn shirt, wrinkled pants, tired shoes. His eyes look distant and distracted one minute, then fiercely intense the next.

Storytelling Hints: Pete's not all there, and sometimes has to struggle to finish a thought or remember to whom he's talking. When he's coherent, he peppers his speech with

Greek and Latin phrases. When he's vacant, he sometimes hums the melodies of Gregorian chants. Pete feels protective and charitable toward his fellow homeless, and tries to look out for them and direct help their way when he can. He maintains good relations with the local police and has many contacts in nearby homeless shelters and social-service offices. Pete's instincts tell him that there's a malevolent force tied to the sycamore tree. He's torn between a desire to confront the problem and the fear brought on by his past experiences. When the characters arrive on the scene, Pete fears they'll involve themselves in matters that they can't handle. He also fears they'll draw him into the struggle he's tried so hard to avoid.

Attributes: Intelligence 3, Wits 3, Resolve 2, Strength 2, Dexterity 3, Stamina 3, Presence 3, Manipulation 3, Composure 3
Skills: Academics (Religion) 4, Empathy 3, Investigation (Enigmas) 3, Occult 4, Stealth 3, Streetwise 4, Survival 3
Merits: Languages (Latin, Greek, French) 3, Iron Stamina 2, Contacts 3
Willpower: 5
Morality: 7
Virtue: Hope
Vice: Sloth
Initiative: 6
Defense: 3
Speed: 10
Health: 8
Derangements: Avoidance, Suspicion

Everett Moth

Quote: "You want my advice? Forget about ghosts and curses and murders and go back to your normal life. If someone had told me that when I was a boy, maybe I wouldn't be sitting here now, penniless and haunted."

Background: Born into a family that had fallen far from a once-privileged position, Everett grew up in an atmosphere of failure and superstition. Perhaps it was stories of the cursed tree that inspired him to dabble in the supernatural, or maybe he was looking for some magical shortcut to bring the Moth name back to its former glory. Whatever the reason, Everett's supernatural dalliances have left him a broken, fearful, miserable man.

Description: Never far from an oxygen tank and an assortment of prescription medication, Everett is frail, sunken and housebound.

Storytelling Hints: Everett alternates between resigning himself to death, and complaining animatedly about the wretched state of his existence. He doesn't want to talk about his past, but does appreciate having an audience to hear his complaints.

Derangements: Anxiety, Suspicion
Abilities: Awareness of surroundings (dice pool 4), Occult (dice pool 6), Filibustering (dice pool 4)

Chapter 5: Holy Ghost

By Matt Forbeck

*This living hand,
now warm and capable*

*Of earnest grasping,
would, if it were cold*

*And in the icy
silence of the tomb,*

*So haunt thy days
and chill thy dreaming
nights*

*That thou wouldst
wish thine own heart
dry of blood*

*So in my veins red
life might stream again,*

*And thou be con-
science-calmed — see
here it is —*

*I hold it towards
you.*

*— John Keats, "This
Living Hand"*

Summary

Some people are blessed with a passion for helping others, whether out of altruism or empathy, or in the name of God. Like any passion, this one can be carried too far and become an obsession, and that's when things can go wrong. When a person is cut down in the pursuit of an obsession, even one as noble as helping those in need, the spirit may refuse to move on to its final reward, no matter the cost to itself.

In "Holy Ghost," the protagonists learn about the existence of a ghost haunting the worst part of town, an area known as Switchtrack Alley. The restless soul is that of the Reverend Isaiah Neely, a pastor who lost his struggle against gang violence in a wash of his own blood. Reverend Neely now exacts his revenge against all sinners who cross his path.

"Holy Ghost" is about thwarted vengeance taken at last, and the redemption of a tortured soul. The players' characters, who can come from nearly any walk of life, play a vital part in this drama.

Variant Locations

This scenario is set in a rotten neighborhood in a city of any size. A large city may seem like a fitting setting, but there's no reason why the story can't take place in any urban environment plagued by violence.

Crimes don't have to be gang related, either. Reverend Neely could just as easily have met his end at the hand of corrupt stockbrokers, a pack of fraternity brothers or even drunken sports fans. Indeed, Neely might have died by the hand of a single person. The important part is that his death was horrific.

Motives

Players can create characters of any sort for this story. It's helpful if they all live in the same town and know each other, but there's no reason why disparate characters can't be drawn together by the actions of Neely's ghost. The following hooks can help you get the characters involved.

• A character knows one of the victims of Neely's vengeance. Not all of his victims are deserving. As his Morality diminishes, Neely loses the ability to recognize degrees of sin. To him, any crime is worthy of the ultimate punishment.

• A character accidentally becomes an instrument of Neely's vengeance. If one of the reverend's intended targets races out into traffic to avoid the ghost, the character hits the person with her car — or nearly does. Either way, the character hears the victim's terrifying tale.

• A character lives or works in the neighborhood and notices that violent incidents plague Switchtrack Alley. She might even witness one of the illusions Neely creates with his Phantasm Numen, or sees the lights or shadows cast by such a display.

- A character knew Neely, or at least knew of him. This character could be a parishioner, neighbor, friend, family member, journalist or detective. A trip to Switchtrack Alley to pay respects on the anniversary of the reverend's death alerts the character that something strange is going on.
- A character is part of a team of professionals that takes care of Neely's victims. This could include police officers, doctors, nurses, social workers or psychologists. If the character pays attention, she spots a pattern among victims' stories. Their horrifying experiences all happen in or near Switchtrack Alley.
- A character is a member of a gang that operates in or near Switchtrack Alley, or simply commits some kind of sin in the area. Neely attacks him directly, but the character escapes… this time.

Preliminary Events

Good stories often start *in media res* — "in or into the middle of a sequence of events." This one truly begins when the players' characters enter the unfolding tale. Before that, however, lots of other things have happened that you need to know.

The Backstory

Three years ago, life near Switchtrack Alley hit the boiling point. As one of the oldest neighborhoods in the city, "the Alley" had a long and proud history that led to ruin and despair. It was once a center of commerce, a place where the railroads that ran through town met at the central switchtrack and warehouse before heading out for destinations across the country.

With the advent of the interstate highway system, railroad traffic diminished and the honest money in the area evaporated with it. As houses and storefronts became older and more dilapidated, people of means abandoned the area to those less fortunate. Only the poor, oppressed and downtrodden remained to call it home.

Before long, gangs came in and ruled the neighborhood. They warred over the best bits of turf and spilled blood, both innocent and otherwise. People outside the neighborhood took to calling it "Switchblade Alley" as a result.

Reverend Isaiah Neely was an African-American leader who grew up in Switchtrack Alley. A man of deep religious convictions, he decided to follow in his father's footsteps as a preacher. Unlike his father Ishmael, however, Isaiah saw wisdom in action as well as words. It wasn't enough for him to exhort parishioners to cling to their faith. He urged them to take a stand.

The young reverend found himself a hero to his people. They looked to him for answers and he led them to success. For a while it seemed like he might manage to take back Switchtrack Alley from the criminals who had set up shop.

Then the fighting began.

The gangbangers decided that they could send a message, too. They targeted the most vocal of Neely's supporters and hit them hard. They threw bricks through windows, slashed tires and set yards on fire.

Instead of telling his people to give up, Neely redoubled his efforts. He led marches on the houses of gang leaders and demanded that they leave. He set up a neighborhood-watch program and members called in every bit of suspicious activity they encountered.

The gangbangers responded by killing Benjamin Pinnon, Neely's young, right-hand man. They found him walking home from church one night, beat him to death, and dumped his body in front of the reverend's church, the Seventh Congregational.

Neely was incensed. He stormed out of the church to confront his friend's killers, rallying his congregation behind him. This show of support didn't stop the thugs, though. Using guns to keep the crowd back, they made an example of Neely.

The gang members dragged him into the middle of Switchtrack Alley and beat him to a bloody pulp as the parishioners watched, none of them courageous enough to come to their leader's aid, despite his desperate pleas.

Finally, Lay-Z, leader of the gang, shot the reverend dead. When it was over, he promised the same fate for anyone who dared to speak out or rise up against his gang.

Lay-Z so cowed the people of Switchtrack Alley that none of them dared turn the killer in. They didn't even call the police. Reverend Neely's own father buried his son, alone. Everyone else was too ashamed to attend the funeral service. The uprising against the gang came to a sudden end.

The Reverend Returns

Reverend Neely was insane with grief and despair when the gangbangers gunned him down. His spirit refused to move on to accept God's judgment. Instead, it remained in Switchtrack Alley and pined for revenge.

With his dying words, Neely cursed his parishioners, his father and even himself for believing in a God that could have made such horrible people for such a horrible world. He saved his worst words for his faith itself, decrying his lifelong belief.

On the anniversary of Reverend Neely's death, his father Ishmael led the congregation to the site of the young preacher's murder. The bloodstains in the middle of the street had never faded or been removed. People were too shamed to do anything about it. This mark on the street became the neighborhood's scarlet letter.

During the anniversary service, Ishmael called on God to forgive the people of Switchtrack Alley, including himself and even Isaiah's killers. He led the people in prayer that they might be healed of this wound and to move on to rebuild their lives.

That night, Lay-Z made his own pilgrimage to the scene of the crime. The part-time rapper and full-time leader of the Switchblade Disciples (also known as the SDs) showed up with a posse of intoxicated gangbangers to piss on the murder site. As they did, Neely's ghost carried out its first act of horror.

The gangbangers' urine turned blood-red and the pool spread as if a dam had broken beneath their feet. The walls of surrounding buildings bled from their mortar. The windows of nearby cars burst out as blood that had pooled in them washed outward.

Lay-Z and his friends panicked in sheer terror. They raced down the street until they reached the next intersection. As they crossed over Prairie Avenue, they exceeded the limits of Neely's reach and the ghost's phantasm vanished. When the gangbangers turned, a semi-truck plowed into them and injured or killed them all.

Lay-Z survived, but his legs were shattered. He wound up in a wheelchair, permanently. The incident crippled the Switchblade Disciples as effectively as it had their leader. Somewhere beyond the veil, Neely's ghost smiled.

Fresh Blood

Neely's ghost had its revenge, at least partially, and it liked the taste. Still, it wasn't ready to move on. For one, it still seethed with anger at the residents of the neighborhood.

Worse yet, Neely's retribution created a power vacuum in the area. Most other gangs backed off after Lay-Z killed the reverend. No one wanted to tangle with someone crazy enough to kill a priest in front of dozens of witnesses. Now, though, with the Switchblade Disciples out of the picture, every local gang wanted to claim at least part of Switchtrack Alley. The gangs moved into the neighborhood like sharks circling a bleeding swimmer. At first they moved tentatively, testing the resolve of the remaining SDs. Then they moved in strong and fast.

Many of the newcomers tasted the unique sense of justice that Neely's ghost served. Every success emboldened the spirit and soon it wasn't enough to take on just the gangbangers. The ghost decided it wanted to do just what it had advocated in Neely's most fiery moments on the pulpit: eliminate sin.

A Haunting Spree

These days, anyone who commits a sin of any kind in Switchtrack Alley, no matter how venal, may find herself the target of Neely's wrath. From killers to blasphemers, the ghost makes no distinction about the degree of the transgression. All sinners are equal in his eyes.

As a result, the neighborhood has experienced a rash of unexplained "accidents" over the past two years, all in the wake of the incident with the Switchblade Disciples. The characters can learn about some or all of these events as you like. They could discover one at a time by poking around the community, or they could get lucky and run into someone such as a reporter investigating a story who knows everything that's happened. Such "accidents" include:

• A drug dealer climbed up the pole of the streetlight overlooking his corner, and leaped to his death. It seems that the cement beneath his feet turned to stone-colored snakes. Everyone assumed he had fallen into the trap of using his own inventory.

• A prostitute broke every one of her fingers as she tried to climb a brick wall in sheer terror. She claims that she had entered an alleyway to service a client. When she turned around to face him, he'd turned into a demon that reached out to hold her in its blazing grasp.

• A pickpocket fell down in front of a little old lady whose purse he'd just stolen. The man claimed that the bag seemed to explode into flames, engulfing him. A moment later, he was fine, but while he writhed on the ground another thief took the bag from him and got away.

• A teenage girl who was cussing while eating started to gag and nearly died before she was brought to the hospital. It seems she thought her food had turned into bugs. Rumor has it she'd just smoked her first rock.

• Head-on collisions have skyrocketed on the street. The victims in each accident claim to have not seen the other cars coming. Some say that they were moving around construction in the street (which didn't actually exist) when a car coming the other way ignored the "signaler."

Life on the Street

Switchtrack Alley is a rotten neighborhood these days. Run-down homes shoulder up next to crack houses, and only a few businesses remain, each of which preys upon local poverty.

As Storyteller, you can include any locations that you like. Here are a few to get you started.

Any building that's still occupied has iron bars over its windows. Those that are abandoned have plywood nailed over their windows or the panes are all broken out. Squatters sometimes live in places for days, weeks or even months at a time. They come and go as they please, so it's next to impossible to know if anyone is in a particular place at any particular time.

Pawn Shop: This shop buys goods for a pittance and sells them for outrageous prices. The owner doesn't care if they're stolen or not, which means that drug addicts often try to get rid of burgled goods here. One way to get characters down here from another part of town might be for their homes to be robbed. The police tell them to try here to reclaim their belongings.

Rent-to-Own: This place rents out furniture and electronics at high prices. After enough payments are made, the goods are owned. The total price is often nearly double what one would pay to buy the same items from a regular store.

Car Title Loans: This place gives loans up to half the value of a car, assuming one owns it free and clear. They charge usurious interest and the vehicle is repossessed if a single payment is missed. A character's car could be repoed accidentally on this place's orders, and she has to come down to sort it out.

Grocery: This is little more than a convenience store, although it offers the basics as well as a small selection of beer and cigarettes. Prices here at least 50% higher than what people in better parts of town pay. Hungry characters may find themselves in here. Neely's ghost might decide to take action if someone gets shortchanged.

Liquor Store: Judging by the number of drunks who hang around out front of this place, caging quarters or taking sips from brown-bagged bottles, it does great business. The number of loiterers has dropped somewhat, though, with the rise in the ghost's activity.

Bar: This is little more than a dark hole in the wall. Business has dropped off since so many people started finding blood in their drinks or worms in the frozen pizzas served.

Check Casher: Show a pay stub and this place gives one an advance on his next paycheck. The place used to get robbed regularly, even though everyone in the neighborhood knew the clerks had little cash on hand. Neely's ghost now discourages robbery by sometimes making the clerks look like angry demons. Unlike the other establishments, this place is located in a steel trailer that has bulletproof windows. The trailer seems to have been dropped in the middle of a vacant parking lot.

Blood Bank: This place offers $30, a glass of orange juice and a sugar cookie for a pint of plasma. Unlike the Red Cross, plasma "donated" here is sold to nearby medical centers at a large markup. Plasma can be given once every few weeks, although desperate souls keep track of which technicians work each day and come in when they know they can fool whoever's on staff.

Pay Phone: One of these sits at each end of Switchtrack Alley, which is only three blocks long (unless you want it to be longer or shorter). There's sometimes a line at each phone, but the call made most often these days is "911." Neely's ghost sometimes makes the phones appear broken to prevent victims from calling for help.

Seventh Congregational Church: The elder Reverend Neely still works at this church. His son's ghost steers clear of the place during services, as memories of it are too painful to endure. Service days are a safe haven from any of the ghost's activities. People seem to have figured this out and attendance has skyrocketed of late.

Culture Clash

Many characters do not blend in well on the streets of Switchtrack Alley. This is a dirt-poor, rock-hard part of town. The majority of people who live here were born and raised here and they may die here — violently.

Most neighbors know each other, for better or worse. They can usually spot an outsider a mile away. This is especially true of wealthy, clean-cut, white outsiders.

The people of Switchtrack Alley don't normally care to talk to outsiders. They silently bear their communal shame over Isaiah's death. They want that burden lifted, however.

If an outsider comes poking around, the locals give her the cold shoulder. They think she's a cop, evangelist or social worker and don't want to have anything to do with her. Worse, aggressive people see outsiders as targets for robbery or violence. Characters can expect constant hassles from the people they might try to help.

If, however, characters reveal that they investigate the ghost, people loosen their tongues. They can't seem to solve the problem themselves, so they're desperate to find someone who can, desperate enough to put aside their taboo against talking to strangers.

To get anyone to open up, a character first has to get that person to believe in his and her intentions. That requires a successful contested action between the character's Presence + Streetwise (or Manipulation + Subterfuge, if the character is lying) and the target's Composure + Streetwise (normally four dice). If the character comes up with a good pretense or story or makes an especially strong appeal, you can grant her player a +1 or +2 bonus.

What the Ghost Wants

Neely's spirit wants nothing less than to eradicate sin in Switchtrack Alley. It's willing to do whatever it takes to succeed in its quixotic quest.

The ghost has only two abilities at hand with which to fulfill its desires. It can manifest and try to scare witness with its proximity, yet it can't communicate directly and prefers to work anonymously. For that reason, it resorts to its other capability of Phantasm.

In one sense, Neely's ghost wants to build a utopia in Switchtrack Alley, to transform it into a place where everyone does naught but good in the eyes of the Lord. That was the reverend's dream in life, though it proved far beyond him to even establish peace in the neighborhood. In death, the ghost has few tools left to it to help attain its lofty aims. And yet, it possesses the kind of determination that only a ghost has, which is strong enough to keep it from going off to its final reward.

Neely's ghost doesn't care about keeping its desires private. In fact, it wants neighbors to live in fear of punishment. He would like them to believe that God Himself is behind all the horrible incidents. The ghost believes that to be true, as he is but a servant of the Lord, granted permission to remain on Earth.

Rising Action

Once the characters arrive in Switchtrack Alley, feel free to let them wander around for a while. Neely's ghost isn't always active and the characters need to explore the various reasons why they've come here.

When you think the characters are ready, hit them with one of the encounters described in this chapter. You don't have to use all of these events if you don't want to, and you don't have to use them in order. Feel free to skip around as much as you like, or to skip entire sections.

If the characters decide to go off in a direction you didn't anticipate, roll with it. Let the characters act as they like. If they stay within Switchtrack Alley, you can use most of the encounters presented here. If they stray further, be sure to read "A Story Interrupted," below.

Wrong Corner

As the characters go about their business, they notice a young man standing on a corner, two blocks east of the Seventh Congregational Church. He's dressed in stylish street clothes, basketball gear in blacks and reds. He spends a lot of time chatting on his cell phone and talking to people who drive by.

Sometimes cars stop and the young man leans over and talks to people inside. He hands over little bags in exchange for fistfuls of cash. He is, of course, selling drugs.

The man standing on the corner sometimes changes, but there is someone there just about any time of day or night. This is one of the prime corners on the main drag through the neighborhood and the drug trade is open for business 24/7.

When the characters pass by, something horrible happens. This is no coincidence. The ghost spots the characters and wants witnesses to its efforts.

A luxury car pulls up. There are two young men inside; white, well dressed, clean cut. They are not from around here.

To the drug dealer's eyes, the buyers transform into police officers. They still talk like young drug users, but they look like patrolmen in full uniform.

The drug dealer panics, drops his goods and runs. The young men in the car get out. Now, to the drug dealer, they look like drug dealers themselves, but their seeming powder-blue clothes mark them as members of a different gang. Confused, the buyers pick up the drugs. As they do, the dealer pulls a gun and fires, shooting both dead. The dealer then races back to inspect his handiwork and realizes that he's just killed two of his best customers. He panics and runs again. As he goes, he trips and hits the concrete hard.

The characters can try to interrupt this drama at any point. If they do, they run the risk of the dealer shooting them in a moment of blind panic. (Use the profile for Lay-Z at the end of this chapter if it comes to this.) And yet, the characters could also save the lives of the young buyers.

Once the scene is over, the characters may have a chance to question the survivors. If they talk to the buyers, learning anything requires a successful contested action between a character's Presence + Streetwise (or Manipulation + Subterfuge if the character lies), and a target's Composure + Streetwise (three dice). A successful contest reveals that it's been getting tougher to buy drugs in Switchtrack Alley. There aren't as many dealers around as there once were. The buyers don't know anything more about the situation.

If the characters catch up with the dealer, he clams up right away. Getting him to talk requires a successful contested action between a character's Presence + Streetwise (or Manipulation + Subterfuge) and the target's Composure + Streetwise (four dice). If the character succeeds, the dealer spills what he's heard about the ghost. He curses the day that Lay-Z got run down. "All the trouble started then," he says.

These conversations may lead the characters to find out more about Lay-Z and his current location. He may be one of the solutions to this puzzle.

If the characters fail to stop the killings, they could have a different set of problems on their hands. They might notice (on a successful Wits + Streetwise roll) that everyone else in the area runs as soon as the shooting starts. Not only do the locals not want to get shot, but they don't want to be known witnesses.

If the police arrive before the characters leave, they stop the characters for questioning. If the shooter is still there, they take him into custody and thank the characters for doing the right thing. Either way, the police bring the characters downtown to get statements from them as witnesses.

The characters are in trouble, though, whether they admit to seeing anything or not. The dealer's gang decides that leaving any witnesses around could be trouble. See "A Story Interrupted" for details.

Bad Confessions

As the characters move along Switchtrack Alley, a woman races out of the front door of the Seventh Congregational Church. An older man in a black suit and white collar follows hot on her heels, yelling for her to stop. This is Reverend Ishmael Neely, and the woman is Ardith Farrer, one of his flock.

Ishmael had been taking the young woman's confession on a non-service day when the ghost struck. Ardith had confessed to not being faithful to her husband. It had been a one-night affair and she was torn up over it. As she

began to weep on Ishmael's shoulder, her tears turned to blood.

Shocked, Ardith tried to wipe the tears, but no matter how hard she rubbed or closed her eyes, the blood kept flowing, staining her white shirt. The woman ran screaming from the church.

The moment Ardith leaves the church, the ghost drops the bloody illusion. The poor woman doesn't realize this, though, and races out into the street. She falls to her knees and prays for God's forgiveness, certain that this is the Lord's way of punishing her for cheating.

The characters can try to comfort the woman. At first, Ardith smacks away any hand offered, but she soon realizes that blood no longer pours from her eyes and she is able to calm herself. When that happens, she falls into the arms of the nearest person, no matter who he is, clenching him until she manages to stop shaking.

Ardith can't explain what happened. It was entirely outside her realm of experience. If someone takes her to a doctor, the physician explains the episode away as an example of hysterical guilt. He gives Ardith some painkillers, stitches up and dresses the scratches on her face, and sends her home.

The characters may ask Ishmael what happened. He saw Ardith's reaction to the ghostly trick and suspects the truth, but isn't ready to talk about it. He tells anyone who asks that the poor woman must have been driven mad by guilt for her actions, but he can't reveal any more due to the sanctity of the confessional.

Savvy characters may be able to tell that the preacher is lying about the source of the problem. Doing so calls for a contested roll of a character's Wits + Subterfuge versus Ishmael's Composure + Subterfuge (three dice). Even if a character succeeds, she cannot tell what Ishmael lies about.

Wrong Way

Pick a character and look at her Vice. As the characters walk down the street, Neely's ghost creates an illusion of something that appeals to that weakness. If more than one character shares the same Vice, all the better. There might appear to be money laying on the pavement, or a prostitute could seem to offer services.

If any character gives in to his Vice, the illusion disappears just as the character is about to enjoy the indulgence. At that moment, a shaft of light spears off the front window of the Seventh Congregational Church and blinds the driver of a passing car. The driver swerves, even driving up on the sidewalk at the distracted character(s).

Players must make successful Dexterity + Athletics rolls for indulgent characters to avoid getting hit. The driver doesn't try to strike pedestrians, so this is not a contested roll. If a character is hit, roll 12 dice (nine for the car's Size and three for its velocity) to determine bashing damage. Injured characters are subject to a knockdown effect (World of Darkness, p. 168), as well.

Whether a character is hit or not, the car plows into a nearby storefront, sending shards of glass flying. The car's airbag goes off and saves the driver's life, but the impact of

the bag hitting her in the face knocks her senseless for a moment.

As the characters sort things out, they notice that there are two other places on the street that seem to have been accident sites. Bricks and glass are broken and still lay where they fell. Spray paint marks remain where investigating police went through the motions. A few strange accidents like this one have occurred in the past few months.

Assuming the characters survive the incident, they can pull the driver from behind the wheel of her wrecked car and ask what happened. Other than being shocked, she is unhurt.

The driver's account may direct the characters to the Seventh Congregational Church and Reverend Ishmael Neely. (That is, assuming they have witnessed and heard enough to believe the neighborhood might actually be haunted.) Ishmael denies knowing anything about the accidents, but this is an opportunity for the characters to ask him about the ghost.

A Story Interrupted

Some characters may decide that the best thing to do is leave Switchtrack Alley alone. If the characters aren't determined souls, Neely's ghost could chase them away.

While that may prove frustrating to you as Storyteller, let them run. Let them think they can hide, that they can forget all about their experiences in the neighborhood.

Then chip away at their conscience and sense of right and wrong. Sooner or later, they'll be back.

Here are some ways to lure characters in again.

• They continue to hear news reports about strange things happening in Switchtrack Alley. These should serve as a reminder of their failure and potential cowardice. If a character has the Virtue of Charity or Vice of Pride, it could be enough to spur her back to the place.

• A character gets a phone call, letter or email from one of the people met in Switchtrack Alley. The person is despondent, terrified or perhaps even suicidal. He makes a direct plea for help, playing to the character's humanity. A character with a high Morality may find it hard to refuse such a request.

• A character may suffer a derangement after a Morality roll is failed in Switchtrack Alley or afterward. If she ends up in psychotherapy, the therapist suggests a field trip to the neighborhood to confront the problem eating at her. If the character is reluctant, the therapist could volunteer to accompany her, only to be caught up in the web of Neely's ghost.

• A family member or good friend is injured or killed in Switchtrack Alley under strange circumstances. The characters may decide that they have to go back to eradicate the threat, whatever it is, so that sort of thing doesn't happen again.

• If the characters witness a crime, the police want their statements and order them to not leave town. At the same time, the criminal or his friends decide to lean on the characters to get them to recant their statements. The thugs could come to the characters' homes to "talk" to them, or could even kidnap the characters and bring them back to Switchtrack Alley for a conversation.

Splitting Up

If the characters refuse to act as a group, you could allow one or more of them to go back to Switchtrack Alley on their own. At that point, you have two options.

You can run the scenario as is, using only those characters. The story may prove too challenging for a small group of characters, especially if they insist on taking an aggressive tact against the ghost. Still, if the characters prevail they should have a strong sense of accomplishment in the end.

Or you can harm or scare brave characters sufficiently that they plead for others to help them. This sort of bonding can be helpful for keeping the group together in the future. If forced to, you could even kill off a friend or family member as a means of drawing the characters closer together.

Putting Things Right

If circumstances in Switchtrack Alley turn sufficiently aggressive or personal for characters, they may feel they have to take matters into their own hands. Say they have a personal stake in the neighborhood, having grown up there or nearby, or are haunted for days or weeks after turning their backs on terrifying events. There may come a point at which complacency or fear makes a smaller demand than responsibility, love or guilt. At that point, the protagonists put themselves aside and seek to do something about the community.

Neely's ghost can be put to rest in a number of different ways, addressed below. If the characters come up with a great idea on their own, something that makes at least as much sense as the resolutions provided here, you can go that route. Let characters (and players) be creative about solutions, and reward their ingenuity if such plans are convincing.

Ghost Identification

Many of the methods characters can use to get rid of Neely's ghost require that they learn who he is. They may use their investigation skills to nose around. If they do, that's great, but it's not necessary. Just about everyone who's lived in the area for more than a year has a good idea of who the ghost is.

Local News

By talking to various locals, the characters can pick up a number of clues about what really happened on that dark night. Here are some examples of the sort of people who might have information and why or how they might impart it.

• Young children hear many more things than adults give them credit for, and they're often not shy about sharing, even if they don't fully understand. All it takes is a small act of kindness (Presence + Socialize), a thinly veiled threat (Presence + Intimidation) or a bit of fast-talking (Manipulation + Persuasion) contested against a child's Composure + Streetwise (two dice).

• Gossipy shop workers are usually happy to have someone to talk to. They see so many people, they sometimes forget that they're chatting with outsiders. This approach requires a contested Manipulation + Socialize roll against the shopkeeper or clerk's Composure + Streetwise (three dice).

• Gang members don't have a lot to say to outsiders. Cracking this code of silence requires a successful contested action between a character's Presence + Streetwise (or Manipulation + Subterfuge, if the character lies) and the target's Composure + Streetwise (normally four dice).

• Working stiffs do live in Switchtrack Alley. They mostly just want to be left alone, but they can open up to those whom they think are on their side, even if temporarily. This approach requires a successful contested action between a character's Presence or Manipulation + Streetwise and the target's Composure + Streetwise (three dice).

• Homeless people wander around Switchtrack Alley. Most folks ignore them, which sort of makes them invisible and allows them to see and hear more than most. Getting them to talk requires a successful contested action between a character's Presence or Manipulation + Streetwise and a target's Composure + Streetwise (five dice). If the characters offer a bribe of money, food or alcohol, a +1 bonus is received.

• Barflies hang out at the different hole-in-the-wall taverns across the neighborhood. They don't like strangers much unless the visitors are buying. Prying open their lips requires a successful contested action between a character's Manipulation + Persuasion against a target's Composure + Streetwise (four dice). A +1 bonus is gained if a character gets the first round — and the second.

Here are the bits of information that locals might reveal. Each is marked to show if it's true or not. Either way, the person relating the info believes it to be genuine.

• Reverend Isaiah Neely of the Seventh Congregational Church died in the center of Switchtrack Alley three years ago. That's his blood still staining the street to this day. (True.)

• A rapper named Lay-Z killed the preacher in front of his congregation and no one tried to stop the gangster. (True.)

• Reverend Neely's father — Reverend Ishmael Neely — held his son in his arms as he died. (False. Ishmael couldn't bear to look at his son until the next morning at the morgue.)

- Lay-Z hangs out at the Alarm Box, a bar on the corner of Wisconsin Avenue and Switchtrack Alley. (True.)
- Lay-Z used to be in charge of the Switchblade Disciples, a local gang. (False. He's still in charge, at least nominally.)
- Switchtrack Alley is haunted by the ghosts of all the people killed there in gang violence. (False. It's just Neely's ghost.)
- The Seventh Congregational Church was built on an old graveyard and they never moved the bodies. (False, but it could send the characters to Ishmael, who can set them straight.)
- Lay-Z is some kind of voodoo-practicing ghostbuster. If it wasn't for him, the place would be overrun with ghosts. (False. Lay-Z doesn't practice voodoo and his only beef is with Neely's ghost.)
- Lay-Z killed the old preacher's wife, which is why Isaiah had it in for him. (The first part is true, although Isaiah didn't know who killed his mother.)

Lay-Z's Story

Lay-Z is a hard man who has spent the better part of his life walking through the rotating door at the local state prison. Like Isaiah Neely, he was born and raised in Switchtrack Alley, but his life took a far different turn.

Lay-Z, born Lazarus Toomes, grew up in a fourth-floor walkup apartment where he lived with his mother and younger sister. His father left when Lay-Z's mother was pregnant with his sister Latisha. Lay-Z was five at the time and he hasn't heard from his father since.

When Lay-Z was 16, he dropped out of school and turned to selling drugs for the Switchblade Disciples. He kept it from his mother and told her he was working at the factory on the outskirts of the neighborhood. They needed the money, and he knew she wouldn't approve of him getting involved in anything but honest work. There weren't any jobs at the factory or anywhere else for a 16-year-old dropout, but the gang took him in with open arms. When Lay-Z's mother found out, she kicked him out of the house, which only forced him further into the gang's embrace.

When Lay-Z was 18, his mentor in the gang, a dealer known as Bug, was arrested. Bug flipped on Lay-Z to the cops, depicting the young man as a top lieutenant in the gang. Bug's testimony put Lay-Z away for 10 years.

While in jail, Lay-Z maintained his mentor's lies to save his life. His fellow inmates assumed he had the kind of power he'd never actually had on the street, and Lay-Z liked it. He grew accustomed to having people follow his orders. When his term was over he made a stab for leadership of the SDs.

Hardened by his time in jail, Lay-Z killed his way to the top and maintained control with an iron fist. And that's how he came to young Reverend Neely's attention. For a while, Lay-Z cut Reverend Neely some slack, as he couldn't stomach killing a man of the cloth. That lack of guts lasted only so long, though. When it seemed that Neely might be a real threat to Lay-Z's position, the gang leader shot the preacher in the middle of the street, a demonstration to everyone of who was in charge.

The incident on the anniversary of Reverend Neely's death convinced Lay-Z that *something* was out to get him. He has no doubt that it's Neely's ghost. He's taken to studying the occult to learn more about the ghost and how he might be able to defeat it. He's made little progress.

The truck that hit Lay-Z crushed his legs and put him in a wheelchair, but Neely's ghost crushed his spirit. He still refuses to give up control of the Switchblade Disciples, which has put the gang at a standstill. In this sense, then, the campaign of Neely's ghost has succeeded.

If the characters decide to talk to Lay-Z, he is reluctant at first. He curses at them and tells them to go away. If they persist and explain that they want to help out with what's happening in Switchtrack Alley, he relents, especially if they mention Neely or a ghost.

Ishmael's Story

Reverend Ishmael Neely knows all about the ghost that haunts Switchtrack Alley. After all, he's the ghost's father.

The elder Neely grew up in the Alley too, but back when it was a much nicer place to live. His family was one of the first African-American permitted to live in the neighborhood, something for which many white neighbors didn't care. As the money left the area, though, the wealthy people moved out to the suburbs and poor folk moved in.

Ishmael had always had a flair for church oratory, so he went to school to study the Bible. When he graduated, he came back to Switchtrack Alley to found the place's first African-American church: the Seventh Congregational. People flocked to it and Ishmael's following grew.

The reverend met and married a lovely young lady by the name of Ruby Stokes. They had a single son, Isaiah, who was the spitting image of his father and grew up determined to follow in Ishmael's footsteps.

When Isaiah was 15, a stray bullet came through the front window of the family home and killed Ruby. Instead of driving the Neely men away, though, the loss only strengthened their resolve to stay the course and do whatever they could to bring peace to their troubled neighborhood.

Isaiah went away to college to study the Bible. When he came back, he joined his father in his ministry at the Seventh Congregational, bringing a new fire to the church's pulpit. While Ishmael had been content to try to save the souls of those willing to join the flock, Isaiah took the battle to the streets.

Father counseled son against this course of action, but Isaiah remained resolute. He didn't want any more children to have to grow up motherless like he did. The violence had to stop.

Today, Ishmael Neely is a broken man. He has lost both his son and wife to gang violence, and he despairs not being able to do anything about it. He doesn't have his son's strength of will, and his parishioners know it. He calls his "path" wisdom, but in his heart he knows it's cowardice.

When Isaiah was murdered, few people left the church right away. Over the subsequent three years, however, many of Ishmael's flock found reason to stop attending services and Sunday mornings became a hollow mockery of what they once were. Since the haunting began, neighborhood folks have intuitively learned that the church is a safe haven from spectral punishment when services are underway. Ishmael therefore presides, but he knows his sermons fall on deaf ears as members of the congregation simply use the church to carry out their own interactions and business. The reverend therefore spends much of his free time in his office, drinking the sacramental wine until he passes out.

Ishmael knows all too well who the ghost of Switchtrack Alley is. He's had several waking visions of his son's death. When they strike him, he falls to his knees, sobbing with grief and guilt. Sometimes in visions, the dying Isaiah reaches out to Ishmael, but the father always forces the phantom back by presenting the golden crucifix he wears on a chain around his neck. The ghost recoils at this, not (as Ishmael suspects) from fear, but from anger at a God who would let such a fate befall a preacher who had dedicated his life to the service.

If someone asks about Isaiah, Ishmael talks about his son with a deep sense of melancholy. He believes that Isaiah could have made a real difference if he hadn't been cut down in his prime. Ishmael openly despairs that he is too old to muster the strength needed to carry on where his son left off.

If anyone mentions Isaiah and the ghost, Ishmael grimaces. He wants to talk about his son's death, but only if he believes some good will come of it. It's up to the characters to convince him that they want to help. A successful contested action of Manipulation + Persuasion against Ishmael's Composure + Subterfuge (three dice) works.

Severing Anchors

The most straightforward way to get rid of a ghost is to destroy or resolve the locations or items that keep the spirit bound to the world. Neely's ghost has three anchors: the spot where he died, the spot where he spent the most important parts of his life, and the man who killed him.

Death's Anchor

Characters who investigate a little should be able to figure out where the first anchor is. Anyone who lived in the area three years ago can point out the exact location. It's marked by a large bloodstain in the middle of the street that seems to have resisted weather and pollution. Local characters might have heard about the murder or even the stain through the grapevine. There are no police records on the killing, and neighbors have kept it out of the press through a code of silence and complacency.

All the locals know that Lay-Z and the Switchblade Disciples were responsible. Everyone calls it a tragedy and most of them shake their heads. No one is willing to admit to being one of the silent witnesses to Isaiah's death, however.

Even if characters have previously led mundane lives and know nothing about how to contend with ghosts, the dried bloodstain strikes them as unusual. In the first place, the fact that no one has had the courage to try to remove it and show Isaiah some respect is appalling. Second, the fact that it persists so many months later suggests that something disturbing is going on with it that's well beyond the norm.

Some characters may decide that the street itself needs to be destroyed to lift its curse. That's a tall order, but they might be able to pull it off. An order from the city to repave the area works if the characters can manage to arrange it.

Perhaps the easiest way to destroy the anchor is to clean the stain or cover it up. A power washer (available at any hardware store) does the trick, as does a 10-gallon bucket of asphalt sealant spread liberally over the spot. Setting a funeral wreath in place also causes the stain to disappear. If you want resolution of this anchor to be as cathartic for the neighborhood as for the ghost, perhaps characters taking the initiative to clean the stain draw out neighbors by the dozens, all of them pitching in to finally absolve their own guilt. Locals could come out of their homes and businesses with buckets, household cleaners, brushes — everything they need to cleanse the street and their own spirits. At that point, the stain means less to Neely's ghost than does final recognition and respect by his old congregation.

If the ghost is freed by some other means, the stain spontaneously fades to nothing.

Life's Anchor

Isaiah is still connected to the Seventh Congregational Church as the focal point of his self-appointed mission in Switchtrack Alley. His soul can't let go of his desire to see the congregation uplifted in thought, deed and spirit.

Utterly blunt characters could seek to destroy the place or have it demolished. The elder Reverend Neely is resigned to sell the building and its land for a fraction of its worth so that he might walk away once and for all, defeated but free. This course permits the characters to do as they will with the building, including hiring a construction crew to raze the place to the ground.

The characters might also try to burn the place. The Seventh Congregational is an old, wood-frame building and fire could destroy it completely. The moral implications of doing so are staggering — certainly enough for a Morality roll. The Storyteller may even impose a derangement on arsonists, regardless of rolls. If there are any witnesses to the crime, they turn the characters in. If the characters are caught, they're sure to face charges and even federal prosecution under the Church Arson Protection Act of 1996 (in the US, anyway). This approach could cause the characters to become fugitives for the rest of their lives. If they are caught, there's no explanation they can offer that a judge or jury would accept.

To be sure the characters understand the repercussions of arson, be sure to warn them. Have a squad car cruise by as they consider this course. Or before they light the match, Ishmael could interrupt them, no matter the time of day or night.

The characters must also watch out for unintended consequences to their actions. Sometimes Ishmael lets homeless people sleep in the church's pews. Other nights find him passed out in his office in the back. If the characters start a fire, they may kill these innocent people. Such tragedies increase the criminal charges against them and should be cause for further Morality loss.

If the characters surreptitiously discuss what might placate Isaiah's spirit in regard to the church, Ishmael suspects there's a way. If the characters can get Lay-Z to attend a memorial service for Isaiah, it might satisfy the ghost and absolve its anger toward the church itself. Or, characters might be able to encourage the congregation to return for the right reasons, to make peace with each other and to honor God. Such renewed, genuine faith restores Isaiah's faith and helps him move on. Characters might encourage locals to resume their old services after the bloodstain in the street is cleansed. A rousing speech along these lines (roll Presence + Persuasion + equipment versus the highest Resolve + Composure of the audience — three dice — in a contested action) might turn the hearts and minds of the congregation. For more on the possibilities of saving the community to free Isaiah, see "A Neighborhood Absolved."

The Living Anchor

Neely's ghost has been haunting Lay-Z since the day it fully awoke (on the first anniversary of the young reverend's death). Sometimes it goes for days or even weeks without bothering the gang leader. Other times it pesters him for days at a time.

Soon after Lay-Z left the hospital in a wheelchair, he realized what was going on. He railed against the ghost, who only laughed in return. Lay-Z decided he had to do something to defend himself, so he's been researching how to get rid of ghosts ever since.

Sadly, Lay-Z hasn't been able to come up with much. He's tried everything he can think of, but none of the traditional abjurations, exorcisms or blessed items that he's learned of or even understood have worked against the spirit. He's willing to go into painful detail about his efforts, but the story always ends the same: failure.

What the ghost wants from Lay-Z is something the rapper has been unable to do yet: repent. To show his sincerity, Lay-Z would have to confess his sins to Ishmael and show true regret for his crime. Until that happens, the ghost isn't leaving.

The other way to destroy this anchor, of course, is to kill Lay-Z, but that requires the characters to murder a man in cold blood, with all its guilt and attendant Morality rolls.

All or Nothing

The characters must take care of all three anchors to banish Neely's ghost. If they manage to figure out and destroy one, the ghost lays low for a few days and then resumes its haunting. It starts out with a few small frights at first, but escalates efforts quickly.

There is a danger that characters might believe their work is done when it's only partly finished. In that case, they get word of new hauntings. It hopefully draws them back to finish the job.

Unfinished Business

Other ways to release Neely's ghost involve helping it take care of lingering goals. Here are some suggested avenues of action for characters to follow, if you want to allow them.

A Neighborhood Absolved

The people of Switchtrack Alley are a sinful lot. Worse yet, they failed to stand beside their spiritual leader when he needed them most. That's what angers the ghost most.

If the people of Switchtrack Alley could somehow manage to repent and ask for forgiveness, the ghost might be appeased. Absolving Switchtrack Alley of sin seems impossible at first. The Neely family and other ministers in the area have fought this battle for years. The ghost has been at it for a couple years and its results have been spotty at best.

The characters aren't as limited in their actions or ideas as a ghost. Put the problem before them and they may well come up with a solution. First, though, they have to identify the problem. They have to learn the story of how Isaiah was killed and that his soul became the ghost that haunts Switchtrack Alley.

The fact that Isaiah haunts the street and assaults anyone for even the smallest violations of the Ten Commandments should tell characters that the ghost is fixated on sin. For instance, the characters could witness or hear about the following events:

• A prostitute falls to her knees on the street, tearing off her wig and clothes. A moment later, she stops. She saw snakes crawling through her clothes.

• A man walks down the street, cursing up a storm as he talks on a cell phone. Then he hurls it to the ground in terror. To him, the phone seemed on fire.

• A child sasses his mother as they leave the liquor store. She starts to yell at him and he blows her off. She is about to give up when the child falls to the floor, screaming in phantom pain.

• A man in a bar pulls a knife and stabs the person next to him. The victim draws a gun and shoots his assailant dead. The two were friends who always went around armed. Word is the guy with the knife spontaneously thought his friend was a cop.

• A man sitting on a park bench harassing (and coveting) women as they go by stands up and walks straight into traffic. His last words are, "What happened to the beach with all the girls?"

• During Sunday services, a drug dealer races into the Seventh Congregational, nearly knocking over the holy water font. She was sitting across the street, eating and making fun of people going to church. Apparently she sought refuge when *something* terrified her.

If the characters can't seem to wrap their collective heads around the ghost's obsession with sin, Ishmael can point them in the right direction. If he hears that the characters are asking questions, he may approach them himself. He wants to lay his son's ghost to rest, but he lacks the courage to do it himself.

Some — including Ishmael — may recall Isaiah's regular plea in his sermons. "Sunday is the day of the Lord. If we can give over just one day to Him, if we could just gather all of his children in His house for one morning to give Him praise, imagine what an accomplishment that would be. Imagine where we could go from there."

For this to work, the characters must round up the people of Switchtrack Alley for a Sunday service. They don't have to get everyone in the area to attend, just pack the church, which holds 250.

If the characters can arrange for a full house, Ishmael rises to the occasion. He delivers an amazing sermon that inspires attendees to make a change in their lives. It focuses on the fact that people are weak, that they're sinners by nature, but the power of God — and people, if they take it up — is forgiveness.

The crowd gets into the sermon, peppering the preacher with amens and hallelujahs. By the end, the entire place is on its feet. The people go forth to tell everyone they know about the church and its fantastic preacher and a new day dawns over Switchtrack Alley. The spirit of Isaiah Neely moves on.

Community Service

The characters could involve the residents of Switchtrack Alley in a community-improvement effort. There are lots of ways to pull this off. In each case, the characters need to do something to help pull the neighborhood together.

• Set up a Neighborhood Watch Association. The gangs in Switchtrack Alley thrive because everyone is too afraid to testify against them. A Neighborhood Watch would encourage people to band together in a united front, something they failed to do under Isaiah's leadership.

• Found a community center. This is a place for seniors to go during the day, and it includes day care and after-school activities. It gives locals a place to come together and do something other than huddle in their homes in fear. It also helps to keep kids off the street and lets parents work decent jobs knowing their kids are safe.

• Host a neighborhood festival or block party. Block off Switchtrack Alley at both ends and provide entertainment, rides, food, vendor booths and more. This is a massive undertaking, but it can both bring money into the area and provide a sense of civic pride that the neighborhood hasn't had for a while.

• Start a "Clean up the Neighborhood Day." The characters can lead the effort to get garbage off the street. If they can get enough people (say, 50) involved, they can make a huge dent in the local mess. Cleaning up the bloodstain in the middle of the street could be a vital element of the effort.

The key to any plan's success is to get the community involved. Switchtrack Alley needs to make a permanent change. If the ghost sees this happening, it realizes that its work is done. Others will carry on without it.

Lay-Z's Rejuvenation

Another development satisfies Neely's ghost: Lay-Z's confession to Isaiah's murder. That would only be a start, however. For the ghost to be appeased, Lay-Z would have to either be arrested or turn his life around with a heartfelt confessional with Ishmael.

Getting Lay-Z to confess is not a simple task. The man feels guilty about what he's done and is terrified of Neely's ghost, but he doesn't want to go back to jail. The characters must convince Lay-Z that telling the truth is in his best interests. Doing so requires a lot of interaction and convincing, possibly backed by a Manipulation + Empathy or Persuasion roll in a contested action against Lay-Z's Composure + Empathy (three dice) or Composure + Streetwise (eight dice).

If the characters can get Lay-Z to confess in front of a law-enforcement officer or get such a confession on video or audio tape, they should have enough to get him put away. Besides the relief of the ghost, the characters earn the gratitude of the police and the district attorney, who have been hoping to nail Lay-Z permanently on one kind of charge or another for years.

It's possible for the characters to convince Lay-Z to go straight. He's been on the fence about it since his first experience with the ghost. However, he's loath to give up control of the Switchblade Disciples while the ghost still haunts the streets. He sees his gang as his best tool and defense against the spirit.

If Lay-Z does have a change of heart, he announces that he's ready to confess, but may agree to do so only to Ishmael. He sees the harm he's done to the community and realizes the only way to put an end to things is to make peace with the surviving reverend.

Ishmael's Reconciliation

Ishmael Neely struggled all his life to be good. He wanted to be a good son, a good preacher, a good husband and a good father. Most of the time he succeeded, but sometimes success meant more to him than truly being good.

Early on in his career, the senior Neely ran afoul of the criminal element in town. He called for aggressive action against the Switchblade Disciples and other gangs that ravaged Switchtrack Alley.

The SDs responded by kidnapping him as he left the Seventh Congregational Church and holding him overnight. They beat him bloody and threatened to kill his wife and son if he refused to give in to their demands.

Ishmael wanted to be good, to be strong, but he was ultimately weak. His love for his wife and son was too powerful to be denied, and the SDs used it to fashion shackles.

When Isaiah was a teenager, Ishmael tried to be strong once again. With his wife Ruby's encouragement, he resumed his crusade against the gangs. He made blistering speeches from the pulpit, encouraging people to stand up to the thugs who were ruining their lives.

Then a bullet came through a window at the family house and cut Ruby down. Ishmael reported it as a stray shot, an accident, but he saw the face of the young man who fired it. The killer was 16-year-old Lazarus Toomes, a boy fulfilling his initiation into the Switchblade Disciples.

Ishmael got the message. He gave up on his fight against the gangs and concentrated on encouraging his son Isaiah to go to college and leave the community far behind.

The fact that Isaiah wanted to come back to take up the fight shocked Ishmael. At first, he tried to dissuade his son, although Ishmael could never bring himself to confess his own weakness. Isaiah's devotion to his ideals was relentless and he eventually wore down his father's objections.

During Isaiah's last days, Lay-Z came to the church to speak to both reverends. The gangbanger told the preachers to back off or they would get the same as Ruby: an early grave.

Isaiah almost killed Lay-Z on the spot with his bare hands. Ishmael pulled the two apart, not wanting to see his son become a killer. Lay-Z left with a final warning to the Neelys to put an end to their anti-gang campaign.

Incensed, Isaiah stepped up his attacks instead. The following Sunday, the parishioners of the Seventh Congregational rose up in arms during the sermon and poured out into the street, ready to demand real changes in their neighborhood.

That night, the Switchblade Disciples murdered Benjamin Pinnon. Isaiah stormed out of the church offices, determined to track down Lay-Z and make him pay. Ishmael followed his son into the street, and folks throughout the neighborhood looked on. They all stood by and watched as Lay-Z murdered Isaiah. When it was over, Ishmael prayed for a forgiveness he knew he didn't deserve.

The ghost now needs Ishmael to beg him, not God, for forgiveness. If that happens, Isaiah's spirit listens to Ishmael's full confession and could release itself from the world.

There are two ways to get Ishmael to confess. The first is for the characters to appeal directly to Ishmael's buried sense of decency. That can be accomplished through roleplaying, but could be supported with a contested action with Manipulation + Empathy rolled versus Ishmael's Composure + Empathy (five dice).

The other solution is to get Lay-Z to confess to Ishmael. No roll is needed for Ishmael's reaction. Being confronted with the penitence of the man who killed his wife and son moves Ishmael to finally confront the deep and utter shame with which he has lived all these years.

Ishmael falls to his knees at the nearest of the ghost's three anchors — the street, the church or Lay-Z — and begs for Isaiah's forgiveness. He then tells his whole horrid story aloud, uncaring as to who might hear him, as long as his son can finally know of his father's long-hidden guilt. At that a palpable weight is lifted from the neighborhood, and Isaiah passes.

Abjuration, Exorcisms and Blessed Items

Any faith-based defenses or weapons that characters might try to turn against Isaiah's ghost have no affect. In its wrath, the ghost denies the authority of a God who could allow such horrid things to happen to the alley.

Denouement

The end of the story depends on how the characters decide to handle the ghost. You don't have too much control over that. More likely, you're along for the ride, filling in circumstances of events that players cannot.

The denouement, however, is more about how the story affects the characters than how they affect it. This is something you need to consider as you craft events with your players.

There are a few possible themes to the story that could be kept in mind throughout. The trick with a theme is that it doesn't work well if the players are aware of it. Never club them over the head with one. Instead, their awareness of theme should evolve naturally from their participation.

Ghosts Represent the Past

Ghosts don't pop up out of no where. They are the personification of past, secret deeds that refuse to remain hidden.

If you want to take a psychological view of it, Isaiah's ghost is fed by the guilt of those who were involved in his death. This includes Ishmael and all witnesses, who quietly blame themselves for not having the courage to stand up to the killers.

The ghost is a muse that spurs others on to uncover the buried tale, to tell the story that others don't want told. To this end, the spirit acts out until it drags in someone who has the courage and determination to see the drama through to its end, no matter how bloody or painful it might be.

The Dead Demand Justice

A ghost story is a murder mystery in which the dead demand punishment of the living. What would have happened if Isaiah's spirit had gone on to the afterlife instead of staying behind as a ghost? Lay-Z and his friends would have gotten away with murder and Ishmael would likely have drunk himself to death in his grief and self-loathing.

A ghost cannot usually ask those close to it for help. Many times, they are the people who had a hand in the victim's untimely demise. If they were going to do something about it, it would have happened already. Instead, the ghost is forced to act out, to reach out to anyone who might be able to understand, to ask someone to pull back the covers and reveal the horrors hidden in the spirit's deathbed.

Crime Affects the Community

The effects of a crime reach far beyond the few people directly involved. A stone is tossed in a pond and ripples reach outward, in this case influencing everyone in the community.

Sometimes this effect is subtle. People may not sit out on their porches as much. They may lock their doors. They cease trusting others, especially strangers.

Sometimes the effect is more direct. The ghost is the personification of these effects. It carries them to a higher level and highlights the ramifications a crime has upon all those around it. Neely does just so by haunting the community and condemning its sins.

Justice has its Own Price

As the characters become embroiled in circumstances, they might ask themselves what their involvement costs them. Is it worth it to them to put an end to the tragedies here, to help put the ghost to rest? It would be easier to walk away, but can they deal with the knowledge that their inaction would allow others to suffer?

These sorts of questions get down to the root of who the characters are. Can they ignore people in distress? Do they shut their windows when they hear a scream? Do they call the police? Do they at least poke their heads out to see what's going on? Are they willing to pay a personal price so that others can receive the justice they deserve?

Variations

If you like, you can put a whole new spin on "Holy Ghost," transforming it into a story that better fits your troupe's sensibilities.

The Spirit of Vengeance

Neely's ghost isn't out to merely punish sinners. It wants to kill them. Switchtrack Alley becomes a war zone in which only looters dare to tread. This pleases the ghost to no end, as those are exactly the kind of people it wants to kill.

Even the police fear to enter Switchtrack Alley these days. None are innocent in the eyes of Neely's ghost. Bodies lay where they fall, and no one is willing to brave the ghost's wrath to recover them.

You might wonder why any of the characters would want to enter such a place, but there are a number of ways to lure them in.

- The characters are looters who aren't put off by ghost stories.
- The characters learn that a pair of young children is trapped in Switchtrack Alley. The ghost appreciates their innocence and doesn't let them leave.
- The characters take a wrong turn and wander into the neighborhood. The ghost haunts fresh game.

Vigilante Justice

Neely's ghost targets actual criminals; real bad people, not the innocent. It kills them in horrible ways, making examples of them for the rest of the neighborhood. The gangs are gone and everyone seems happy, but local security is not real. Everyone lives in fear that they'll be next.

In this variation, Switchtrack Alley is a kind of paradise, but one that's enforced by murderous means. Once the characters discover this reality, they must decide whether they can stomach it. Is making the streets safe by any means acceptable?

Even if locals don't kill criminals themselves, they condone the ghost's actions by their own compliance. The ghost patrols the streets all night long and little escapes its notice. Few indiscretions can be kept private from it. People live as well and honestly as they can out of sheer terror of being caught doing wrong.

The characters must decide if such supernatural tyranny is wrong. Can they leave the place behind with a clear conscience? If not, they may find that many locals stand ready to stop them from harming their ubiquitous protector. They remember what Switchtrack Alley was like before, and don't want to go back. Are the characters prepared to hurt others — and invoke the ghost's wrath — to do what they think is right?

Voodoo Rites

The creation of Neely's ghost was no accident. Lay-Z is a powerful practitioner of Palo Mayombe, an ancient African religion based on themes of death. Lay-Z stumbled across the faith while in prison and has since become a Tata (father) in it, complete with his own Prenda (a consecrated cauldron). He pays tribute to Zarabanda, the Nikisi (ancestral spirit) of war and vengeance.

Lay-Z ripped Isaiah Neely's heart from his chest and placed it in his cauldron to create the ghost and force it to do his bidding. Under Lay-Z's direction, Neely's spirit destroyed all of the other gangs encroaching on the Switchblade Disciples' turf. Lay-Z then turned the ghost against anyone in the community who dared to stand against him. That included the police, who now fear to enter what they call "Lay-Z's Town."

This all comes to a head when Ishmael finally finds his backbone and tries to rally the people against Lay-Z and his mystical help. The ghost refuses to cross the threshold of the church, so Ishmael and his parishioners are safe while they stay there, but those who leave are fair game.

Cast Members

The basic profiles for the main antagonists of this story appear below. Feel free to modify these as much as you like to suit your needs.

The Right Reverend Isaiah Neely

Background: Isaiah Neely was once a devout man of God, an evangelist who tried to take his message to the streets and restore peace, order and prosperity to the neighborhood. He paid for his hubris with his life.

Neely's spirit rested uneasily and refused to move on. For a full year, it waited, enveloped in its grief, until his murderers desecrated the site of its death.

Description: Neely's ghost rarely manifests visibly. It prefers to create images of itself with its Phantasm Numen. These images are usually an idealized form of what Neely looked like in life. He appears as a handsome, young, African-American man with short-cropped hair and a preacher's black suit and white collar.

When it does manifest visibly, the ghost looks like Neely as he was at the moment of his death. This is a man beaten in every sense of the word. His skin is dark and sallow where it is not bruised or broken. A ragged hole passes clear through his chest, larger in the back than in the front.

In either case, freezing cold and the scent of blood and wine accompany the ghost's manifestations. When the ghost is around, the entire street effectively becomes his grave and reflects the chill of such a place. The wine represents the sacrament Neely administered during services while alive. The blood stands for the blood of Christ, into which the wine transmutes during services, and for Neely's own spilled blood that still stains the street.

Storytelling Hints: If Neely was unbalanced just before his death, the actual murder sent him over the edge. If the ghost could talk, it would be a raving madman who went on endlessly about how the righteous could triumph over sinners only by administering their own form of blessed justice.

The ghost's insanity makes it ignore shades of sin. It punishes them all with equally savage delight. A truly horrible transgression, however, can distract it from bothering with a lesser one, at least for a little while.

The ghost spends much of its time moping about how horrible things have become in Switchtrack Alley. Because of this, its interventions against lesser sinners are often irregular. Despite its intent to punish all equally, it sometimes can't muster the indignation to deal with minor crimes. Any major sin, however, sets it off.

Anchors: Neely's ghost is anchored to Switchtrack Alley itself, and that's where it haunts. Deep down, the ghost knows its own sins are as bad as anyone else's, but it figures its own punishment is the afterlife in which it is trapped. The only thing it believes it can do to expiate its sins and leave this purgatory is to carry out the Lord's wrathful will. The ghost typically manifests at night, when the streets are nearly abandoned. Only the bravest or most dangerous people prowl after dark, and those are exactly the kinds of victims for which the ghost hunts.

Attributes: Power 2, Finesse 5, Resistance 3

Willpower: 5

Morality: 4 (Derangement at 5: Fixated on sin)

Virtue: Faith

Vice: Wrath

Initiative: 8

Defense: 5

Speed: 17 (species factor 10)

Size: 5

Corpus: 8

Numen: Phantasm (dice pool 7)

Lay-Z (Lazarus Toomes)

Quote: "I didn't have nothin' to do with it."

Background: Lazarus Toomes was always more ambitious than the other kids. He just wasn't imaginative enough to find a way out of Switchtrack Alley. Instead, he joined what seemed to be the best of the gangs: the Switchblade Disciples.

For his initiation, he murdered Ruby Neely. Later, his mentor in the gang framed him for a crime he didn't commit and Lazarus spent 10 years in jail. When he got out, remade as Lay-Z, a wannabe rapper, he dedicated himself to taking over the Switchblade Disciples, a position he holds to this day.

Description: Lay-Z is a handsome, light-skinned African-American who keeps his head and face shaved smooth. His arms bear prison tattoos that mark him as one of the Switchblade Disciples. He wears a professionally made one on his right shoulder. It depicts two switchblades in the form of a cross. He is 30 years old.

Back when he could walk, Lay-Z stood over six feet tall, but he slouched so much it was hard to tell. Now, as then, his clothes are always in the latest hip-hop style and he drives a new Lexus SUV with gold trim. The windows are tinted to almost black. As it passes through the streets, its subwoofer rattles nearby windows.

Lay-Z wears black sunglasses with shiny black lenses at all times. He sneers when he talks. He never does drugs

and he despises those who do. He's happy to have his people sell them, though.

Storytelling Hints: Lay-Z is proud of how far he's come and that usually makes him arrogant. Right now, though, he's scared for his life. He's never seen anything like what happened to him the night of the anniversary, and he hopes he never will again. He considers giving up the SDs for good, although he knows that he has nothing else.

Lay-Z portrays himself as tough and vengeful, but he's desperate for help. If the characters show they believe in ghosts and might be able to help, he does everything he can for them — short of putting himself in jail.

Attributes: Intelligence 2, Wits 3, Resolve 3, Strength 3, Dexterity 2, Stamina 2, Presence 4, Manipulation 4, Composure 4

Skills: Athletics 2, Brawl 3, Drive 2, Firearms 2, Intimidation 3, Investigation 3, Larceny 3, Persuasion 2, Socialize 2, Stealth 2, Streetwise 4, Subterfuge 3, Weaponry 2

Merits: Allies (Criminals) 3, Brawling Dodge, Contacts (Criminals, Occult) 2, Fast Reflexes 1, Inspiring, Resources 4, Status (Criminals) 3

Flaws: Crippled (permanently)

Willpower: 7

Morality: 3

Virtue: Fortitude

Vice: Greed

Initiative: 7

Defense: 2

Size: 5

Speed: 3 (1 if other actions performed)

Weapons/Attacks:

Type	Dmg	Range	Shots	Dice Pool
Glock 17	2	20/40/80	17+1	6

Health: 7

Reverend Ishmael Neely

Quote: "God bless you for trying to help."

Background: Ishmael Neely once had high hopes. He had a flock of people who respected him, a church of his own and a loving wife and son. Today, he has lost his family and he seems to be doing his best to drink the rest of his life away.

Ishmael once considered himself to be a shining knight of God, ready to fight all the evils the world could throw at him. Over the years, he's realized that he's a coward who doesn't have the stomach to stand up to those who threaten him — or the ones he loves. Even now that he has little left to lose, he has trouble finding it in his heart to do what's right.

Description: Ishmael Neely is a short, thin African-American man with dark, wrinkled skin and thin, wire-rimmed spectacles. At 60, what little hair he has left has gone gray, fading to white in the back. Before his son's death, he kept himself well groomed, but these days he seems disheveled and a bit out of focus.

Ishmael wears a black suit and black shirt with a preacher's white collar. His clothes are usually rumpled from sleeping in them, and his collar sometimes shows a red stain from spilled sacramental wine. His glasses are bent at the temples and slightly off-kilter.

Storytelling Hints: Ishmael is a shattered man. He often starts to say something and catches himself before he finishes. He constantly second-guesses himself, often trailing off in mid-sentence.

Sometimes Ishmael shows flashes of his former glory as a great orator who could move a room of people, but they are rare. They come only when he is worked up enough to forget his grief and shame.

Attributes: Intelligence 3, Wits 3, Resolve 2, Strength 1, Dexterity 2, Stamina 1, Presence 3, Manipulation 2, Composure 2

Skills: Academics 2, Brawl 1, Drive 1, Empathy 3, Expression 3, Intimidation 2, Investigation 1, Medicine 1, Occult 1, Persuasion 2, Politics 1, Socialize 2, Streetwise 2, Subterfuge 1

Merits: Allies (Religious) 3, Contacts (Religious, Political) 2, Resources 1, Status (Religious) 3

Flaws: Embarrassing Secret: Coward

Willpower: 4	**Vice:** Pride	**Size:** 5
Morality: 7	**Initiative:** 4	**Speed:** 8
Virtue: Faith	**Defense:** 2	**Health:** 6

coming next

Antagonists